Kabbalah

Cover art by

Jane A. Evans

Kabbalah

An Introduction and Illumination for the World Today.

Charles Poncé

This publication made possible with the assistance of the Kern Foundation.
The Theosophical Publishing House
Wheaton, Ill./Madras, India/London, England

First Quest edition, 1978, published by the Theosophical
Publishing House, a department of the Theosophical
Society in America.

Library of Congress Cataloging in Publication Data
Poncé, Charles
    Kabbalah.

    (Quest Books)
    Reprint of the ed. published by
Straight Arrow Books, San Francisco.
    Bibliography: p.   Includes index.
    1. Cabala — History.   I. Title.
(BM526.P57   1978)   296.1'6   78-7385
ISBN 0-8356-0510-8

Printed in the United States of America

For David
On the occasion of his coming into manhood

For Jabir
That another door may be open for now
and all eternity

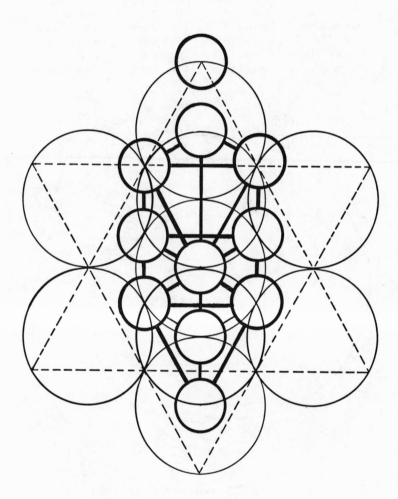

"God with-
out all Na-
ture & Crea-
ture. The
Unformed
Word in
Trinity with-

out all Na-
ture. The
Eternal
Unity, or
Oneness,
deeper than

any Thought
can reach. . . .
The Trinity
Unmanifest
or rather,
that Triune

Unreachable
Being, which
cannot be an
Object of
any created
Understanding."

represented by this finer Circling Line: Which Lubet goes along with (but secretly and inconprehensibly to) the Lubet (yet not mixed nor

Desire represented by this Grofs and Dark Circling Line: Which Desire is turning out, together with

This, Abyssal, Nothing will introduce it self into Something viz. into Nature: that is into Proper- ties: and through Nature, into Glory & Majesty. This now is done

by a Soft, Meek or Tender Lubet. . . . Lubet . . . by a Sharp, Keen or Strong

(Desire, through

The first in a
series of illus-
trations of
the Deep
Principles of
Jakob Bohme.

From *The
Works of Ja-
cob Behmen*,
Volume II,

left by the
Rev. William
Law, Lon-
don, 1764.

Title page:
File from
Robert Fludd,
*Utriusque Cos-
mi Historia*, Op
penheim, 1617.

Contents

The Kabba-
lists built-up
a system of
symbolic cor-
respondences
between the
manifesta-
tions of di-
vine powers,
letters, num-
bers & the
different
parts of the
human body.
Shown here
are the
hands, each
bearing six-
teen letters
correspond-
ing to the
thirty-two
ways of wis-
dom of the
first *Sefirah*,
the Crown,
or *Kether*.

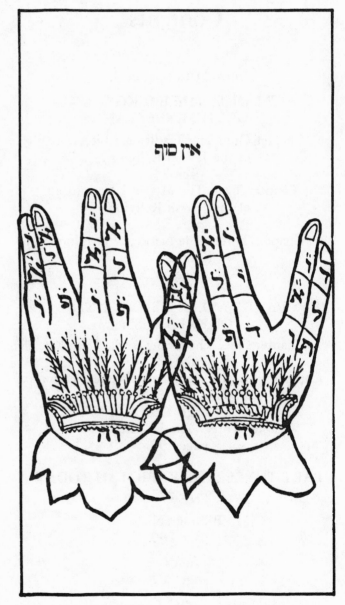

אין סוף

Introduction

THE TERM *KABBALAH* translates literally into tradition, & refers us specifically to the tradition of Jewish mysticism. Although the term itself did not come into prominence until the twelfth century of our era, there were mystical currents in existence within Judaism before that time which can also be called Kabbalistic since they contained the basic principles of what eventually became identified as *the* Kabbalah, *the* tradition. In the section on mystical literature, therefore, no rigid distinction is made between those mystical works preceding the twelfth century & those which follow it, even though the latter generally, & the famous *Sefer Zohar* or *Book of Splendour* in particular, have for some time been erroneously identified as comprising *the* Kabbalah.

The difference between Jewish mysticism & Jewish religion is analogous to that to be found between the religion & mysticism of other peoples. Mysticism can be thought of as an extension & amplification of traditional religious views. It attempts to go beyond or behind traditional & established dogma, in order to satisfy the needs which certain individuals have to experience the Divine directly, without the intercession of an appointed body of 'fathers.' The number of these individuals, the frequency

Twenty-eight of the seventy-two seals of the chief spirits of the Goetia, the Book of Evil Spirits From W. de Laurence, *Lesser Key of Solomon*, Chicago, 1916.

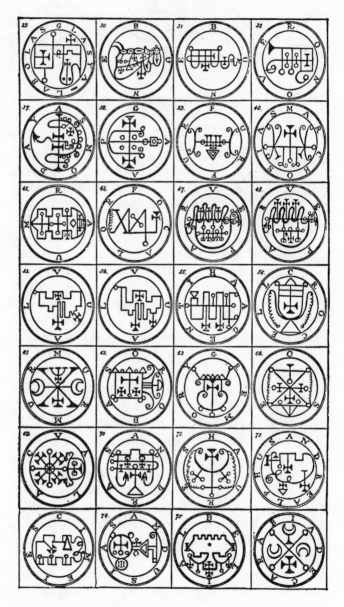

quency of their appearance in history & their tenac-
ity all suggest that mysticism takes its strength
from deficiencies of established religious practice.
It is as if mystics fill up the holes in the over-
scrubbed fabric of religious tradition.

The Kabbalah, the main compendium of Jewish
mystical thought, differs from rabbinical Judaism
in proposing that:

1. The creator God of the Bible is a limited God
& that he is subordinate to yet a higher, limitless
& unknowable God, the *En-Sof*.

2. The universe is not the result of creation *ex
nihilo*, but the result of a complex operation performed by the emanated attributes of the *En-Sof*,
the *Sefiroth*.

3. The *Sefiroth* are a bridge connecting the finite
universe with the infinite God.

There are two main subdivisions under which Kabbalism falls: the speculative & the practical. The
speculative branch deals essentially with philosophical considerations, whereas the practical, sometimes
also called the magical, stresses the mystical value
of Hebrew words & letters. It is this last description
which has gained for Kabbalism and Judaism in
general a great misunderstanding, which must be
discussed here briefly.

Jewish magic has never been anything but the
invocation of the benefic powers through the vehicle
of the holy names of God and his angels. The Talmud was the first to make a distinction between
black & white magic; the black variety was forbid-
den by the Bible in a number of places under penalty
of death. So-called white magic, the variety which
allowed the employment of sorcery to further *religious* needs, was in many cases condoned. The famous

Black magic
& white
magic

The relationship of the seventy-two spirits (or kings) of the Goetia to the cardinal points.

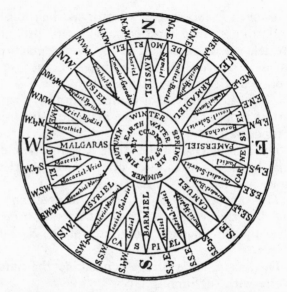

Magic seals used in ceremonial magic for the invocation of the various good & evil powers, from the *Lesser Key of Solomon.*

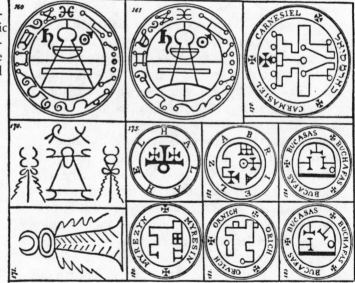

Sefer Yetsirah was often employed in such a manner. By the time of the Mediaeval period there were many texts containing various incantations, formulaes, & rituals. In other words, Jewish magic existed long before the appearance of what is now called Kabbalism. One of the most famous of these texts was the *Testament of Solomon* (not to be confused with the infamous *Key of Solomon*) which listed the names of the demons responsible for a variety of illnesses, along with the cures.

The Star of David, Solomon's Seal

The mediaeval Christians, owing to their thorough misunderstanding of the principles which underlay early Jewish magic, were at one & the same time terrified & fascinated by such texts. Magic had existed for some time in Christendom, but the Christians, already hostile to the seemingly strange ways of Judaism, were quick to call the Jews master magicians; not just a few Jews here & there, but all Jews. Did their Old Testament in so many words not say that King Solomon was a magician? The only problem with this questionable Christian praise was that they awarded the title of master magicians to the Jews within the context of their own understanding of magic.

The Christian treated magic as infernal, as an art of the Devil, taught by the Devil. In every instance the magic practiced by the non-Jews of Europe was deliberately blasphemous of the Church. The magic of the non-Jew was a paean to the Devil, and the practices were considered more effective the more obscenely they were performed. Magical powers were conferred on the practitioner by the Devil himself or his demons, & practically all the powers conferred can today be described within the context of psychopathology. This state of affairs

Magic as the art of the devil

The form of the magic circle of Solomon, "the which he made that he might preserve himself therein from the malice of the evil spirits."

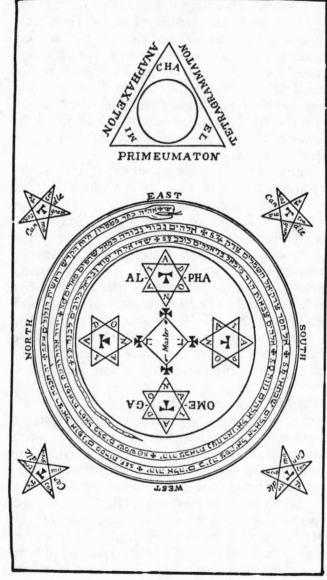

was promoted by the Church itself in its obsessive concern with sex & its demeaning attitude towards women.

A cursory examination of the *Malleus Malleficarum* *(The Witches' Hammer)*, that famous handbook of the Inquisition so thoughtfully prepared by the two Dominican priests, Sprenger & Kramer, will bear this out. The Devil worked through women & women worked their evil through sex. It has been estimated that by the time the Inquisition had run its course throughout Europe several million people had been executed for the practice of witchcraft, the sister of magic. We can only assume many Jews met the flames.

Torturing of Jews accused as heretics and perpetrators of Black Magic. From a woodcut, 1475.

In contrast, the practice of magic by the Jew was always performed *within* the framework of the Jewish religion, & was never satanic. True, as history moves on we find satanic texts bearing the names of Hebrew demons, & even the name of God, but close examination reveals that such products were the invention of non-Jews borrowing the terminology of Jewish magic, but not its intent.

Therefore, the few instances in this book where the term magic appears should be understood against the background of what has just been said. This point must be emphasized for there still exists today the idea that the magic of Kabbalism is the magic of the Christian kind. There is a similar problem with what, for want of a better term, I call Christian Kabbalism.

There exist innumerable texts in the West purporting to outline the fundamentals of Kabbalism, which actually obscure its principal theories. This is not to say that a great deal of Christian Kabbalism is not without merit & invention, but rather that

it abounds with topics generally foreign to Kabbalism & which on the whole have come to dominate
its characteristically Jewish elements.

Christian Kabbalism embellishes Kabbalistic doctrine with Christian dogmas such as the concept of the
Christ & the Trinity. Add to this an insatiable involvement with astrological matters, a topic to be found in
Jewish Kabbalism but of secondary or tertiary importance, & a curious disregard for Old Testament scripture & its Kabbalistic interpretation, a prominent feature of later Jewish Kabbalism—& you have a good
thumbnail sketch of what Christian Kabbalism looks
like.

Because so much attention has been given in other
works of Kabbalism to topics quite alien to Jewish
mysticism, this work will attempt to concentrate
on Kabbalism as a Jewish phenomenon alone. For
this reason the reader will find at the beginning
of the book a section unknown in practically every
work on Kabbalism printed in the past two centuries: an outline of the literature of the Jewish
religion.

What I will attempt to give in this book is a
simple presentation of the Kabbalah as it emerged
in the history of Jewish mysticism and an outline
of the basic doctrines of Kabbalism with as little
interpretation as possible. The background, literature & history of Kabbalism will occupy the first
part. Included will be an outline of the mystical
significations of the Hebrew alphabet given us in
the *Sefer Yetsirah* or *Book of Creation*, & an account
of the emanationist doctrine of the four worlds.
§Part II, chapter 1 will be a detailed presentation
of two concepts central to the whole of Kabbalism:
the *En-Sof* & the *Sefiroth*. Part II, chapter 2 will
contain information generally ascribed to the practi-

cal or magical branch of Kabbalism: the various forms of alphabetical permutations employed by the Kabbalists. The final chapter of Part II will deal with the essence of man, the soul & the *Shekhinah*.

I have kept Part III, entitled The Kabbalah Today, for most of my interpretative remarks. There I have attempted to discuss the relevance of the Kabbalah to twentieth-century man, in the hope that the reader may discern its implications.

The six-pointed star of creation

"The three first. (Salt, Sulphur, & Mercury.) The Triangle in Nature. The inferior, restless Part of Nature. The Properties of Darkness. The Root of Fire. The Wheel of Nature . . . The Hellish World, if in a Creature divorced from the Three on the Right . . ." Number two in a series, from *The Works of Jacob Behmen*.

Part One
The Background of the Kabbalah

The Ark
within its
cherubim,
the beings
supposedly
seen by
Moses kneel-
ing at the
footstool of
God. In gen-
eral appear-
ance it is
probable that
they re-
semble the
famous cher-
ubim of Eze-
kiel. From
Calumer, *Dic-
tionary of the
Holy Bible,*
London,
1800.

Chapter One. The Traditional Literature of the Jewish Religion

ECAUSE this book is intended as a handbook for the student of Kabbalism, an attempt will be made to provide the reader with as much as possible of the material he will need for his preliminary excursions. For this reason included here is a very brief outline not only of the literature of the mystical tradition of the Jewish people but that of the Rabbinical tradition as well.

The basic doctrines of Kabbalism

The principle literature we must outline will be that of the *Torah, Talmud, Mishna, Gemara, Midrash, Halakhah & Aggadah*.

THE TORAH
§The term *torah* (law) refers to a written Law & an oral Law. The written *Torah* is comprised of The Pentateuch, the first five books of the Old Testament, that is, the Books of Moses. This designation distinguishes the *Torah* from the other two main divisions of the Hebrew Bible—the *Prophets (Neviim)* & the *Hagiographa*. The *Hagiographa* is composed of the following eleven books: Psalms, Proverbs, Job, the Five Scrolls (Song of Songs, Ruth, Lamentations, Ecclesiastes, Esther), Daniel, Ezra, Nehemiah & Chronicles. The *Torah* covers the judicial, moral & ceremonial areas

The written Law & the oral Law

Noah & his Zodiacal Ark, a symbol & allegory of the early Holy Catholic Church. The ark is divided into eleven main sections, subdivided into three stories (Heaven, Man, Earth), making the sacred number thirty-three. Two openings are shown in the ark — the main door through which the animal lives descend into physical existence, & a small window at the crown of the head through which the spirit gains liberty. From Isaac Myer, *Qabbalah,* Philadelphia, 1888.

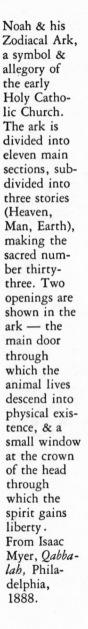

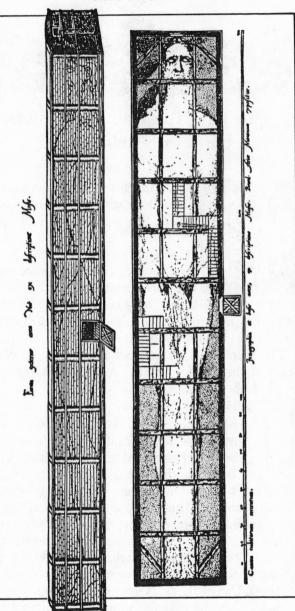

of Judaism, the rules & regulations by which the whole of Jewish life was guided.

It was believed that when Moses received the written Law (*Torah she-bi-khetav*) on Mount Sinai, he was also given the oral Law (*Torah she-be-al-peh*). In Rabbinical tradition the two *Torahs* are thought of as one, each dependent on & completing the other. The oral *Torah* constitutes everything that has been said by scholars or sages in their discussions of the written *Torah*. What is particularly to be noticed for the purposes of our study is the fact that the *Torah*, long before the recording of mystical speculations on the book took place, was thought of as containing a magical structure. This idea became the central point for later Kabbalistic speculation.

Moses ben Nahman (Nahmanides), the Spanish Talmudist, Kabbalist & Bible commentator (1194-1270) wrote that the entire *Torah* was composed of the names of God & that the division of the words contained in it could be further divided to yield esoteric names. Another Spanish Kabbalist, Moses de Leon, wrote that the entire *Torah* was the single holy & mystical name of God. (It was believed generally that the order of the *Torah* actually contained the secret life of God.)

But the most striking statement about the creation of the written *Torah* is to be found in a statement made by the founder of the Hasidic movement in Poland & Russia, Baal-Shem Tov. He proposed that the *Torah* existed originally as an incoherent jumble of letters & that the phrases, sentences, words, sections & chapters which now exist came into existence at the time that the events described took place. For example, the written passage describing the creation of Adam automatically arranged itself into its present form as his creation took place. If any of the events which took place in the creation of Adam had been different, the written account would have been different as well. Historical events, in other words, were not predetermined by God. What was predetermined, however, were the number of coordinates or letters contained in the written *Torah*. Because not so much as a vowel point can be added or subtracted from the *Torah*, & because it is thought of as a living organism reflective of the secret life of God himself, what we have is a receptacle for divine energy. The number of the coordinates represents a quantum of energy, of spirit. That is to say, the creation had allotted to the written *Torah* a specific quantum of spirit, & that the spirit allotted it is only one aspect of divinity. We shall, during the course of this book, discover that this aspect is the feminine

The thirty-two characters or co-ordinates of the Hebrew alphabet.

principle of God.

Furthermore, it was believed by the later Kabbalists that the *Torah* contained 600,000 different meanings & aspects, one for each of the 600,000 primordial souls present in every generation of Israel. To each of these souls one letter of the *Torah* is assigned as their own property. This letter is the individual's root & determines the way in which the *Torah* will be revealed to him. Its meaning is reserved specifically for him & no one else.

Several chapters could be devoted to discussing the theories which grew up around the existence of the *Torah* in both rabbinical & mystical traditions within Judaism, but this brief outline is not the place for it.

THE TALMUD

§ The word *Talmud* is a comprehensive term for the *Mishna* & the *Gemara* (to be discussed below) when the two are thought of as a unit. In this sense the *Talmud* is a compendium of sixty-three tractates containing the discussions & interpretation of Biblical laws by the rabbinical community. In essence, it is a history of the national & religious experience of the Jews covering a period of one thousand years.

A history of national & religious experience

There are in existence two *Talmuds*: the Palestinian *Talmud* & the Babylonian *Talmud*. The Palestinian *Talmud* was completed in the fourth century of the Christian era (300-400 c.e.), the Babylonian *Talmud* about a century later. Neither of them as they exist today are complete. The Babylonian recension (revision) has received more continuous & intensive study than the Palestinian & is by far the larger of the two—2,500,000 words to the Palestinian's 750,000.

The Mishna §The Hebrew word *mishna* is derived from the root meaning 'to repeat,' & is extended to mean 'to learn' or 'to teach' by repetition. The term *mishna* came to have the meaning of teaching by oral repetition:

'For upon the first day of the first month began he to go up from Babylon, & on the first day of the fifth month came he to Jerusalem . . ., For Ezra had prepared his heart to seek the law of the Lord, & to do it, & to teach in Israel statues & judgments.' (Ezra *vii*, 9-10).

The return of Ezra & his companions from the Babylonian Exile marked the beginning of a new tradition of religious study. It was Ezra's decision to make the *Torah* the foundation stone of Judaic life that eventually led to the voluminous produce of later commentators of the *Torah*. Around him arose a band of teachers whose sole purpose was the interpretation & teaching of the Law in the belief that it ultimately had to be the basic authority in the life of the community if they were to survive. In order for this to take place, it was necessary that the written Law of Moses become supplemented by oral explanation, or oral Law. It was their task, they felt, to effect the transition from the word to the act by means of interpretation & discussion. The *Torah* was not to be added to, but enlarged upon. The first attempt at this is recorded in Nehemiah *viii*:

'And all the people gathered themselves together . . ., And Ezra the priest brought the law before the congregation & . . . read in the book in the law of God distinctly, *and gave the sense, & caused them to understand* the reading . . . Also day by day, from the first day unto the last day, he

read in the book of the law of God.' (*my italics*).
In this manner the oral Law rapidly expanded
into a moral & legal system exclusively entrusted
to memory. There are some indications that early
attempts were made to record the teachings of the
teachers, but many felt that such notations, because
they were in writing, actually constituted an addition to the *Torah*, rather than an amplification.
Because it was understood that the Law was complete, many retreated from what they believed
would be a blasphemous act. It was thought that
the recording of the oral Law would place it on
an equal footing with the written *Torah*. However,
another & far stronger reason was that once the
oral teachings were recorded they would lose the
vitality of the spoken word & would in time bring
an end to oral discussion. But it was only a matter
of time before the interpretations of the *Torah* by
the teachers would reach proportions too great for
even the ablest of memories. This oral · tradition
finally evolved into exegetical methods which in
themselves demanded a computer-like memory in
that they subsequently came to the grand total of
thirty-two. The bewildering accumulation of many-
faceted interpretations finally became recorded by
rabbi Judah ha-Nasi at the end of the second century
of the Christian era in a work called the *Mishna*.
The *Mishna* was thought of as a textbook rather
than a code. Its purpose was to make available
the essence of the oral Law as it was then taught.
It is not a running commentary on the *Torah*, but
rather a structure of Law not associated with specific
scriptural verse or passage. Verses from the *Torah*
may at times be cited as proof in a particular argument, but the resulting legalistic statement was

not to be understood as a commentary on the passage quoted.

The *Mishna* is composed of six main divisions or orders, each order including a number of tractates or volumes, the total of which is sixty-three. Each tractate in turn is divided in perakim, or chapters. The six orders are as follows:

1.*Zeraim* (Seeds) §Containing eleven tractates mainly concerned with agricultural laws.

2.*Moed* (Appointed Times or Festivals)§Containing twelve tractates dealing with laws of sabbath, high holy days, passover & the paschal sacrifice & other laws having to do with feasts.

3.*Nashim* (Women) §Containing seven tractates dealing with marriage, divorce, unfaithfulness, etc.

4.*Nezikin* (Damages) §Containing ten tractates having to do with phases of criminal & civil law.

5.*Kodashim* (Holy Things) §Containing eleven tractates dealing with various forms of temple service.

6.*Toharot* (Purifications) §Containing twelve tractates dealing with laws of ritual purity & impurity.

Gemara §No sooner was the *Mishna* completed than it was felt that a considerable portion was no longer applicable to the times. Whereas the *Mishna* had been created to complement & enlarge upon the wisdom of the Bible, the rabbinic community now felt it necessary to comment & enlarge upon the *Mishna* itself. Where the *Mishna* was given to concise statements without rhetoric or ornamentation, the *Gemara* consists of complete transcripts of the discourses which took place in the academies, much of it non-legal in character & ancedotal. The text of the *Gemara* is composed of questions & answers.

MIDRASH

§The *Midrash* is the rabbinical commentary dealing in the main with the biblical books & is an extension of the oral Law. Essentially, the *Midrash* is a running commentary on biblical verse which it uses as a starting point for amplification. In contrast to the *Mishna*, it does not attempt to set up legalistic interpretations which could stand independent of the *Torah*. Its aim is a literal interpretation, extension & reconstruction of Scripture.

HALAKHAH & AGGADAH

§*Halakhah* translates into law, *Aggadah* into lore or legend. A negative definition of *Halakhah* is 'anything which is not *Aggadah*.' The literature of the *Halakhah* stems from the Talmudic & later periods & deals with religious, ethical, civil & criminal law. It is the abstract formulation of Jewish law & rests upon the Judaic premise that God is the law-giver. It

א	ב	ג	ד	ה	ו	ז	ח	ט
Aleph	Bayt Vayt	Ghimel	Dallet	Hay	Vav or Waw	Zayn	Hhayt	Tayt
1	2	3	4	5	6	7	8	9
י	כ	ל	מ	נ	ס	ע	פ	צ
Yod	Kaf Khaf	Lammed	Mem	Noun	Sammekh	Ayn	Pay Phay	Tsadde
10	20	30	40	50	60	70	80	90
ק	ר	ש	ת	ך	ם	ן	ף	ץ
Qof	Raysh	Seen Sheen	Tav	final Khaf	final Mem	final Noun	final Phay	final Tsadde
100	200	300	400	500	600	700	800	900

The letter numbers: The Hebrew alphabet & its numerical values.

was the Halakhic tradition which eventually gave birth to such compendiums as the *Mishna* & *Gemara*.

The *Aggadah* constitutes the non-legal portions of the *Talmud* & *Midrash* & there is little Aggadic material in the *Mishna*. The traditional literature is made up of theological speculation, legends, folklore, moral & ethical teachings, prayers, interpretations of dreams & philosophical considerations about man's relationship to the cosmos. It is from this tradition that the Kabbalists sprang.

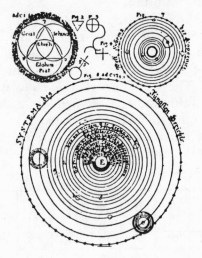

Chapter Two The Mystical Literature of the Jewish Religion

THE EARLIEST recognized form of Kabbalistic literature is to be found in the tradition of the *Merkabah* mystics. These mystics concerned themselves with the *Merkabah* or Throne Chariot of God which they believed they could reach in a shamanistic ascent, or in some cases descent, through a series of heavenly halls. During the period of the Second Temple (circa 538 b.c.e.-70 c.e.) an esoteric doctrine concerning the first chapter of Genesis & the first chapter of Ezekiel was current. The doctrinal statements of this school presently exist in scattered fragmentary form, some of it in brief tracts, the entire body indicating that they are only a portion of a voluminous output. What is left is the product of editors working sometime between the fifth & sixth centuries. The greater portion of the tracts are called *Hekhaloth Books* & contain descriptions of the heavenly palaces or halls (*hekhaloth*) through which the mystic was believed to have passed on his way to the *Merkabah*. The most important of these works are the *Greater Hekhaloth* & *Lesser Hekhaloth*.

The tractates falling under the general category

The literature of Merkabah mysticism

The Vision of Ezekiel was the central fable of *Merkabah* mysticism, the descriptions of the *Merkabah* or Throne Chariot being the focus point of all meditation. From *The "Bear" Bible*.

of the *Lesser Hekhaloth* have as their principal speaker rabbi Akiba & appear to be earlier in origin than the *Greater Hekhaloth*. The emphasis in the former is on the ascent of the mystic in his travels towards the heavenly halls. Those falling under the general category of the *Greater Hekhaloth* describe the mystic's jorney through the seven palaces lying beyond the seven heavens which he would have earlier had to traverse in his movement towards the *Merkabah*.

The *Lesser Hekhaloth* & the *Greater Hekhaloth*

These works also contain lengthy descriptions of the secret names and seals the initiate had to have either upon his person or in his mind. These guaranteed his safe transition through the heavenly halls, each stage of his ascent demanding a different seal & sacred name with which he could combat the demons of the newly entered portal. It is in this body of literature where the last stages of the mystic's upward flight are also outlined. There we find descriptions of what he may expect to encounter as he passes through the sixth & seventh gates of the halls. The majority of these descriptions are presented as the discussions held between the gatekeeper of the hall & the mystical traveller. The principal speaker in the tractates of the *Greater Hekhaloth* is rabbi Ishmael.

One of the most famous & familiar of *Hekhaloth* books is the *Book of Enoch*,[1] edited and translated in 1928 by a Swedish scholar, Hugo Odeberg. This work contains legends centering on the person of Enoch who, according to tradition, was a cobbler. Because he dedicated his life to piety, God took him up into the heavens where he was raised to the first rank of angels & turned into an angel himself, called Metatron, The Prince of the World, an angel with flesh of fire, eyelashes of lightning

[1] Hugo Odeburg, *3 Enoch* or the *Hebrew Book of Enoch*.

[2] G. H. Box & R. H. Charles, *The Apocalypse of Abraham and the Ascension of Isaiah.*

& eyes of flaming torches.

Another work which falls into the tradition of *Merkabah* mysticism is the *Apocalypse of Abraham*,[2] translated & edited by Box & Charles in 1918. This is a record of how Abraham ascended to the *Merkabah* itself & heard the voice of God commanding him to ascend further.

The literature of the *Merkabah* mystics is extensive but most of it is still unpublished, & very little of that is translated. Once this formidable task is accomplished, however, our knowledge of Jewish mysticism will be considerably advanced. In the meantime the student who wishes to pursue the study of this tradition of gnostical speculation should make use of Gershom G. Scholem's small but thorough *Jewish Gnosticism, Merkabah Mysticism, & Talmudic Tradition.*

THE SEFER YETSIRAH OR BOOK OF CREATION

§ Many Kabbalists consider that this work is the foundation stone of their study & that without it the mysteries of Kabbalism may not be understood. The *Sefer Yetsirah* is one of the books which arose from *Maaseh Bereshith*, the esoteric discipline dealing with theories of cosmogony & cosmology. Early rabbinic tradition warned that such information was not for the public's eyes & that, ideally, the information contained in such speculative considerations should be passed from master to disciple by word of mouth. This prohibition was imposed on the *Sefer Yetsirah* because the gnostic material which it contained, if interpreted incorrectly, could be taken as heretical.

The ten *Sefiroth* & the Hebrew alphabet

The date ascribed to the writings which comprise

the *Sefer Yetshirah* is somewhere between the third and sixth century c.e.[3] The *Sefer Yetsirah* has only six chapters & even in the fullest editions contains no more than sixteen hundred words.

The doctrine outlined within it was revealed to the Patriarch Abraham. After he perceived & understood the nature of the revelation, he recorded it. Then & only then did God reveal himself to the Patriarch making at that time his covenant with him. Rabbinical legend tells us another version: Abraham did not commit the revelation to writing but instead transmitted it orally to his sons. Whichever is the case, the final chapter of the *Sefer Yetsirah* reveals plainly that its creation was the result of a visionary experience.

The first part of this two-part vision concerns itself with the ten *Sefiroth* or numbers, while the second is devoted to the establishment of the Hebrew alphabet as a divine instrument of creation which in its totality is the foundation of all things. Because we shall spend an entire chapter discussing the *Sefiroth* & their place in Kabbalistic thought we shall here concern ourselves only with the nature of the divine alphabet.

It is with the second chapter of the *Sefer Yetsirah* that the exposition begins:

'The twenty-two letters & sounds comprise the Foundation of all things. There are three mothers, seven doubles & twelve simples. These three Mothers are *Aleph, Mem & Shin*—Air, Water, & Fire.'[4]

The three primordial substances of air, water, & fire were believed to constitute the whole of creation. Air was the spirit which mediated between the heavens which were composed of fire, & earth which

[3] The first publication of this seminal work was in the Latin of Gulielmus Postellus, Paris, 1552. The first publication was in Mantua, 1565, in which edition the text was accompanied by five commentaries, purported to have been written by Moses Nahmanides, Abraham B. David, Eleazer of Worms, Moses Botarel & Saadia Gaon, (see Bibliography).

[4] Westcott, *Sefer Yetsirah*, p18.

was composed of water. The reasoning behind this association with the three letters *aleph, mem, & shin* lay in the following considerations:

The letter *aleph* is an aspirate, a letter pronounced with a silent breathing, so the element air is assigned to this letter.

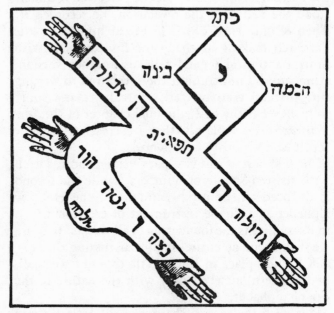

The letter *Aleph* is symbolic of air & may be thought of as a breath-spirit. From Athanasius Kircher, *Oedipus Aegyptiacus*, Rome, 1652.

The letter *mem* belongs to the class of mutes, letters which are not accompanied by any sound in their production. The pronunciation of this letter is a pressing together of the lips. The reasoning behind the associations of this letter with the element water is more difficult to see at first sight: in all creation the creature most symbolic of silence or muteness is the fish, & the fish is the chief occupant of water. In addition to this the first letter of the Hebrew word for fish is *mem*. Hence, the assignment of the letter *mem* to the element water.

The letter *shin* belongs to the class of sibilants. Letters in this class are pronounced with a hissing sound. 'fire' in Hebrew is *esh*, spoken with accent placed on the two consonants.

These three letters represent the divisions into

which the twenty-two letters of the Hebrew alphabet naturally fit: mutes, sibilants & aspirates. They are the mothers of the remaining nineteen letters of the alphabet. By associating the three mothers with the three elements, the *prima materia* of all things, one obtains the mystical statement that the creation of the cosmos is the result of the creation of language. The alphabet is the instrument of creation itself.

'The three Mothers are *Aleph, Mem & Shin*. The

Kabbalistic & magic alphabets were invented by early philosophers to conceal their tenets & doctrines from the profane. Probably the most famous is the *Malachim*, supposedly derived from the constelations. From Francis Barrett, *The Magus*, London, 1801.

Shin: the head; fire; summer season

Mem: the stomach; water; winter season

Aleph: the chest; air; spring & autumn seasons

[5] Wescott, *Sepher Yetsirah,* p. 19.

heavens were created out of the substance of Fire; the earth from Water, & the Air from the Spirit which mediates between the two.'[5]

In addition to being symbolic of the elements, the three mothers also define the temporal year: the element fire (*shin*) corresponds with the summer season; the element water (*mem*) corresponds with the winter season, & the element air (*aleph*) corresponds with the seasons of spring & autumn. A further correspondence assigned these three letters are the three divisions of the human body: the head was formed by fire (*shin*), the stomach by water (*mem*), and the chest by air (*aleph*). This makes man a microcosm.

Besides the three mothers there are seven double letters typifying the opposites which go to make up the cosmos. The letters are called double because they represent two different sounds, the one positive & strong, the other negative & soft. The seven double letters are *beth* (B), *gimel* (G), *daleth* (D), *kaph* (K), *pe* (P), *resh* (R), & *tau* (T, TH). Each letter in turn represents a bipolar unit: life & death, peace & war, knowledge & ignorance, wealth & poverty, grace & sin, fertility & sterility, & power & slavery. They also represent seven positions in space: above, below, east, west, north, south & the holy palace in the midst of them.

In addition to these significations we are told that with the aid of the seven double letters God produced & formed the planets, the days of the week, & the gates of the soul. The gates of the soul are the two eyes, two ears, two nostrils & the mouth.

The remaining letters of the alphabet, according to the *Sefer Yetsirah*, are twelve simple letters corresponding to the senses & their various states, &

to the points of the compass. The twelve letters are: *he* (H), the foundation of sight; *vau* (V or U), the foundation of hearing; *zain* (Z), the foundation of the sense of smell; *cheth* (CH), the foundation of speech; *teth* (TH), the foundation of the taste & digestive organs; *yod* (Y), the foundation of sexual

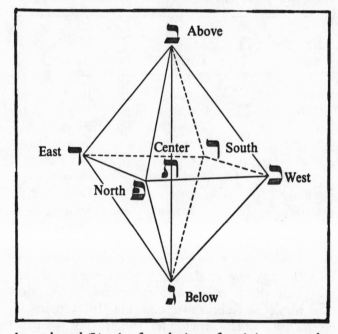

The seven double letters give birth to the directions of space, thereby causing order to appear in the midst of the original chaos.

love; *lamed* (L), the foundation of activity or work; *nun* (N), the foundation of movement; *samekh* (S), the foundation of anger; *ain*, the foundation of mirth (O); *tzaddi* (TZ), the foundation of imagination, & *qoph* (Q), the foundation of sleep. The assignment of these letters to the compass points in this instance is unusual in that it suggests the existence of two spaces. Furthermore, because the designations of the above referring to the macrocosm and the below referring to the microcosm or profane world lie within the range of the human body (the various senses & moods are associated with them), it follows that man is intimately connected with the universe. Furthermore, the twelve simple letters are emblematic of the zodiacal signs:

The twelve
simple letters
& the zodiac

he		Aries	♈	March
vau		Taurus	♉	April
zain		Gemini	♊	May
heth		Cancer	♋	June
teth		Leo	♌	July
yod		Virgo	♍	August
lamed		Libra	♎	September
nun		Scorpio	♏	October
samèkh		Sagittarius	♐	November
ain		Capricorn	♑	December
tzaddi		Aquarius	♒	January
qoph		Pisces	♓	February

In closing, the student should take note of the fact that the *Sefer Yetsirah* in no way represents the whole of Kabbalistic doctrine. In it there is no mention of the other chief principles of Kabbalism: the *En-Sof*, Adam Kadmon, or the *Shekhinah*. Technically speaking, it does not even contain mention of the *Sefiroth* as they are understood in the fully developed sense. What it speaks of in its first chapter are the operations of numbers, or what will eventually be understood as the numerical operations of the *Sefiroth*. Nowhere is there any mention of the rich system of mystical meanings which arise in the fully developed doctrine of the *Sefiroth*. This

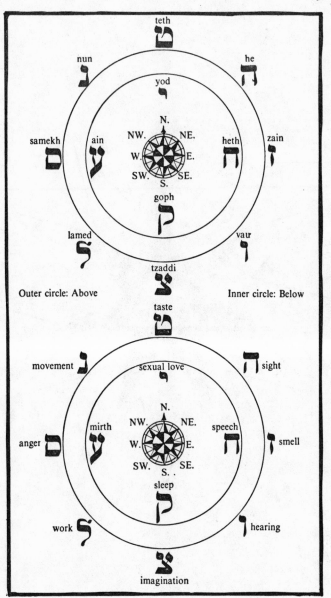

Outer circle: Above

Inner circle: Below

The twelve simple letters correspond to the entire range of sensate experience.

A fanciful depiction of a passage in the *Sefer Yetsirah.* The triangle contains the three mother letters which give birth to the double letters, symbolic of the planets & the heavens.

will be dealt with at length in chapter 1 of Part II. Meanwhile, we will continue this introduction to the literature of the *Kabbalah* with the second of its two major works, the *Zohar*.

THE SEFER ZOHAR OR BOOK OF SPLENDOUR

§The full title of this work is the *Sefer Ha-Zohar*, which translates into *Book of Splendour*.[6] It has become a canonical text. For many centuries it ranked beside the *Talmud* & the Bible in importance & was the only Kabbalistic text to have been awarded this status by the rabbinical community. The nature of its authorship has been for several centuries a point for scholarly argument, but it has now been satisfactorily shown that the author of this monumental work was Moses de Leon (Moses ben Shemtob de Leon) who first began to circulate editions of the book in Guadalajara sometime between 1280 or 1290. He claimed that it represented the writings of Rabbi Simeon bar Yohai of the second century c.e. It is a commentary on the first five books of Moses & for this reason is also known as *The Midrash of Rabbi Simeon bar Yohai*.

The published editions of the *Zohar* occupy some 2,500 pages & are broken down, after Scholem, into the following books or parts:

1. A large untitled section primarily made up of commentaries on passages from the *Torah*. This material makes up a portion of the Simon & Sperling English translation.

2. '*Sifra di-Tseniutha*' or 'Book of Concealment.' ('The Book of Concealed Mystery' in Mathers' translation.) In its original this section is only six pages long. This book concerns itself with the manifestation of the *Macroprosopus*, the Greater Countenance,

[6] The first edition of the *Sefer Zohar* was published in Mantua in 1558. It was followed by two more editions in Cremona, 1560 & Lublin, 1623. (See Bibliography p. 284).

The nineteen parts of the *Sefer Zohar*

יהוה

The *Tetra-grammaton*

The nineteen parts of the *Sefer Zohar*

which came into being as a symbol of harmony after the equilibrium of the universe had been established. This *Macroprosopus* is ever-concealed but expands itself to yield the *Microprosopus*, or Lesser Countenance who is known by the *Tetragrammaton*, *IHVH*. The *Macroprosopus* is known only by the exclamation, 'I am,' (*yah*).

The idea of the *Macroprosopus* as a *deus absconditus* or hidden God is suggested by the depiction of this God only in profile. The archetype which is representative of, but not reflective of, the manifest God, is shown full-face under the form of *Microprosopus*. 'The Book of Concealed Mystery' comprises the first part of Rosenroth's *Kabbalah Denudata*, as translated by Mathers.

3. '*Idra Rabba*' or 'The Greater Assembly.' This section is a development and explanation of the information contained in the preceding chapter and is presented as a record of the discourse of rabbi Simeon bar Yohai to a congregation of his disciples. Much of this section deals with the description of each feature of the *Macropropus*. The ecstatic tension caused by the rabbi's revelations increases to the point where, at the end, we are told three of his disciples die in ecstatic trance.

'The Greater Assembly' comprises the second part of Rosenroth's *Kabbala Denudata*.

4. '*Idra Zutta*' or 'The Lesser Assembly'. This section is a recapitulation of 'The Greater Assembly' with much speculation on the *Sefiroth*. It is at this time that Rabbi Simeon bar Yohai himself dies in an ecstatic trance leaving behind the surviving six disciples to record his revelations.

This section comprises the third and last portion of Rosenroth's *Kabbalah Denudata*.

5. *'Idra di-be-Mashkana'* or 'The Assembly before a Lecture on the *Torah*.' This section is an exposition on the mystical aspects of prayer. It does not exist in translation at this time.

6. *'Hekhaloth'* or 'The Palaces of Light.' This section is a description of the structure of the seven halls of light of *Merkabah* mysticism that a soul perceives either after his death or during devout prayer.

The title page of *Kabbala Denudata*, Sulzbach, 1677

7. *'Raza de-Razin'* or 'The Secret of Secrets.' This section deals with physiognomy, chiromancy & the soul's connection with the body.

8. *'Sava Demishpatim'* or 'The Discourse of the Old Man.' In this section an old donkey driver discusses the doctrine of metempsychosis with the rabbi. This, together with the following two sections, is included in the Simon & Sperling translation.

9. *'Yenuka'* or 'The Discourse of the Child.' Here, a young student thought of as ignorant by his parents is sent by his mother to receive benediction at the hands of the Rabbis. He goes, only to reveal to the Rabbis profound mysteries of the *Torah*.

10. *'Rev Methivtha'* or 'The Academy Head.' A record of a journey through paradise undertaken by some members of the Academy, & a lecture by the head of the Academy on the destiny of the soul.

11. *'Sithre Torah'* or 'The Mysteries of the Torah.' General allegorical & mystical interpretations of passages from the *Torah*.

12. *'Mathnithin & Tosefta'* or 'Small Additional Pieces.' Again, a general discussion of various Kabbalistic topics.

13. 'Commentary on the Song of Solomon'

14. *'Kav Ha-Middah'* or 'The Standard of Measure.'

Discourse on the meaning of Deuteronomy vi, 4.

15. '*Sithre Othioth*' or 'Secrets of Letters.' This section concerns itself with the mystical letters composing the name of God.

16. '*Midrash Ha-Neelam*' or 'The Mystical Midrash.' A discussion of the destiny and nature of the soul, along with a general explanation of certain scriptural passages by the science of number.

17. '*Midrash Ha-Neelam Midrash Ruth*' or 'On the Book of Ruth.' A commentary on the Book of Ruth.

18. '*Raya Mehemna*' or 'The Faithful Shepherd.' This & the following section are later interpolations & are not the creation of Moses de Leon. ·

In this section we find the rabbi in discourse with the Faithful Shepherd, Moses, & the prophet Elias. Of all the supplementary texts of the *Zohar* this is the longest and most popular. Its content is primarily an interpretation of the Mosaic commandments along allegorical lines.

19. '*Tikkune Zohar*' or 'New Supplements of the Zohar.' A commentary on the first book of the *Torah*.

What should be borne in mind for our purposes is that the Mathers translation of Rosenroth's *Kabbalah Denudata, The Kabbalah Unveiled*, is composed of sections 2, 3 & 4. The Simon & Sperling translation contains section 1 & 8-10. Sections 1-17 were written by Moses de Leon while 18 & 19 are later supplements by another hand.

THE OTHER MAIN WORKS OF KABBALISM

§ The Thirty-Two Paths of Wisdom § In 1642, Joannes Stephanus Rittangelius translated from the Hebrew a text dealing with the paths formed by the emanation of the divine principle through the *Sefiroth*. The nature of these paths as discussed in this little work will be dealt with in our chapter on the *Sefiroth*.

Pardes Rimmonim ('Orchard of Pomegranates') §Written by rabbi Moses Cordovero in 1548 & first published in Cracow, 1591, & then in Munkacs, 1906, this little work is a detailed exposition of Kabbalistic doctrines. Another work of Cordovero was *Shi'ur Komah* (which means measurement of height), Warsaw, 1883. In this latter work the system & theory of the *Sefiroth* was laid out in full. Unfortunately, there is no English translation of either work available.

Aesch Mezareph or Purifying Fire §Apart from a mention of this work in 1706 by Claverus in his work *Observations on the Most Useful Things in the World*, we have no way of being sure that it is *A Chymico-Kabbalistic treatise collected from the Kabbala Denudata of Knorr von Rosenroth* (the subtitle of the 1714 English translation of the work). If it were not for this early reference I would have been tempted to ascribe it to the hand of W. Wynn Westcott, the editor of the 1894 reprint & eponymous 'Sapere Aude' who conveniently added notes to this American edition.[7]

The *Aesch Mezareph* is an alchemical treatise & it is unclear whether it is the product of Hebrew or Christian Kabbalism. It sets out the system of the *Sefiroth* in alchemical terms, but was probably intended more as meditational instrument than as textbook of practical alchemy.[8]

Sefer Bahir or Book Bahir §Before ending this very brief survey of the major works of the Kabbalah, we must consider this obscure but influential work. The Book *Bahir* was compiled from earlier Kabballist

[7] W. Wynn Westcott, ed., *Aesch Mezareph or Purifying Fire.*

[8] See below, Part Two, ch. 1, p.166.

ist writings in Provence sometime during the last half of the twelfth century. It is important, from our point of view, because it contains the theory of *gilgul* or reincarnation & serves as a link between the neo-platonist doctrines of the early gnostics & the speculative theories of the mediaeval Kabbalists.[9]

[9] See below, Part Two, ch.3, pp. 201, 215-16.

The *Hekhaloth* books, the *Sefer Yetsirah*, the *Sefer Zohar* & the *Sefer Bahir* constitute the written core of what the Kabbalists themselves regard as *the* Kabbalah. There are countless other works, & we have mentioned only three of them. The reader who is interested in finding a more extensive selection should consult the bibliography in Gershom Scholem's *Major Trends in Jewish Mysticism*.

The manifestation of the Universal Monad known as *En-Sof*.

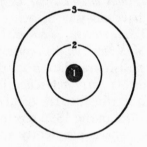

Chapter Three. The Nature & Origin of Kabbalism

HERE ARE two main branches of Kabbalistic thought: the speculative & the practical. The speculative branch concerns itself solely with the operations of the spiritual dimension of the universe, in an attempt to discover how it meshes with this world. Speculative Kabbalism aims also at revealing how man may find a place in both dimensions at one & the same time. The practical Kabbalah is primarily concerned with winning the energies of the spiritual world for the purposes of magical control. By employing the names & offices of the angels one may control the whole of nature & its powers. Practical Kabbalism greatly influenced the magic of Western Europe during the Mediaeval period, with the ambiguous results which were discussed in the introduction.

The roots of these branches may be traced back to two schools of mystical activity: that which concerned itself with the *Maaseh Bereshith* (History of Creation) & that which concentrated on the *Maaseh Merkabah* (History of the Divine Throne or Chariot). The latter, as has been seen, centered around the mystical adoration of the throne chariot of God as described in the first chapter of Ezekiel. These doctrines were carefully guarded during the Talmudic

"The Fourth Property of Eternal Nature. The Magic Fire. The Fire World. The First Principle. The Generation of the Cross. The Strength, Might & Power of Eternal Nature. The Abyss or Eternal Liberty's Opening in the dark World, breaking & consuming all the Strong Attraction of Darkness." Number three in a series, from the *Works of Jacob Behmen.*

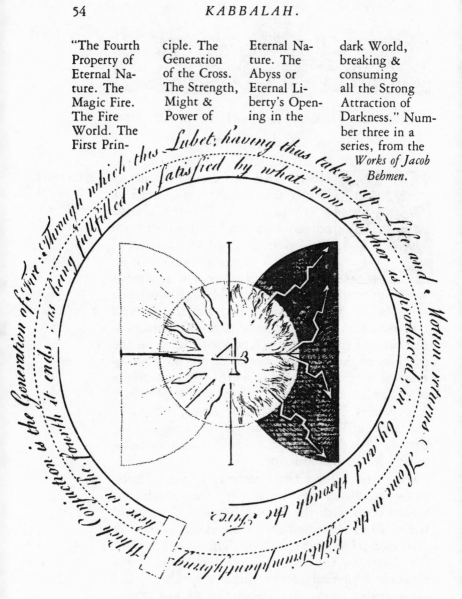

mudic period (135 b.c.e.-1035 c.e.), lest they be revealed to the uninitiated & in doing so lead to misunderstandings which could only lead to heresy. It is mentioned that rabbi Jochanan ben Zakkai was the father of *Merkabah* mysticism, & Rabbi Akiba that of *Maaseh Bereshith* mysticism. By the time of the establishment of the Gaonic Institution the city of Palestine had become the chief center of *Merkabah* mysticism, & Babylon the center of *Bereshith* speculations.

P RACTICAL KABBALISM
§ 'And above the firmament...was the likeness of a throne, as the appearance of a sapphire stone: & upon the likeness of the throne was the likeness as the appearance of a man above it ...This was the appearance of the likeness of the glory of the Lord. And when I saw it, I fell upon my face, & I heard a voice of one that spake.' (Ezekiel *i*, 26-8).

The journey
of the *Merka-bah*-rider

This scriptural passage was to serve as the keystone for the first & longest phase of Jewish mysticism, *Merkabah* mysticism, covering roughly the period 100 b.c.e. (before christian era) to 1000 c.e.

The term *Merkabah* means God's throne-chariot, and refers us to the chariot of Ezekiel's vision. The *Merkabah* mystic, or *Merkabah*-rider as he was sometimes called, had one goal: entry into the throne-world of the *Merkabah*, but this was no simple task, for the devotee had to pass through not only seven heavens to accomplish his ends but through seven *hekhaloth*, heavenly halls or mansions, before reaching the *Merkabah* itself in the seventh and last *hekhaloth*.

The preparation for this journey was the simplest of shamanistic techniques—fasting & repetitious

"The three Exalted, Tinctured, or Transmuted Properties of the Right Hand. The Kingdom of Love, Light, & Glory. The Second Principle. The Second Temperature . . . The Trinity manifested, which only now can be an Object of a created Understanding. Byss. Wisdom, Tincture." Number four in a series, from *The Works of Jacob Behmen.*

recitation of hymn & prayer. Once a state of trance was achieved, the *Merkabah*-rider then had to send his soul upwards—*downwards* according to later *Merkabah* mystics—in an attempt to pierce the veil surrounding the *Merkabah*. In order to protect himself from the demons & evil spirits which would attempt at every turn to destroy him, the devotee had to have prepared beforehand talismans, seals & magical incantations. Each successful passage through one of the seven palaces demanded yet more magical devices, & the devotee had to have at hand, in memory, incredibly long & difficult incantations to insure his safety.

Throughout the entire experience he was threatened with death. At one point he is caused to stand erect in space without his feet. The gate-keepers he would meet standing before each palace were enormous beings, taller than mountains, with lightning flashing from their eyes, scorching coals falling from their mouths & spheres of brilliant fire roaring from their nostrils, their dragon-like horses standing by drinking their fill from rivers of fire. It was to these beings that the devotee had to present his amulets, seals & secret passwords.

A mysticism of ecstasy

Much of the magical rituals of later Kabbalism had their origin in this early mysticism. *Merkabah* mysticism is the simplest form of Jewish mysticism we will discuss. It is quite simply a mysticism of ecstasy. The devotee sought nothing more than the vision of the *Merkabah*. No explicit doctrinal statements beyond accounts of their journeys into the heavens grew out of the experience, nor do we find the slightest hint of a developed system beyond that of simple shamanism & the later involvement with magic. The *Merkabah* rider did

"The four first figures were . . . to show . . . the Generation of Eternal Nature, which has a Beginning without Beginning, & an End without End. This fifth represents now, that this Great Royal Residence . . . was replenished at once with innumerable Inhabitants, All Glorious Flames of Fire . . ." Number five in a series, from *The Works of Jacob Behmen*.

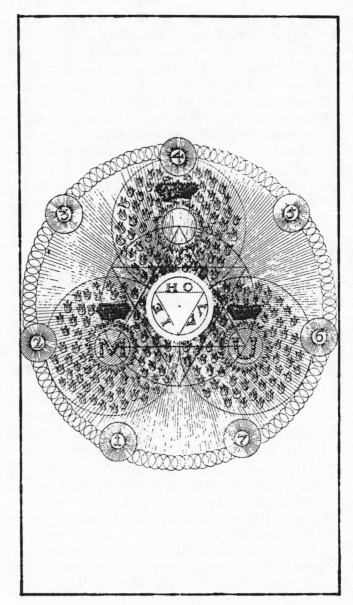

not attempt to see beyond the throne-kingdom or question its nature & origin. It was there. It was to be experienced, & nothing more. Clearly, the successful entry into the deepest realms of the seventh *hekhaloth* was efficacious for the spiritual development or completion of the devotee. However, no specific mention is made about the precise nature of the transformation which the *Merkabah* rider underwent.

No one in fairness can point to the sophistications of later Jewish mysticism & say this mystical school was a small event in the history of Jewish mysticism. These men who threw themselves headlong into the fire of the universe for no other reason than the desire to experience the Divine in all of its radiance set a courageous example which later mystics would have to follow. Lacking in philosophical or eschatological theories though *Merkabah* mysticism may be, it is not without that knowledge of the love of God which runs like a thread of fire through all later Kabbalism. That for close to a thousand years men were content to risk their lives & their minds for so seemingly simple a reason as the confirmation of a small passage in Biblical scripture only emphasizes the need man has to witness the Divine.

Man's need to witness the Divine

It was out of the mystical tradition of the *Merkabah*-riders & their involvement with angelology, talismans & magical incantations, not to mention the ritual putting on & taking off of sacramental robes, that the branch of practical Kabbalism originally sprang.

According to Eleazar of Worms (1165-1238), one of the earliest German Kabbalists, the literature of practical Kabbalism was introduced to Italy in

917 c.e. by a Babylonian scholar, Aaron ben
Samuel. Almost immediately upon his arrival he
imparted his mystical knowledge to the scholarly
Kalonymus family. When they moved to the Rhine-
land in 917 c.e. they established what is now referred to as German Kabbalism by some, and Early
Hasidism by others. Until the time of Eleazar of
Worms, the mystic doctrine transmitted by Aaron
ben Samuel had been considered the private property
of the Kalonymides. It was Judah ha-Hasid, the
Pious (died 1217), a member of the Kalonymides
family, who directed his pupil Eleazar to reveal
the oral & written doctrine of practical Kabbalism
to a larger audience.

The German branch of Kabbalism, practical Kabbalism, was ecstatic in nature & used as its primary
vehicle prayer, supplementing it with meditation
& contemplation, & adorning it with magical ritual.
Here we must remember that this branch of Kabbalism had its beginnings in *Merkabah* mysticism &
that much of its symbolism & theory was taken
directly from that tradition. The important difference between *Merkabah* mysticism & practical Kabbalism is that the latter no longer concerned itself
with the mystic's ascent to the throne of God, but
on prayer. The magical efficacy of the *word* took
precedence in this mysticism. The *Merkabah* mystic
had not concerned himself exclusively with fixed
formulae, but had instead lent himself to the spontaneous expression of his feelings while in trance.
Admittedly, magical incantations had to be learned
& recited by heart, but such practices were subsidiary
to the central objective of meditating on the divine
throne itself.

The German Kabbalists were, in contrast, concerned

cerned primarily with the esoteric meanings of fixed terms, & so much so that their counting & calculating of every word in their prayers & hymns eventually gave rise to three techniques of mystical speculation familiar to every student of Kabbalism: *Gematria, Notarikon,* & *Temura*, about which we will have much to say in a later chapter.[10] All in all, German Kabbalism, or Early Hasidism, was essentially an attempt to bring to the *Merkabah* tradition a new interpretation & focus.

The essential doctrines of this German school of mysticism may be broken down into three theories.

The first element in their thinking was the idea that God is too exalted for the mind of man to even begin to comprehend. His holiness & greatness is thought of as formless & may only be comprehended as that presence of God which is *hidden* in all things. But in order that he might be visible to angels & those men who have cultivated a constant awareness of God's presence, he allowed his glory to take shape in the form of a divine fire or light which only the prophets or mystics may know. This glory of God is called the *Kavod* & is understood by the mystics of this period to be not the creator himself, but the first creation, the *Shekhinah.*

Unable to approach God himself directly, the mystic could unite himself with his glory. The most striking point of this theory is that the *Kavod* was two-fold: one aspect was invisible & the other visible or *inner*, believed to be present in all creatures but without form, existing only as a voice.

The second element in German Kabbalism was the characterization of the figure believed to be seated on the Chariot Throne of the *Merkabah* mystics

Three themes of early Hasidism

[10] See below, Part Two, ch.2, pp.169-74.

tics: the cherub. This cherub is the *emanation* of God's invisible glory, his *Shekhinah*, whose flame encircles God & causes to come into being not only the cherub & the throne upon which he sits, but the human soul. Master of all forms, it was from the cherub's transformation into a human form that the model of man in the likeness of God was made.

Finally, the German mystics held that there were four worlds or domains: the domain of God's glory, the domain of angels, the domain of the animal soul & the domain of the intellectual soul.

These mystical pleasures could only be enjoyed if the devotee led a life of saintliness & humility & conducted his life in the path of self-abnegation & altruism. His duties to God were at no time allowed to supersede his duties to the community. Because of his connection with the *Kavod* he became all the more responsible to the spiritual needs of his people. The dynamism of this branch of Jewish mysticism lasted from about 1150-1250.

The Kabbalism of Provence & Spain

SPECULATIVE KABBALISM
§Speculative Kabbalism had its origins in Babylonia but the spark which lit its fuse was the *Sefer Yetsirah* or *Book of Creation*. There were other works important to speculative Kabbalism, but none so dynamic in its effects as this one. Twelfth century Provence was the birthplace of this branch of Kabbalism, which attained its height in Spain during the fourteenth century.

Whereas the Jews of Germany sought refuge in the practical application of their mysticism from the devastating oppression & serfdom they were forced to suffer, the Jews of Provence & Spain during this period were much less deprived & so far better

The scheme of the Four Worlds, contained within *En-Sof* (circle
X1). The power of the "rings" and their vibration decrease
towards the center, for power is measured by the things controlled & each ring controls those rings within it. The outer rings

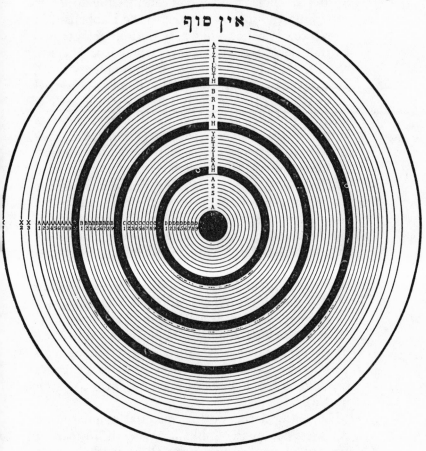

(the area from X1 to the boundary of A1) constitute the boundary
of the original dot, the first establishment of individualized existence. The other forty rings are the lower universe within the dot
(D10 being the lowest sphere of creation) evolved from, yet contained within, the nature of the first Crown, *Kether.*

able to enjoy the luxuries of speculation. They had no need to turn to talismanic & ecstatic arts in àn attempt to transform their condition.

Modern scholarship has had considerable difficulty in tracing the sources of speculative Kabbalism in Provence. What is known is limited & obscured by traditional Kabbalistic legend which names Issac the Blind as its originator. The arguments for & against the truth of this legend will not be rehearsed here. What is known for certain is that the earliest literary product of speculative Kabbalism was a work entitled *Masekheth Atsiluth*, (*Treatise on Emanation*), written by Jacob ha-Nazir sometime during the beginning of the twelfth century. At the time of this book's appearance, the Kabbalah was not a topic of general study. Only the elect had access to its secret doctrines, to the limited stock of which the *Treatise on Emanation* added the doctrine of the four worlds through which God manifested Himself; (the first three of which had already been intimated in the *Sefer Yetsirah*.) The presentation of this doctrine in the *Treatise on Emanation* is a simple one, but because of the intricate embellishments added by the later Kabbalists, & because of its central position in Kabbalistic thought, I will here present the doctrine as it is generally understood today & not as first laid down by Jacob ha-Nazir.

The cause of the world's material manifestation is understood by the Kabbalists to be the immanent activity of God. This materialization took place on four planes, or worlds, simultaneously.

The first world is called *'atsiluth*, the world of emanation in which God manifests himself in the form of archetypes. It is in this first world that

The four
worlds of the
*Treatise on
Emanation*

the *Sefiroth* originally manifest themselves & reside. Just as the system of the *Sefiroth* is explained as a process occurring eternally in God, so too must the four worlds, inasmuch as they are the materiali-zation of God's activity, be understood as a process taking place within him. The first world represents the hidden God's first form of activity: a raying-out of his inexhaustable energy in the form of ideal or archetypal representations which will in time become the models for all things in the world.

The four worlds

It is in this world that the union of God & his *Shekhinah*, his feminine counterpart takes place. The three worlds which follow are fruit of their union. The first world takes its name, *'atsiluth*, from the Hebrew verb in Numbers *xi*, 17: 'And I *will take* of the spirit which is upon these, & will put it upon them.'

The second world is called *beri'ah*, the world of creation in which the *Merkabah* takes form from the emanations of the lights of the *Sefiroth* which stream from the first world. Here reside the pure spirits of the truly pious & the highest ranking angels of the universe. When the emanation of the unformed *Shekhinah* penetrates this world from above these are the angels who joyously gather them-selves about her light to form her body. The name of this world, & those of the two worlds to follow, are taken from the three Hebrew verbs in Isaiah *xliii*, 7: '*I have created* him for my glory, *I have formed* him; yea, I *have made* him.'

The third world is called *yetsirah*, the world of formation, & is the abode of ten angelic hosts: Malachim, Arelim, Chajoth, Ophanim, Chash-malim, Elim, Elohim, Benei Elohim, Ishim & Seraphim. These angels are presided over by the great Metatron, the Prince of the World, the Angel of Presence. Although this angel's name is nowhere to be found in the Old Testament, the rabbis tell us that he is the one referred to in the following passage from Exodus *xxiii*, 20.1:

'Behold, I sent an Angel before thee, to keep thee in the way, & to bring thee into the place which I have prepared.

'Beware of him, & obey his voice, provoke him not; for he will not pardon your transgressions: for my name is in him.'

The rabbis tell us that the name contained in this angel is *Shaddai* (Almighty) & that because its numerical value of 314 corresponds with those Hebrew letters which form the name Metatron, it is this angel that has been sent to keep order in the world. This angel, legend tells us, was originally the pious man Enoch, who was raised after his death to the highest rank among the angels. His eyeballs were turned to torches, eyelashes to lightning, veins to fire & his flesh to brilliant flame. God placed him next to the throne of glory which he protects to this day. The throne he protects is the second world, *beri'ah*, & the world he stands guard in is the place where are found the *hekhaloth*, the seven heavenly halls through which the *Merkabah* mystics had to journey in their attempt to reach the throne of God.

Each of the preceding worlds diminishes in quality as the original emanation which began their formation becomes grosser. Eventually the ensuing impurities of its passage gather to form the fourth world, which is the world of matter & of the evil *kelippoth*, the world of nature & human existence.

The name of this world is *asiyah*. This term translates into the world of making, & not into the
world of action by which it has commonly come
to be known. It is in this last world where the
Shekhinah lives in exile—among men & the evil

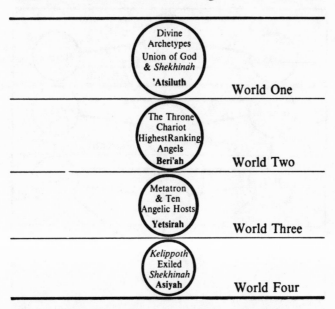

Divine
Archetypes
Union of God
& *Shekhinah*
'Atsiluth

World One

The Throne
Chariot
Highest Ranking
Angels
Beri'ah

World Two

Metatron
& Ten
Angelic Hosts
Yetsirah

World Three

Kelippoth
Exiled
Shekhinah
Asiyah

World Four

The Diminu-
ition of the
Four Worlds
as they be-
come mani-
fest.

spirits which constantly vie for their souls.

The schema for the four worlds is presented in
the figure above. There are other schemes used in
this tradition. We shall mention & provide diagrams of two of them.

The first alternative scheme of the four worlds
has as its major difference the idea that the ten
Sefiroth appear again in each one of the four worlds,
their qualities & essences diminishing as they
approach their final formation in the fourth world.

The second alternative scheme is more complex

but far more rewarding from a speculative & meditative point of view. In this scheme the *Sefiroth* are distributed throughout the four worlds: *Kether*, *Hokhmah* & *Binah* in *'atsiluth*, the first world; *Hesed*, *Gevurah* & *Tifereth* in *beri'ah*, the second world;

The Distribution of the ten *Sefiroth* through the Four Worlds.

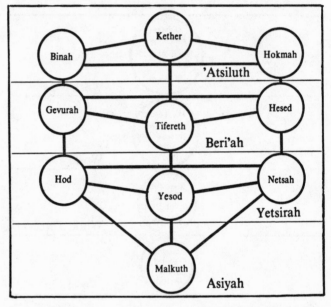

Netsah, *Hod* & *Yesod* in *yetsirah*, the third world; & *Malkuth*, comprising *'asiyah*, the fourth world.

11 See below, Part Two, ch. 3.

The principle triple division of the soul[11] also figures in this scheme. The highest degree of the soul, *Neshamah*, corresponds to the *Sefirah Kether*, & therefore with the world of *'atsiluth* which in this instance would correspond with the intellectual world. The second aspect of the soul, *Ruah*, the moral element which determines the nature of good & evil, corresponds to the *Sefirah Tifereth* located in the moral world. *Nefesh*, that aspect of the soul which corresponds to animal life and desires, corresponds to *Yesod*, located in the third world, the material & sensuous world, with the *Sefirah Malkuth* located in the fourth world.

Another topic which figures in this doctrine is

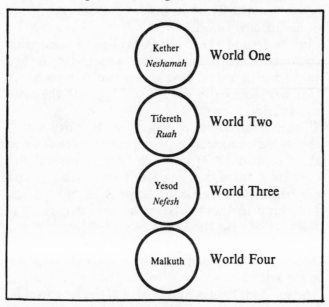

Kether
Neshamah — World One

Tifereth
Ruah — World Two

Yesod
Nefesh — World Three

Malkuth — World Four

The Four Worlds & their correspondence with the divisions of the Soul.

the emanation of the *Torah* as an instrument of creation. In our section on the relevance of the *Torah* to the Kabbalah it was mentioned that the book was thought of as a living organism. Its order & organization were reflected in the created world. All things have as their prototype the *Torah*. The unfolding of this divine order is of course traceable in the unfolding & progression of the four worlds as well.

In the beginning, when the hidden God first considered revealing himself through the agencies of both the oral & the written *Torah*, all the linguistic possibilities were gathered in germ. In this form the *Torah* existed as a sequence of all possible combinations & permutations of the consonants of the Hebrew alphabet. It is in this seemingly chaotic order that the *Torah* exists in *'atsiluth*, the world of divine emanation.

In the second world, the world of creation, that combination of the consonants contained in the first world which would best reveal the holy names of God were selected & made fast along with the pious souls residing there.

The angelic names & powers of the third world, the world of formation, compose the *Torah* in its third immaterial & invisible form. Up until this time the word of the book is but an intricate pattern of emanations woven into a fabric of beatitude accessible only to those mystics & masters capable of reaching beyond the limits of themselves.

It is not until the fourth world, the world of making, *'asiyah*, that the *Torah* becomes what we know know.

Adam & the four worlds — Adam, too, figures in this plan of the four worlds. In the first world we find him as the upper Heavenly Man, the archetype not only of the forms to follow but of man himself. The second world reveals Adam as he first appears in Genesis *i*, 27. The third world contains the Adam of the Garden, when he was composed of a garment of light instead of flesh. The Adam of these first three worlds was androgynous. The Adam of the fourth world is the Adam of the expulsion, the Adam of flesh traversing the desert of his exile, & the Adam capable of reproducing himself now that he is no longer androgynous. The four Adams outlined in the four worlds in turn compose the universal man, the *animus mundi*. In this schema his brain is located in the first world, his heart in the second world, his breath in the third world & his genitals in the fourth world.

The next work of speculative Kabbalism of considerable prominence was the *Book Bahir* which appeared in Provence around 1180. Some ascribe it to Issac the Blind but this ascription appears to be composed of more legend than fact. It is in this work that two doctrinal statements of speculative Kabbalism appear which in the centuries following it will effect all Kabbalistic thought: the relating of the *Sefiroth* to a clearly delineated structure of intelligible primal principles, & the identification & deification of a feminine principle in God, the *Shekhinah*, who not only represents the spiritual body of Israel, but the soul of man itself.

Many scholars have commented on the book's poor writing & badly organized structure, leaving some to find in the author's statement that the *Sefiroth* emanate all at once to be a contradiction of the very theory of emanation originally allegedly professed by the author. How on the one hand can we have a series of gradual transitions or emanations from the infinite to the finite, & on the other an instantaneous emanation? The answer to this question is to be found in chapter I, verse 6 of the *Sefer Yetsirah* where we are told that the ten *Sefiroth* have the appearance of a lightning flash. The author has simply taken a meteorological observation & applied it to metaphysics. Any child will tell you that lightning travels from above to below but that its movement is so swift its appearance in the sky is instantaneous. So too if a series of bulbs on a single circuit are turned on, regardless of the fact that we know that electricity travels *through* points A, B & C, they light up instantaneously. Again, one will immediately, without thought, pull back one's hand from a hot stove without giving thought to the very intricate & graduated series of chemical impulses which conspire to effect the reflex. What the author was trying to suggest, & what all Kabbalists have known since the suggestion was made, is that as God himself is invisible, so too is his *process* of emanation.

In Hebrew, *Shekhinah* simply means indwelling, & refers us to the Biblical usage of the word to indicate the presence of God, the manifestation of his divine presence in the world & in man. It was most probably thought of as the type of feeling one has of another's presence in a room one had thought to be empty. That feeling could be thought of as a synonym for the feeling of the presence of God—his *Shekhinah*.

The *Ecclesia* & the *Shekinah*

In the *Book Bahir* things take a new turn. The *Shekhinah* is not only spoken of as a divine entity in its own right, a *portion* of God himself, but as a feminine power. Furthermore, the mystical *Ecclesia* of Israel, the religious community, *is* the *Shekhinah* as well. The community of Israel had always been thought of as a divine community of individuals, & though always separate from God, *under* God. Here, the author tells us that not only is the *Ecclesia* a part of God, but by virtue of the fact that Israel had always been personified as a daughter & bride, the community is also, in spiritual reality, both his wife & daughter!

The ramifications of this identification of the *Ecclesia* with the *Shekhinah* as a divine personage in its own right has been brought out by Scholem where he points out that the *Talmud* explicitly states that whenever the children of Israel were put into exile God's *Shekhinah* was with them. In the original sense it simply meant that God's presence was there with them. In the light of the statement from the *Book Bahir* it comes to mean that whenever the children of Israel went into exile, a portion of God himself went into exile as well.

The *Shekhinah*, moreover, is the *neshamah*, the soul of man. Because we shall discuss the soul in a separate chapter all that we need point out here is that the mediaeval Jews thought of the soul as having been hewn from the Throne of Glory & that by being sent down into the body of man it not only suffered the state of finiteness, but of possible contamination through mortal sin. Through the eyes of the *Bahir's* author a portion of God himself became finite & open to contamination.

The *Book Bahir* in its entirety is only thirty to forty pages long, but its doctrinal statements altered the course of Jewish mysticism forever.

Another significant product of the speculative branch of Kabbalism was *The Commentary on the Ten Sephiroth*, by Azriel ben Menachem (c. 1160-1238), the leading disciple of Isaac the Blind of Provence. The historical research on this period is not complete & it is difficult to say with any certainty that the concept of the *En-Sof.* or of God as absolute infinity, appears for the first time in this work. I am tempted, however, to attribute Azriel with the creation of this doctrine.

The concept of the En-Sof

According to Azriel, the world & all of its manifestations was contained in God, the absolute & infinite being, the *En-Sof*. But because of the imperfections

tions

tions & finite state of the world, the world cannot be thought of as having directly come into being out of the perfection of the Absolute. The Infinite, by definition, is perfect & without end. How, then, could something finite & imperfect have been born of it? Through the medium of the *Sefiroth* was Azriel's answer. The *En-Sof* emanates the qualities which compose the universe in much the same way that the sun radiates its light & heat without diminishing its essence. This energy then filters through the *Sefiroth* who then emanate it through the world.

Abraham ben Samuel Abulafia

THE REVIVAL OF PRACTICAL KABBALISM

§In the midst of this speculative activity there appeared a mystic whose aim was the supplanting of speculative Kabbalism with the doctrines of the earlier practical Kabbalists of Germany. This mystic's name was Abraham Abulafia. Abulafia not only railed against the doctrine of the *Sefiroth* & their emanations but swore to reinstate the prophetic, visionary system of letter & number mysticism. Because we shall refer to his doctrines in the chapter on number & letter system later in this work, I take the opportunity here of outlining his life. It is a typical visionary's life & one that the reader should keep in mind while reading mysticism in general. There is a tendency to think of visionary mystics as recluses, hidden away in small rooms, refusing to deal with life's difficulties. When we read the writings of these men we tend to forget that they actually lived in the world, sometimes with feverish & frightening courage. Their lives have inevitably been tragic.

Abraham ben Samuel Abulafia was born in Spain in 1240. The immediate impression one receives of

this visionary prophet is one of extreme uprooted-
ness. He was constantly on the move either because
he was being pursued by those who wanted to
destroy him, or because he himself was in constant
pursuit of redemption. He first left Spain & jour-
neyed to the Near East in the hope of finding the
stream Sambation where legend had it the ten lost
tribes of Israel might be found. He returned from
this search shortly afterwards & for a space of ten
years lived first in Greece, & then in Italy. By
the time he returned to Spain in 1270 he had already
become fully competent in the doctrines of Kabbalism. He reports that in the year 1271 he was granted
visions by which he learned the nature of God's
true name.

This then must be regarded as the turning point
of his life. All of his doctrines grew out of the
experiences of that year. We find him returned
to Italy three years after what must have been a
singularly solitary career of proselytizing in his
homeland. He was never to set foot in Spain again,
& one can only wonder if the years spent attempting
to find hearts & ears sympathetic to the doctrine
revealed to him in vision had been bitter enough
to make him renounce his birthplace forever.

The streetcorners on which he stood proclaiming
the message of his Lord were in Christian lands.
His own people turned to the rabbis for the word
of the law. Those without rabbinic training were
looked upon as heretics, if not madmen. Either
or both were dangerous.

It is necessary, however, that such restraints as
religious orders be established. There are few who
can survive the blast of the cosmos. Even Abulafia
shows symptoms of having suffered from this, &

there must, somehow, be a balance or limit. If everyone were to experience the Divine, no one would experience the mundane. The mundane is the place to which we have all been exiled. The mundane is in its own right a 'sacred' place because it is an Other. Inasmuch as it is *not* divine it too is distinctive & unique.

Abulafia, the self-styled Messiah

Continuing his efforts to put forth the word of God Abulafia published, in Urbino, Italy, in 1270, his conversations with God. It must have been shortly after this time that it was revealed to Abulafia that *he* was the promised Messiah. One of the first tasks the Messiah was to perform upon his arrival on this earth was the release of his people from bondage. This involved a direct confrontation with the Pope & Abulafia accordingly set out for Rome.

Pope Nicholas III received news of the imminent approach of this self-styled Messiah & issued an order that when the man who called himself Raziel (Abulafia had adopted the name) arrived in the Holy City he was to be led out of town & burned.

Abulafia learned of the Pope's plans in advance but set out on the road to Rome anyway, certain of his task & of its completion. Shortly before reaching Rome he had a vision in which he saw two mouths growing on the Pope. He felt it was not necessary for him to fathom the meaning of this vision, but its meaning was revealed the next evening upon his arrival at the city-gate, where he learned that the Pope had mysteriously & quite suddenly died the evening before. There must have been a great deal of confusion, for what was done with Abulafia in no way met with the Pope's orders. He was imprisoned for twenty-eight days, & then set free. The imprisonment gave him time to think things over. Upon his release he left Rome & never again tried to confront a Pope.

After this episode he set out with a band of his disciples for Sicily where God gave him the final word on his messiahship. Abulafia had this message published in 1274. One might have assumed that people would have grown accustomed to him by this time & that another of his numerous pamphlets would have gone unnoticed. But this pamphlet contained a prophecy close to every Jew's heart, one which caused hope to override sensibility: the restitution of Israel. Abulafia promised that this would come about sometime in 1296, a short twelve years away. Thousands prepared themselves for the journey home.

There were others, however, who had grown weary of Abulafia, his doctrines & his newly won power over the people. Having had much opportunity in his life to know danger when he saw it, Abulafia decided that he had arrived at the end of his good fortune. He set sail for the island of Comino where he settled down to a peaceful life of contemplation & writing. Death came to him sometime around 1292, four years short of his prophecy. We can be sure that he died in the certainty that it would come about on schedule.

The bizarre & seemingly psychopathic side of Abulafia's personality is something we must leave to the probings of historians of medicine & psychopathology. What is of value to us here, & to the study of the Kabbalah in general, are the doctrinal statements of Abulafia which so incensed many of his contemporaries. They contradict & appear to balance his fanaticism. They make of his personal loneliness a small payment to the powers which quickened his native intelligence with the light of wisdom.

LATER DEVELOPMENTS IN KABBALISM

§It is not until the appearance of the *Zohar* in Spain sometime between 1280-1290 that the two branches of Kabbalism—practical & speculative—became united. When people mistakenly speak of *the* Kabbalah they inevitably have this work in mind.

Practical & speculative Kabbalism become united

When the Jews were exiled from Spain the *Zohar* was carried by them to all the countries they were forced to settle in. But it was at Safed in Palestine that the teachings of the *Zohar* became firmly established. The tomb of rabbi Simeon bar Yohai, the scholar to whom Moses de Leon ascribed the creation of the *Zohar*, was close at hand. There, in Safed, we find two of the most prominent Kabbalists in the history of Kabbalism: Moses Cordovero & Isaac Luria.

Moses Cordovero (1522-1570) was born in Cordova where he became one of Europe's leading Kabbalists & exponents of the *Zohar*. His brother-in-law, Solomon ben Moses ha-Levi Alkabetz, was the primary instrument in his mystical education. Alkabetz was a Kabbalistic poet of considerable stature, & his *Lekhah Dodi* ('Come my Beloved') was one of the last poems to be included in the Hebrew Prayer book. It is still recited in synagogues at the beginning of the Sabbath.[12] Cordovero, along with many other Kabbalists, made Safed his home after the terror of the Spanish Inquisition. He was strictly a speculative Kabbalist & his major concern was the relation of the *En-Sof* to the *Sefiroth*. Cordovero's

[12] S. Singer, trans., *Authorized Daily Prayer Book.*

vero's insistence that God is in all things influenced Spinoza's theory of pantheism.

There is a legend in Safed according to which Moses Cordovero was one of three angels of the Lord of Hosts—the other two were Joseph Caro & Isaac Luria—sent to this world to help mankind with secret teachings. At his death it is said that a pillar of fire shot up from his bier.

The other Safed Kabbalist of prominence was Isaac Luria (1533-1572) whose speculations gave birth to modern Kabbalism. It was his doctrine that the later Hasidim employed in the construction of their system. While being an exponent of the *Zohar* he was primarily interested in the practical side of Kabbalism in direct contrast to Moses Cordovero. As the influence of his school spread, so too did the creation of amulets, the juggling of numbers & letters, & the conjuration of devils. Aside from all this Lurianic Kabbalism contains some of the most exciting & far-reaching doctrines in the whole of Kabbalism. The most striking of which is the concept of *tsimtsum*.

The term *tsimtsum* originally meant 'contraction' or 'concentration,' & appeared in the *Talmud* where it was used to describe God's projection & concentration of his divine presence, his *Shekhinah*, at a single point. In Luria's use of the word *tsimtsum* means withdrawal or retreat from a single point. The original concept appears in a few Kabbalistic treatises prior to Luria's reformulation of it. It does not, however, appear in the *Zohar*.

The concept of *tsimtsum*

This voluntary contraction on the part of God, the *En-Sof* in this case, is the act which causes creation to come into existence. Without this act there would have been no universe. Because the

En-Sof was limitless, in all things & all places, a plenum of divinity, it was necessary that a primordial space, *tehiru*, be established. It was necessary therefore that the *En-Sof's* first creative act be a withdrawal or contraction into Himself. In so doing He permitted to come into being the primordial space which was necessary for the creation of the finite world. But the space created was not entirely empty. In much the same way that the fragrance of perfume lingers in an empty bottle, so too did a *divine presence* remain behind in primordial space. Once this space existing outside of & separate from the *En-Sof* was established, the second act of creation began to take place.

The first act of creation

The first act of creation was an act of limitation: the second, that of emanation. At this time the *En-Sof* rayed out a single beam of light to form the first configuration ever fashioned, the body of Adam Kadmon (the primordial man), from which there then burst forth from his eyes, mouth, nose & ears the lights of the *Sefiroth*. The *Sefiroth*, themselves light concentrated from the original beam, were at this stage totally undifferentiated, without the qualities presently assigned to them. In this form they did not require special light-made bowls to contain them. The plan of creation that the *En-Sof* had in mind demanded that the *Sefiroth* become differentiated & contained so that they might receive the more heavily concentrated beams of light emanating from the eyes of Adam Kadmon. Since these bowls or vessels were constructed out of varying mixtures of light, the heavier lights streamed forth from the primordial man's eyes & were received without difficulty into the first three *Sefiroth: Kether, Binah,* & *Hokmah*. When it came time to fill the bowls of the lower *Sefiroth* the light suddenly burst forth with such intensity that it broke the vessels designed to contain it.

The principle of the *shevirah*

This brings us to Luria's second doctrinal principle: the *shevirah*, or breaking of the vessels, which has its roots back in an *Aggadahic* saying that before the creation of this world God had created & destroyed many others which had not been to his liking. Moses de Leon employed the information of this saying as an explanation of Genesis *xxxvi*, 31: 'And these are the Kings that reigned in the land of Edom, & who died.' According to Moses de Leon's interpretation there was a time when God employed only the forces of *Gevurah*, the *Sefirah* of stern judgment, & by so doing caused the destruction of those worlds by the excessive weight of the *Sefirah*. As he points out, the world may only exist in a state of balance, a condition of equilibrium brought about by the modifying of stern judgment with the compassion of mercy or grace, represented by *Sefirah Hesed*. This is the state of things as they are now.

In this doctrine, Isaac Luria equates the bursting of the vessels with the death of the primordial kings of Edom. This death, Luria adds, came about because of a lack of harmony between the masculine & feminine elements of the *Sefiroth*. That is, the feminine & passive *Sefirah* of stern judgment, *Gevurah*, did not allow itself to be approached by the masculine & active *Sefirah Hesed*, Mercy or Grace. When the light pouring out of the eyes of Adam Kadmon shattered the vessels of the *Sefiroth*, the light which composed the vessels themselves shattered into sparks & fell into the realm of the demonic *kelippoth* or shells, the evil powers created out of the residual waste of the primordial kings.

With the breaking of the vessels everything suddenly fell into a state of chaos. The lights from the eyes of Adam Kadmon rebounded upward or crashed downward into the realm of the shells. The divine machinery came to a stop & a new blast of light issued forth from the *En-Sof*. This light then burst forth from the forehead of Adam Kadmon in an attempt to stop the chaos from blossoming & re-order the elements which had been torn asunder by the catastrophe.

Instead of the original plan, therefore, according to which the whole of creation would have been illuminated by the light of *En-Sof,* now only certain portions are lit by the sparks, & other portions are left in total darkness. This darkness is the realm of the shells, the evil in creation which would have been redeemed if all had gone as planned. Instead, the sparks which fell into the darkness become ensnared by the shells. This mingling of the sparks led to the present reality where there is no evil which does not contain some good, no good which does not contain some evil. It is at this point, the point where the *En-Sof* streams forth again, that the *Sefiroth* take on the attributes they now have. This reformation of the *Sefiroth* begins the work required of the *tikkun,* the restoration.

The work of *tikkun*

The only way in which the sparks may be retrieved from the dark realm of the shells is by the work of *tikkun*, part of which is undertaken by God. But the restoration of the original order became complicated by the Fall of Adam. All the souls that were ever to exist existed in Adam's soul, & after the Fall his size was diminished to the size of man. His soul was exiled from his body; so too are our souls in a state of exile. They are the sparks hidden in the darkness of the shells. The recovery of the original unity cannot come about without the aid of man, for which purpose he was created & sent down into the place of the shells which is our world. The restoration of the original unity is a collective venture each individual must set out & accomplish for himself, for the restoration of his exiled soul is his own responsibility.

These are the bare outlines of Lurianic Kabbalism. Even in as simple a presentation as this one cannot escape being struck by the scope of Luria's vision. This Kabbalism is the most exciting of the many systems. The works of Luria's foremost disciple, Hayyin Vittal Calabrese (1543-1620) spread the doctrine of Lurianic Kabbalism throughout the world. What is needed now is the translation of the major Lurianic works & a commentary.

At about this time the study of the Kabbalah began in Poland, but with considerable opposition on the part of the Talmudic authorities. The spirit of Kabbalism which had been sparked centuries earlier was all but dead & would not be revived in Germany until the arrival of the Kabbalists coming out of Poland in the eighteenth century. By that time the Kabbalah had spread throughout Poland to such a degree that no rabbi could think of neglecting Kabbalistic studies. The doctrine studied in Poland was Lurianic Kabbalism.

In eighteenth-century Europe, Judaism operated solely on Talmudic prescription. The academies of learning spent their time on & applauded the successful performance of *pilpul*, hair-splitting. The intellectual fervor associated with Talmudic studies left little room for the emotional undercurrent of

"Here now one of those three Hierarchs, even the most glorious of them, because he was the Created Representative of God the Son, commits High Treason, revolts, lets his dark, proud Will-Spirit . . . out of his own Center fly up on high, Above God . . ." Number six in in a series, from *The Works of Jacob Behmen.*

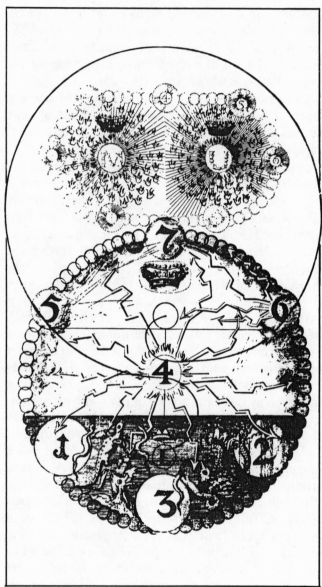

Judaism & had little to do with reality. Those who were not Talmudic scholars, the *Am Aratzim* or uncultured & crude masses, were looked upon with extreme contempt. The last thing the scholars of that period would have expected would be the emergence of a mystical theology parented by a peasant whose sole possession was a horse given him by his brother-in-law, & who supported himself & his family by digging lime out of ravines.

Israel ben Eliezer, the famed Baal-Shem Tov (Master of the Holy Name), after years of humble praying & sporadic teaching in the heart of the Carpathians, returned to the 'Civilized' living of Miedzyboz & unobtrusively established a following. Perhaps not so unobtrusively, however, for it did draw the attention of the Talmudic authorities who were quick to express their dislike of his doctrine. The arid scholasticism of the rabbinical tradition, available to the privileged few, was challenged by the Baal-Shem's proposal that joy & prayer alone united one with God.

The hair-splitting arguments of the scholar could not lead one to God's presence; 'where we find much learning, there we shall find little piety.' This revival of Hasidism was the revolt of the unlearned multitude who had been shut out of the garden of rabbinical Judaism by their 'ignorance.' In short, the entire movement symbolized the democratic idea that God is not the sole property of an aristocracy but of the people. This, coupled with the idea that study was worthless, eventually led to the subordination of learning to ritual after the Baal-Shem's death. Fervor replaced devotion. This branch of Jewish mysticism remains with us today as a legimated form of Jewish religion. Even

The revival
of Hasidism

though these two branches of mysticism are technically at odds with one another, many Hasidic scholars adhere to certain Kabbalistic Doctrines.

The central concept in the new Hasidism (from *hasidim* or pious ones) has to do with the idea that God is present in all things & that meditation on the theological proposition 'There is no place empty of him,' is all that is necessary to dispel sadness & fear. Once one understands that God is in all things one can then come to understand that the evil & unhappiness existing in the world is only man's faulty view of things & not in the things themselves. The joy & celebration through prayer of the Hasidim has to do with their recognition of God being everywhere. One must live fearlessly & cheerfully for in all things, no matter how incomprehensible they may be to our intellect, God works. To the hard-pressed peasant of the period this doctrine was a salve which served to kindle the spirit of the masses.

The *Zaddikim* & the Hasidic community

As central as this pantheistic concept of God is to Hasidism, that of Zaddikism is even more prominent. The idea of the *zaddik* (righteous) was not new to Judaism. It referred simply to a man who was in some mysterious way united or connected with God in such a way that he was present to not only his mystery, but capable of acting in his behalf. The true *zaddik* was a righteous man, one who is beloved by God because of his firm adherence to his faith & prayer & who in every instance has his prayers answered. In Hasidism this general concept became extended. There we find the *zaddik* as one who has lost his sense of individuality in attaining union with God. Endowed with the gift of prophecy which such an act affords, the *zaddik* was thought of & treated as a prophet. The *Zaddikim* were holy beings capable of acting as intermediaries between God & the community of Israel. Believing them to be endowed with miraculous powers of healing, the diseased, infirm, childless, & impoverished approached them for their blessings, paying them with either money or goods for their services. This practice eventually led to excesses on the part of some of the *Zaddikim*. Some of them lived in opulence which was excessive in the eyes of their own people. In addition to this, the institutionalizing of the *zaddik's* office as a gift of heredity inevitably brought about the appearance of many false *Zaddikim*. All of this resulted in a growing distrust of the office of the *zaddik* & gave cause for the rabbinical fathers to become actively hostile to the Hasidic community in general.

Scholem has pointed out[13] that the major development in Jewish mysticism to be found in Hasidism lies in the fact that all of the secrets of the divine realm are presented as a mystical *psychology*. It is through a descent into one's own self that a person penetrates the spheres separating man from God. The Kabbalistic doctrines which the *Hasidim* included in their mysticism become aspects of a surprisingly accurate system of psychological analysis. On the other hand, regardless of the inclusion of many Kabbalistic doctrines, Hasidism, as Martin Buber in his book, *Hasidism*, has pointed out,[14] may in no way be compared with Kabbalism. Kabbalistic doctrine is looked upon by its practitioners as esoteric dogma, for those who have ears & eyes to see in a special way, for those with *gnosis*. The *Hasidim*, with their belief that God & his mysteries are open & available to all men, could not,

Hasidism & Kabbalism

[13] Gershom Scholem, *Major Trends in Jewish Mysticism*, p. 341.

[14] Martin Buber, *Hasidism*, p. 137 ff.

therefore, think of themselves as Kabbalists. Nor could they side with the Kabbalists in their practice of freeing themselves from the contradiction of the opposites by seeing through it with the aid of *gnosis*. For the Hasidic master it is his duty to endure & survive the tension of the world's contradictions & in that way alone redeem the opposites.

The Christian mystics

During the eighteenth century the Jews of Western Europe began to put aside their mysticism. It was fortunately kept alive for them by Christian mystics who, as early as the thirteenth century, had become attracted to its teachings. The list is long—beginning with the Spanish mystic Raymond Lully & ending with the English scholar E.A. Waite. Admittedly, most of the interest was more with the practical side of Kabbalism than with the speculative side. The exceptions are the geniuses of mysticism like Jacob Boehme. The most famous of the practical Christian Kabbalists—those who concerned themselves exclusively with the magical aspects—was Heinrich Cornelius Agrippa of Nettesheim (1487-1535) whose chief work, *De Occulta Philosophia*, is still referred to today by those who work in this particular area of Kabbalism.

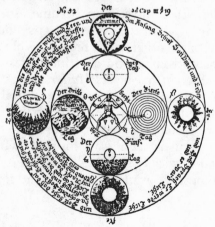

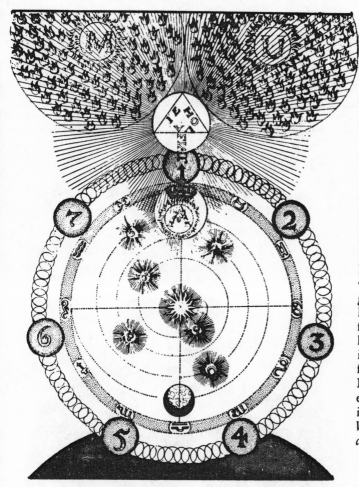

"When Lucifer by his Rebellion had brought the whole extent of his Kingdom into such a desolate condition, that it was . . . without Form and Void, & Darkness was upon the Face of the Deep, that whole Region was justly taken away from under his Dominion, & transformed . . ." Number seven in a series, from *The Works of Jacob Behmen.*

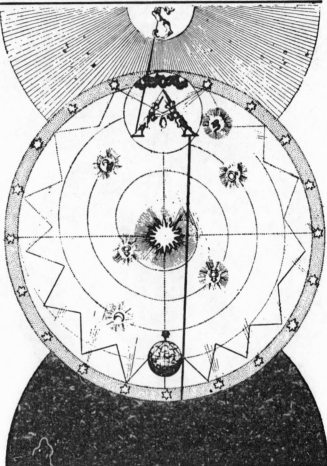

"This ADAM, though he was indeed created in a State of Innocence, Purity, Integrity and Perfection, could not yet stand on that Top of Perfection which he was designed for . . ." Number eight in a series, from *The Works of Jacob Behmen.*

Part Two
The Doctrines of Kabbalism

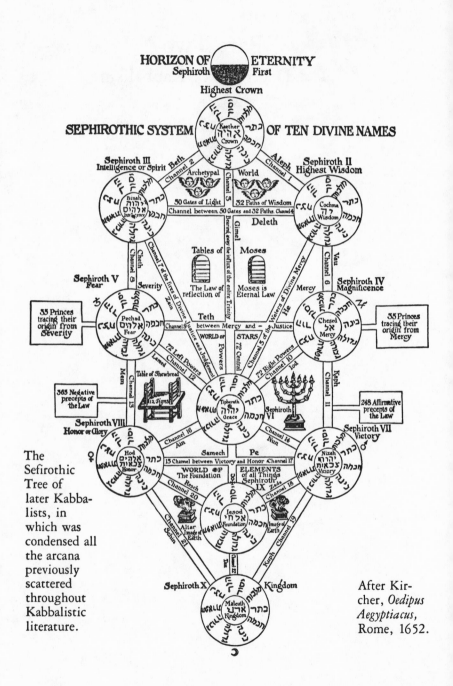

The Sefirothic Tree of later Kabbalists, in which was condensed all the arcana previously scattered throughout Kabbalistic literature.

After Kircher, *Oedipus Aegyptiacus*, Rome, 1652.

Chapter One. The *En-Sof* & the *Sefiroth*

THIS CHAPTER will deal with the two concepts which are at the center of all Kabbalistic thought. No matter how much one Kabbalist may differ from another in his theoretical speculations he will agree that without the concepts of the *En-Sof* & the *Sefiroth* there is no Kabbalism. He might even add that with these two concepts the whole of Kabbalism may be understood without further commentary. Comprehend the *En-Sof* & you comprehend the meaning of divine being. Comprehend the system of the *Sefiroth* & you understand the meaning of Being in general. I cannot think of any aspect of Jewish mysticism which, in the last regard, does not have as its foundation-stone at least one of these two concepts.

A language capable of communicating the quality of the transcendent realm in which the *En-Sof* & the *Sefiroth* reside must be symbolic. Without symbols nothing can be said. The Kabbalists accordingly devised an array of descriptions which they felt best described what was beyond perception. These were men who had glimpsed the divine pattern of manifestation with the interior eye of dreams & intuitions or by means of the powers of vision

The Kabbalistic Seal of Agrippa. From Henricus Cornelius Agrippa, *De Occulta Philosophia Libri III*, Antwerp, 1533.

with which they had been touched. In the following pages, therefore, we should not expect to come any closer to a full understanding. At most, we can satisfy our *philosophical* appetites.

The concept of *En-Sof*

THE EN-SOF

§ The term *En-Sof* translates into limitless or boundless (*E*=without, *Sof*=end). It is the name for the God of Kabbalism which symbolizes total unity beyond comprehension.[1] It is in Him that all opposites exist in complete ignorance of their differences, in a unity beyond unity, which knows no possibility of differences. In the minds of the Kabbalists the *En-Sof* is no-thing, does not exist, is not fathomable & cannot be discussed

sed

sed at all in terms of Being or Non-Being. The *En-Sof* is so much *not* a part of human experience that as rational beings we cannot even begin to discuss its existence, much less its non-existence. Because it is something beyond comprehension, it is also something beyond classification. The very most we can say is that it exists in its non-existence, & that in its non-existence it exists. If the material body of the universe, the sun, the planets, the solar systems, were compared to a tree, the *En-Sof* would be the sap of that tree. Even this simile is not appropriate. Let us instead say that the sap of the tree would be the vehicle of this force called *En-Sof*, this spiritual nonentity.

Many commentators have tried to postulate the *En-Sof* by what he is not, hoping by misdirection to find direction out. The many examples from Jewish mysticism are reminiscent of Pseudo-Dionysius' definition of God:

'The cause of all things is neither soul nor intellect; nor has it imagination, opinion, or reason, or intelligence; nor is it reason or intelligence; nor is it spoken or thought. It is neither number, nor order, nor magnitude, nor littleness, nor equality, nor inequality, nor similarity, nor dissimilarity. It neither stands, nor moves, nor rests. It is neither essence, nor eternity, nor time. Even intellectual contact does not belong to it. It is neither science nor truth. It is not even royalty or wisdom; not one; not unity; not divinity or goodness; nor even spirit as we know it.'

But this avenue of approach continually refers us back to something until we arrive at a basic concept of what he is: nothing or no-thing, yet another explanation of some commentators. Even this fails.

[1] There are different conventions for the transliteration of Hebrew words into the Roman alphabet. אין סוף *Ain-Sof, Ayin-Soph* and *En-Sof* are all equally correct versions of the same Hebrew term which we have chosen to transliterate as *En-Sof* because it is the most favored by scholars in the field.

nothing or no-thing is comprehensible, the human mind through assiduous discipline (such as that to be had through *yoga*) can train itself to comprehend & perceive no-thing. That the concept of nothing is within the range of human comprehension is suggested by the fact that infinity, another imponderable concept which is usually conceived negatively, may not only be conceived positively, as a reality extending without end, but has even been sufficiently comprehended in this way for there to exist an 'axiom of infinity' in the science of formal logic. But the *En-Sof*, by definition, cannot be comprehended. So he can be neither understood by what he is not, nor by the idea of nothing. Neither approach works.

The *En-Sof* comes before the creator God. Even this does not explain Him. He cannot be localized in space or time. The only thing that may be said with some certainty is that the *En-Sof* was not the cause of this world. He stands even beyond the impetus of cause, desire. He is without desire, without non-desire. He is Himself. He is *En-Sof*, a plenum of emptiness.

The Kabbalists played on this difficulty of expressing the inexpressible by pointing out that the 'nothing' (*ain*) signifying God had the same letters as the personal 'I' (*ani*), emphasizing that the last of the emanations from the *En-Sof* (the *Sefiroth*, to be discussed below) is represented by the personal 'I'. I imagine what I am trying to convey here is the idea that a section or even a chapter on the *En-Sof* should be by definition non-existent. All the words of a language cannot explain Him. Not even the silence of a language can reveal Him. The *En-Sof* is something beyond human comprehension

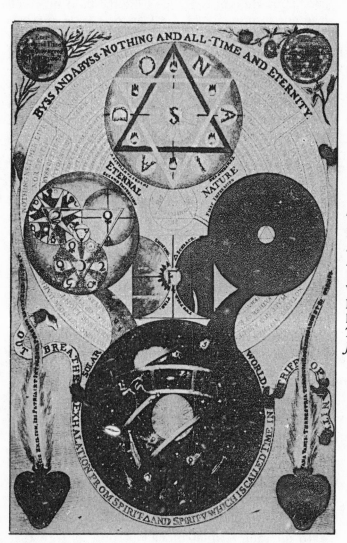

The True
Principles of
All Things.
A watercolor
by the Rev.
William
Law, trans-
lated from
*The Works of
Jacob Behmen.*

The concept
of *En-Sof*

sion, but He is at the same time the fluid in which
the entire universe of the *Sefiroth*, the emanations
of His totally uncommitted affluence, reside.

If there is one other thing that might be said
about the *En-Sof* it is this: the *Sefiroth* are the result
of its emanation. Some Kabbalists add that the
En-Sof is to be found in each *Sefirah*, but even then
He is an invisible & unapproachable being. His
presence in the *Sefiroth* may be known but not comprehended. His life, His movement within Himself,
are gradations of the *Sefiroth*. That is to say, the
life of the *En-Sof*, thought of as activity, may be
experienced indirectly by means of the movements
& relationships of the ten *Sefiroth*. In a way these
constitute a field which could be thought of as
His body, if He had a body.

Above all it is important to understand that the
En-Sof of the Kabbalah stands above the creator
God of the Old Testament. The *En-Sof* is 'nothing'
&, if, as the Old Testament has it, He created
things in his own image, He would create nothing.
The only activity, if we could call it that, of the
En-Sof was the emanation of a ray of light. Nothing
more.

[2] See above,
Part One,
ch. 3, pp.79-
83.
It is in the Kabbalistic system of Isaac Luria[2]
that we find an extremely intricate description of
the activity of the *En-Sof* in the universe prior to
the creation. Luria tells us that the infinite being,
En-Sof, retreated from the arena of the universe,
contracted into Himself, & left behind Him, in
that space which was defined as Him, an emptiness.
It was by the *En-Sof's* retreat from infinite space
into an infinitesimal monad of pure energy that
the world comes into being. If the *En-Sof* had not
contracted Himself there would have been no space

for the activity of Genesis to take place. The world comes into being only after this contraction. It was then that the *En-Sof* sent forth a beam, an emanation of Himself into the space created by His contraction. It is on the 'surface' of that space that the first spark was struck, the pinpoint of light which was to become the *Sefiroth*.

In order for a creation to be possible there must first be a contraction, a concentration of all energies at a center. Then, an expansion must occur; the gathered energies must be sent forth in concentrated form as a ray or beam of energy.

The activity of the *En-Sof* as outlined by Luria immediately brings to mind the method of yoga in which the yogin is called upon to retrieve the energies bound up with the sense-organs, dispersed in the world, & concentrate them on a center located in his body. In the Chinese yogic text called *The Secret of the Golden Flower*[3] we are told that in order to create the flower, or subtle body, we must take the energies which normally flow outward into world through the eye (*i.e.,* the senses or general involvement with the world of the senses) & cause them to 'flow backward'. This withdrawal of energies might be likened to the *En-Sof's* contraction of Himself.

Again, in the Tantric discipline of Kundalini Yoga the purpose behind the retrieving of energies is awakening the bundle of spiritual energies slumbering at the base of the devotee's spine. After the initial contraction there is then a release of energies. But, as in most yogic systems, the newly found & released energy follows a specific path or course. So too does the expression of the *En-Sof* after its contraction take on a course or series of paths.

[3] Cary F. Baynes, trans., *The Secret of the Golden Flower*.

The concept of *En-Sof*

4 Westcott, *Sefer Yetsirah*, Pt.I, p.15.

5 Swami Madhavanda, trans., *The Brhadaran-yaka Upani-shad*, p.337.

6 Quoted in J. Abelson, *Jewish Mys-ticism*, p.137

7 Westcott, *Sepher Yet-sirah*, vs.6 &7, p.16.

Facing page: Representa-tion of the Four Worlds based on the idea that the ten *Sefiroth*, appear in each of them, their quali-ties & es-sences dimin-ishing with each world (see diagram on page 63).

'In thirty-two wonderful Paths of Wisdom did Jah, Jehovah Sabaoth, the God of Israel, the Elohim of the living, the King of sages, the merciful & gracious God, the exalted One, the Dweller in eter-nity, most high & holy—engrave his name by the three Sepharim (means of expressions)—Numbers, Letters & Sounds. [4]

These thirty-two paths refer us to the twenty-two letters of the Hebrew alphabet & the ten *Sefiroth*, which means, literally, 'numbers'. These paths & these *Sefiroth* are generally thought of as residing outside of the *En-Sof*. That is, the *Sefiroth* & their systems are always diagrammed as being a unit separate & divorced from their origin. But I would have the reader consider the possibility that the emanations of the *En-Sof*, the *Sefiroth*, are actually stages or operations contained & operating within Him. This is not to reverse my earlier statements to the effect that the *En-Sof* is without active con-cern. The glands within the human body operate & function without our consideration or awareness —so too do the *Sefiroth* operate within the *En-Sof*.

Later Hasidic theory relegated the activity of the *Sefiroth* to the plane of the human mind. The only conclusion these two proposals can lead us to is the idea that the Self, the transpersonal portion of unity contained within each of us in potential, is that referred to in the theory of the *En-Sof*. Furthermore, because each *Sefirah* is assigned a moral & ethical value, & because these qualities are pecul-iar to the human condition, what we are now about to discuss is not just speculation on the universe in general, but a theory of the operations of the human mind at the deepest level where it merges with the soul.

The *En-Sof* & its emanations, the *Sefiroth*, are inseparable. The *Sefiroth* are the internal psychic organs of God. Once they have come into being, they cannot be divorced from Him. They are Him, they are *En-Sof*, as much as the nerves of our bodies are in their own way representative of us. *En-Sof*, I would further suggest, is the meaning in creation, the limitless meaning which our scientists seek to discover in their attempts to unveil the origin of the universe. *En-Sof* is what they seek.

'The form of that 'being' is as follows: Like a cloth dyed with turmeric, or like grey sheep's wool, or like the scarlet insect called *Indragopa*, or like a tongue of fire, or like a white lotus, or like a flash of lightning. He who knows it as such attains splendour like a flash of lightning. Now therfore the description of Brahman: 'Not this, not this.' Because there is no other & more appropriate description than this 'Not this.'[5]

THE SEFIROTH

§He made ten lights spring forth from His midst, lights which shine with the form which they have borrowed from Him, & which shed everywhere the light of a brilliant day. The Ancient One, the most Hidden of the hidden, is a high beacon, & we know Him only by His lights, which illuminate our eyes so abundantly. His Holy Name is no other thing than these lights.'[6]

The ten lights are the *Sefiroth*. The idea of their luminescence has its origin in the *Sefer Yetsirah*,[7] where they are referred to as lightning flashes & flames of a burning coal, the *En-Sof*. The Kabbalists depict the *Sefiroth* visually according to the diagram.

The *Sefiroth* are understood as abstract entities

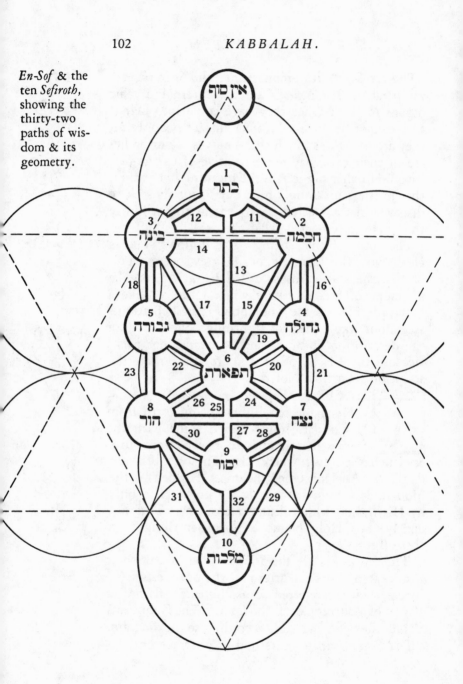

En-Sof & the ten *Sefiroth*, showing the thirty-two paths of wisdom & its geometry.

through which all change in the universe takes place. A point that is rarely considered, however, is that they are composite figures with two-fold aspects. In their first aspect they stand as vehicles through which change & transformation take place, & in this aspect they are symbolized as 'vessels'. In their second aspect they represent what is eternally constant or unchangeable, & in this aspect they are symbolized by light. The manifestation of the divine power of the *En-Sof* as light takes on different qualities or 'colors' as it is captured by & passes through each of the *Sefiroth* acting in their role as vessels. The quality of each *Sefirah* is thought of as a translucent colored glass vessel. At the same time, the *Sefiroth* are themselves vessels made of light; that is, the quality of their light although originally derived from the *En-Sof* is dynamically different.

It is this distinction which is referred to by those mystics who refer to the light of God & the light in nature. The former speaks of the numinosity of God as He is in Himself & the latter of the numinosity which is revealed to His creatures. The frequent Kabbalist image of the *En-Sof* in manifestation as water poured into different colored bottles is actually a statement about this distinction. The colored bottles, or *Sefiroth*, are the manifold qualities which constitute the known reality. It is only through these differing aspects that the unknowable may be perceived. We cannot see the source, the fount of this outpouring, we can only see its effect in manifestation.

Furthermore, there are differing degrees to which His manifestation may be perceived. One may see only one of the vessels, one aspect, or several. The

The ten lights of the *Sefiroth*

Beauty as the bearer of all the Powers; Beauty as the foundation of all the Powers; Beauty as the Source.

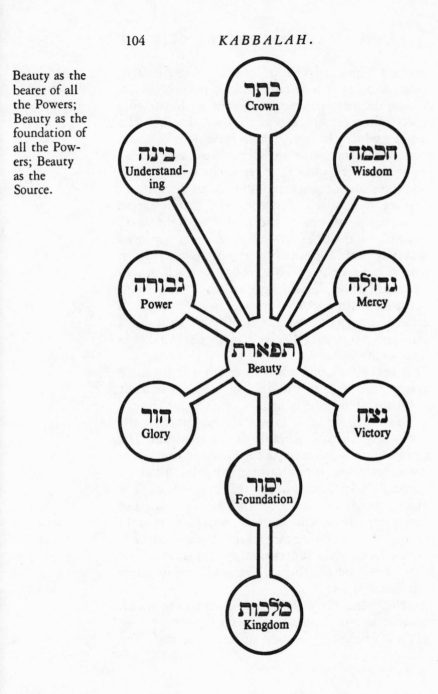

aim is to become capable of seeing all of the parts & their functions in unison. If one can fathom the relationship of the ten *Sefiroth* and their operations in the world as well as in themselves, one will perceive the full brilliance of the light in nature. It is from *this* light that the world gains its substance.

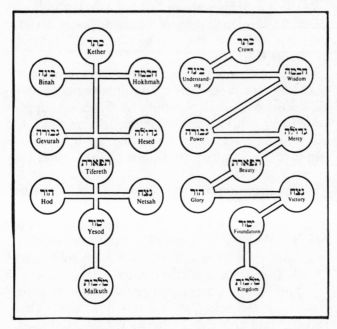

The relationships of the *Sefiroth* to each other are manifold. Through contemplation of these relationships, however, the fullness of the *En-Sof* may be experienced.

The *Sefer Yetsirah* which contains the first literary expression of the theory of the *Sefiroth* speaks of this idea in its first chapter. Immediately below, the reader will find this chapter of the *Sefer Yetsirah* in its entirety. It should also be pointed out that although this famous work is always referred to in conjunction with the theory of the *Sefiroth*, only this first chapter discusses them:

The *Sefiroth* according to the *Sefir Yetsirah*

The *Sefiroth* according to the *Sefer Yet-sirah*

'1. Jeohovah, through thirty-two Paths, engraved his name using the three forms of expression called Letters, Numbers, & Sounds.

2. There are ten Sacred *Sefiroth*. The Foundation of things are the twenty-two letters. Of these, three are Mothers; seven double & twelve simple letters are the remainder.

3. The Sacred Sefiroth are Ten as are their numbers. They are the ten fingers of the hands, five corresponding with five. But in the middle the Sefiroth are knotted in Unity.

4. There are ten Sefiroth. Ten & not nine; ten, & not eleven. If one acts & attempts to understand this Wisdom he shall become wise. Speculate, apply your intelligence, & use your imagination continually when considering them so that by such searching the Creator may be re-established upon his throne.

5. The beginnings of the Sefiroth have no ending & a boundless origin; they are each vast distances & pits of good & evil of immeasurable depths & heights; they are composed of infinite distances to the East & the West, North & South, ruled only by the Lord from his holy throne.

6. Their countenance is like the scintillating flame flashing in lightning, invisible & boundless. They race outward from the throne, away from their Lord, but return to fall prostrate in holy adoration before his throne, & the Word they speak comes as if out of a whirlwind.

7. Their ending is as their beginning. They are as brilliant flame flowing upwards from the surface of a roaring coal. *IHVH* is great in his unity, there is none like Him.

8. When you think of the ten Sefiroth cover your

heart & seal the desire of your lips to announce their Divinity. Yoke your mind. Should it escape your grasp, reach out & bring it back under your control. As it was said, 'And the living creatures ran & returned as the appearance of a flash of lightning,' in such a manner was the Covenant created.

9. The Sefiroth reveal the Ten numbers. In the first the Spirit of the God of life, more resplendent than the Living God. The sound of the Voice, the Spirit & the Word are of this Spirit.

10. The second: God produces Air from the Spirit & turns it into twenty-two sounds, the letters of the alphabet: three of them are mothers, seven of them are double letters, & twelve of them are simple. But even above these does the Spirit stand in worth. Third: the Waters were formed from this Air by Him. He traced designs on the stillness of their faces. Out of the boundless void of clay & mire he formed the Waters, hewing them into the matter which is of the Foundation. Fourth: And he formed fire out of this water so that he might fashion the Merkabah. And Auphanim, Seraphim & Kerubim were his assisting angels. It was with the aid of these three that the Place sheltering Him was completed. So it is written: 'Who maketh his angels spirits; his ministers a flaming fire.'

11. From the simple letters three were chosen & sealed so that they may be formed into a Magnificent Name, *IHV*. With this name was the universe sealed in six directions by Him.

Fifth: Height was sealed with *I H V*. This he did while looking above.

Sixth: Depth was sealed with *I V H*. This he did while looking below.

The *Sefiroth* according to the *Sefer Yetsirah*

יהוה

יהו
יוה

היו
היו
ויה
והי

[8] Westcott, *Sepher Yetsirah*, pp.15 -17.

[9] F. Lelut, ed., *L'Amulette de Pascal*, p.156.

Seventh: The East was sealed with *H I V*. This he did while looking in front of Him.

Eighth: The West was sealed with *H V I*. This he did while looking in back of Him.

Ninth: The South was sealed with *V I H*. This he did while looking to the right.

Tenth: The North was sealed with *V H I*. This he did while looking to the left.

12. Look! The Spirit of the Air, Water, Fire, Height, Depth, East, West, North, & South emanate out of the Ten Divine Sefiroth!'[8]

The major point of this passage is that the limitations of the creation, the elements which compose the world, its height, depth & direction, have as their essence & foundation the *Sefiroth* whose 'countenance is like the scintillating flame flashing in lightning.' This is the light that Paracelsus, Jacob Boehme & the alchemists perceived in their meditations. It is the fire which Pascal hailed in his concealed amulet, the piece of paper which served as a record of his moment of enlightenment:

'From about half-past ten in the evening until about half-past twelve, midnight, FIRE. God of Abraham, God of Isaac, God of Jacob, not of the philosophers nor of the Wise. Assurance, joy, assurance, feeling, joy, peace.'[9]

This light in nature, these *Sefiroth*, are the representations of forces active in the *En-Sof* itself. To the extent that the substance of reality is the *Sefiroth*, the creation & all that followed it is merely the external development of God, a reflective manifestation of something inexpressible through a medium by which its effects might be perceived. In addition to this, by virtue of the fact that the *Sefiroth* are intimately connected with the Hebrew alphabet,

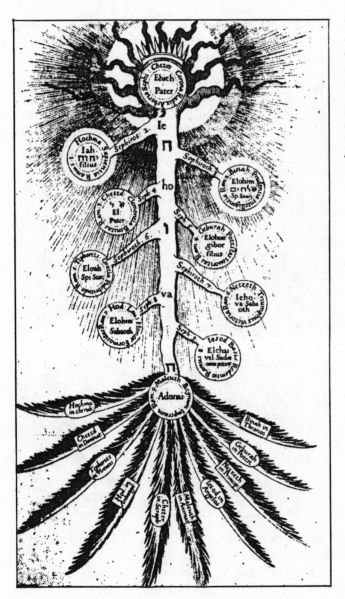

The divine outpouring of the philosophical tree of Jewish mysticism. By Johannes de Bry from the *Works of Robert Fludd.*

they are also the names of the *En-Sof* as is suggested by section 11 from the chapter of the *Sefer Yetsirah* quoted above, as well as what is meant by the

The Sefi-rothic Tree, from Paulus Ricius, *Porta Lucis,* Augsberg, 1516.

PORTAELVCIS
Hçc est porta Tetragrãmaton iusti intrabũt p̃ eam.

passage in the *Zohar* which reads, 'His Holy Name is none other than these lights.'

These sefirothic lights manifest themselves in three triads, each triad representing a particular value as was originally contained in the *En-Sof in potentia*. The first triad is composed of the *Sefiroth Kether*, *Hokhmah*, & *Binah*. This is the most important of the three triadic divisions of the *Sefiroth* for it symbolizes the dynamic function of a thought process anterior to the world, & therefore an archetypal model. It represents, in other words, the thought process of God.

The prominence of the activity of these three *Sefiroth* may be seen in the fact that the Kabbalists have left us more information, specific information,

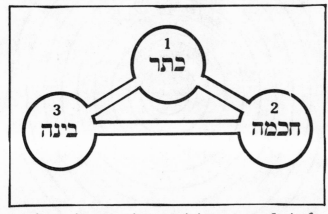

The first triad, *Kether, Hokhmah* & *Binah*. The Kabbalists used the flame-like points of the letter *Shin*—

on them than on the remaining seven. It is for that reason that the discussions to be had about the last two triads will at first sight appear to be wanting. This is not because they are any the less significant, but rather because they are representative of the sacred operations of the *En-Sof* in the world. The abundance of information to be found on the operations of that realm beyond human comprehension is strange. Yet this paradox is not peculiar to Jewish mysticism. For some reason the unknown & incomprehensible is always better

(above) to conceal this first trinity of the *Sefiroth,* the union of the Crown, the Father & the Mother from which are produced the worlds & the generations of living things.

The *Sefiroth* are shown here in the form of the Solar System. The outermost ring is the orbit of the all-inclusive *Kether*, the inner those remaining *Sefiroth* surrounding the Kingdom or physical universe. The orbits are thought of as decreasing in dignity and power as they decrease in size. From Thomas Maurice, *Indian Antiquities*, London, 1800.

explained & better outlined than the mysteries of our own immediate reality. The explanations of the activity of the divine & its operations in the world are generally more complex & confusing, if they are given at all.

It is at this juncture that philosophers & mystics

begin to diverge. About the beginning there is much agreement; about its result, the world, little. All of which appears to indicate that the mystery, as well as the answer to the mystery, is to be found here, in the world. It is as if the purpose of contemplation, & contemplation of the Divine in particular, is the understanding of the world. In short, such contemplation serves as a mirror by which we may perceive the totality of being.

Kether - The Crown §In its act of emanation the *En-Sof* stands in relationship to the first *Sefirah*, *Kether*, as a cause to its effect. It is in this first *Sefirah* that the plan of the entire universe is contained & in which the concept of unity as our intelligence is capable of understanding exists.

This *Sefirah* is also referred to in Kabbalistic works as 'The Old or Ancient One,' 'The Primordial Point or Monad,' 'The Ancient of Ancients,' 'The Smooth Point,' 'The White Head,' 'The Inscrutable Height,' & 'The Vast Countenance' or 'Macroprosopus.' This latter designation figures prominently in Kabbalistic speculation, so it would do us well to briefly discuss it & its origin.

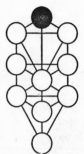

Kether is the Crown of Knowledge.

The Hebrew name of the *Macroprosopus* is *Arikh Anpin*, which translates into 'The Long Face' or 'The Greater Countenance.' Some Kabbalists feel that the term more accurately translates into 'The Long Suffering.' In order to understand the significance of this latter designation it is necessary to realize that each *Sefirah* is sometimes thought of as containing within it ten lights, each light in turn containing another ten, & so on *ad infinitum*. Every *Sefirah* has at least one of these lights illuminated, but those which have all ten burning at the same time constitute a special class, the configurations known as *Partsufim*, 'Countenance,' (*Partsuf*, singular). *Kether* constitutes the first *Partsuf*, *Arikh Anpin*; the *Sefirah hokhmah* constitutes the *Partsuf Abba* (father); the *Sefirah Binah* constitutes the *Partsuf Imma* (mother); the fifth & last *Partsuf* is *Nukba*, the *Sefirah Malkuth*. The six *Sefiroth* immediately following gather the potencies of their luminosity under the *Partsuf* known as Zair *Anpin*,

'The Lesser Countenance,' also known as 'The Short Face,' or 'The Impatient,' the *Microprosopus*.

When the *Macroprosopus* is given us in illustrated form it is in accordance with the Kabbalistic statement that he is partially concealed & that 'in him is all right side.' In the *Zohar* the first chapter of 'The Book of Concealed Mystery'[10] is dedicated to a complete description of him. There we are told that his skull has as its primary substance the light of the *En-Sof*, & contained within that a crystalline dew. The brightness of this skull, we are told, extends into 40,000 worlds superior to this one, & the interior of it contains an additional 13,000 myriads of worlds. The dew in which these worlds float flows down from his head & is the elixir which reawakens the dead for the world to come, the manna of heaven. It is this crystalline dew, white in color, in the skull of the *Macroprosopus* which the Kabbalists believe is referred to in Exodus *xvi*, 14: 'And when the dew that lay was gone up, behold, upon the face of the wilderness there lay a small round thing, as small as the hoarfrost on the ground.'

The membrane of the brain of *Macroprosopus* has an outlet which leads to the worlds below, the *Sefiroth* below, so that His brain can send out along thirty-two paths a shining white emanation. It is for this purpose that the skull has a small hole at its base. This refers us to the thirty-two paths mentioned in the opening stanza of the *Sefer Yetsirah*: 'Jehovah, through thirty-two paths, engraved His name.' The Kabbalists also see in this idea the meaning of Genesis *ii*, 10: 'And a river went out of Eden to water the garden.'

His hair, which is made of a substance as fine

[10] S.L. MacGregor Mathers, trans. *Kabbalah Unveiled,* pp. 43-66.

& as white as wool, is composed of 7,500 hairs which radiate the lights of the fountains contained within each of them into 410 worlds (410 being the numerical value of the word 'holy'.)

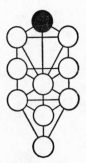

Of his one eye which is visible to us, the Kabbalists, citing Psalm *cxxi*, 4 ('Behold, he that keepeth Israel shall never slumber nor sleep.'), say it is eternally open & that if it should close but for a fraction of a second nothing could exist. It is for this reason that the *Macroprosopus'* eye is depicted as being lidless.

Kether, the Long Suffering and the Smooth Point.

From his nostrils, which are described as being the size of enormous galleries, the spirit issues forth to the lower worlds.

His beard, as white as the wool of his hair, is divided into thirteen parts—thirteen being the number expressive of unity. 'The Book of the Greater Assembly' in the *Zohar* dedicates one chapter to each portion of his beard.

One cannot help recalling, while holding this picture of *Macroprosopus* in mind, a section from 'The Book of Daniel' in the Old Testament where we are told he saw in vision the 'Ancient of days' whose garment was white as snow, & the hair of his head like the pure wool: his throne…like the fiery flame, & his wheels as burning fire.' (Daniel *vii*, 9.)

The appearance of the *Sefirah Kether* is just the first impulse of *En-Sof* towards manifestation. It is the first expression of God's primal will, a will to will, an impulse & nothing more as yet. *Kether* is the effect of *En-Sof* & only in this regard can we distinguish a difference between the two concepts. Within this *Sefirah* reside all opposites in peaceful union. They exist in a state of potential separation. It is not until the two following *Sefiroth* come into being that the idea of balance appears.

Kether represents equilibrium as a force or power residing at the central axis of a fulcrum. It is that point where two contending & opposing forces are counterbalanced. This is the significance of *Kether's* attribute of 'The Primordial or Smooth Point.' It is not a point in the normal sense of the word, a dot on a piece of paper; it is a monad of pure energy in which is contained the power of the opposites in unity. Its first appearance in the *pleroma* of space is as a spark tearing an opening in space itself, a brilliant shining point out of which will eventually emerge the remaining *Sefiroth*. Some Kabbalists, when thinking of the 'vessel' aspect of this *Sefirah*, state that it was made manifest by the *En-Sof* for the sole purpose of shielding this world from the initial outpouring of its Light.

The energies of the second & third *Sefiroth, Hokhmah* & *Binah,* in that they are representative of all that is extreme in polarities, are contained by *Kether* in a point. It is the intensity of these powers residing together in one space which cause *Kether* to 'suffer' as it were. It is essential, however, that this suffering be not understood as stemming from the energies contained in *Hokhmah* & *Binah* in an antagonistic or hostile form. In the West the opposites traditionally are thought of as warring elements, antagonistic towards one another until they are united, at which point they no longer are thought of as antithetical but as one. This characteristically Western view is a simplification of the matter, & yields little philosophical substance or meaning, especially when applied to the two *Sefiroth* under consideration here. What is particularly significant is the fact that the relationship of *Hokhmah*

& *Binah* represents a high stage of development.

To understand this statement it is necessary that the relationship of the opposites, any opposites, be viewed as one which develops in a three-fold pattern. In the first stage the opposites exist in ignorance of or indifference to the existence of the other. Examples of this type of antithetical relationship are such units as night & day, black & white, above & below, North & South. This first stage is one either of ignorance or innocence rather than of indifference. It is in such a state that we find the supreme biblical opposites, Adam & Eve, in the Garden of Eden. Both are defined as antithetical beings, but both are ignorant of their differences until they eat of the Tree of Knowledge. It is at that time that they notice they are naked, at that time that they first perceive their differences, here expressed through the medium of sexuality.

The second stage in the development of the relationship of the opposites is expressed in terms of conflict, abhorrence or contradiction. Here the opposites are openly hostile towards one another.

Finally, the third & final stage in the relationship of the opposites is where they exist in a state of harmony, distinct from one another but mutually co-operative, in love. This is the state in which we find the *Sefiroth Hokhmah* & *Binah*, the 'wisdom' & the 'intelligence' of God.

Hokhmah - Wisdom §The second *Sefirah* is masculine & has the attribute of the father. It is in this *Sefirah* that the will to create first manifests itself, & that which the *Zohar* refers to when it states that after the initial breakthrough of the divine power in the *pleroma*, the establishment of *Kether*, there suddenly appeared a shining point

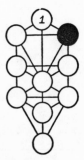

Hokhmah is the Wisdom of the Knower.

which was called *Reshith*, 'Beginning,' the first word
of creation. This *Sefirah* & that immediately following it, *Binah*, are parallel emanations of *Kether*,
the Crown. I cannot help feeling that this first
trinity, its format & the metaphysical statements
surrounding it, have their origin in Job *xxviii*, 10-
12:

'He cutteth out rivers among the rocks; & His
eye seeth every precious thing. He bindeth the floods
from overflowing; & the thing that is hid bringeth
he forth to light. But where shall wisdom be found?
& where is the place of understanding?'

In order to see the relationship between this passage & the quote from Job it is necessary that I
bring out what appears to be another 'borrowing,'
this one appearing in the *Zohar*.[11] There we are
told that the source of the sea is *one* (*Kether*) &
the current which issues forth from it, *two*
(*Chokhmah*), which was formed as a vessel as small
as the letter *Yod* which was called 'The Wisdom-
Gushing Fountain.' *Kether*, whose eye (singular)
'seeth every precious thing,' then cuts out a channel
in the earth into which the waters of 'The Wisdom-
Gushing Fountain' flow & fill up. This channel,
or large vessel, he then called 'Sea,' the third *Sefirah*,
Binah, Intelligence or Understanding. He finally
smites it 'into seven streams,' (Isaiah *xi*, 15), the
seven remaining *Sefiroth*.

So the first three *Sefiroth* & their creation are
intimately connected with each other in many ways,
if we take the passage from *Job* as the source for
the theory of their operations. It is *Kether* who cuts
out the rivers from the rocks, his one eye overlooking
everything. And it is *Kether* who receives the first
flow of the *En-Sof's* emanation, stemming the flood

[11] Paul P.
Levertoff,
trans.,
The Zohar,
vol. 3, p.129.

of numinosity & keeping it from overflowing. And what he brings forth is an aspect of the divine *En-Sof*, his unity, in a symbolic anagram which is comprehensible to the human mind: the union of the opposites. At least, this is one way of interpreting 'that is hid.' A simpler interpretation would be that it is *Binah*, the third *Sefirah*.

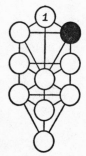

Hokhmah, the Wisdom-Gushing Fountain, water of the wise.

Hokhmah, the *Sefirah* of God's wisdom contains within him, in potential, the whole of creation set within the catalyst of a will to create. In *Kether* we had the plan as intimated to him by the *En-Sof*; in *Hokhmah* we have not only the plan but the impetus, the 'current,' the bursting desire to put forth the plan of creation. But maybe this is too romantic an interpretation. It is not so much a desire as a readiness to express, a willingness to let go. In *Kether* we find a 'will to will.' In Wisdom we find a willingness to *express* that will. The manifestation of God's wisdom is as yet unexpressed, undifferentiated & unknown, but it is full to the bursting point. It is, if nothing else at this time, the essence of the creative aspect of the *En-Sof* as transmitted through *Kether*. It is an aspect of the dynamic portion of the Divine which, if perceivable, would appear static rather than dynamic. But this, too, might be said of a tree.

Hokhmah is the father of all created things, which is to say that the wisdom of God is the father of all created things. One aspect of Wisdom looks upwards towards the Crown (*Kether*) to perceive the plan received from *En-Sof*, & another aspect looks or beams downwards in an effort to teach men what is engraved there. ('O Lord, how manifold are thy works! In wisdom hast thou made them all: the earth is full of thy riches.', Psalms *civ*, 24; 'The

Lord by wisdom hath founded the earth; by understanding hath he established the heavens.', Proverbs
iii, 19).

The reader by this point might have noticed that
Wisdom has all of the attributes of *sophia*, a feminine
principle. Those readers versed in the Hebrew language will have also been confronted with the contradiction inherent in the idea that *Hokhmah* is a
feminine noun. This is the source of much confusion
for the student of the Kabbalah, especially when
he comes across passages in Kabbalistic writings
which refer to *Hokhmah* as *she*.

The difficulty is ironed out, quite simply, by
Mathers in his introduction to *The Kabbalah
Unveiled*.[12] He points out that every *Sefiroth* is
androgynous to a certain degree in that it stands
in a relationship of receptivity (femininity) to the
Sefirah which immediately precedes it, & transmis-
siveness (masculinity) to the *Sefirah* which
immediately follows. The exceptions to the case
are *Kether*, which has no *Sefirah* preceding it, &
Malkuth, the last *Sefirah*, which has no *Sefirah* following it. Only *Kether*, therefore, is purely masculine,
& only *Malkuth* is purely feminine. This explains
why, for example, in Book III of the *Zohar*[13] we
are told that *Kether* (the masculine principle) was
moved to come into union with *Hesed* (Mercy, but
also Love) which is in the same passage not only
referred to as masculine, but as the place of circumcision. All of the *Sefiroth*, from this point of view,
must be regarded as residing in a state of receptivity
(femininity) when we refer them to *Kether*, & all
of the *Sefiroth* should be regarded as being actively
transmissive (masculine) when we refer them to
Malkuth. Once this is understood it will not seem

[12] Mathers,
*Kabbalah Un-
veiled*, intro.,
p.26 ff.

[13] Lever-
toff, *The Zo-
har*, vol.3,
p.113.

[14] Mathers,
*Kabbalah Un-
veiled*, p.273.

[15] Mathers,
*Kabbalah Un-
veiled*, p.284.

contradictory that *Hokhmah*, the spirit which issues from the nostrils of the *Macroprosopus*, is feminine:

'And that Spirit issues from the concealed brain. She is called the Spirit of Life & through Her do all men understand Hokhmah, Wisdom, in the time of the Messiah.'[14]

This *Sefirah* is the archetype of fatherhood, for he is referred to as the 'father of fathers,' & it is within this context that it might be understood why he is also synonymous with Eden.[15] Eden was the prototype of the world, the model after which the world would pattern itself. It was 'masculine' in that it did not extend itself but remained as a closed unit, inaccessible & isolated from 'mother earth.'

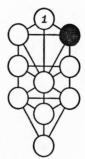

Hokhmah, the Father of Fathers.

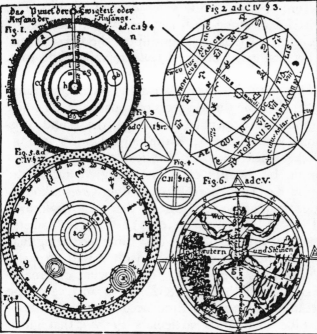

One of the Kabbalistic charts reproduced in Giorgius Von Welling, *The Magical Quabbalistical, & Theosophical Writings on the Subject of Salt, Sulphur & Mercury*, Frankfort 1735, showing amongst other things, the solar system accordiing to Genesis (Fig. 1).

Binah - Intelligence or Understanding §*Binah* is the Supernal Mother, *Imma*, within whose womb all that was contained in Wisdom finally becomes differentiated. It is out of her that the remaining *Sefiroth* proceed. The union of *Hokhmah* & *Binah*, Wisdom & Understanding, yields a son, *Da'at*, Reason, although this son is not counted amongst the *Sefiroth*.

According to the symbolism of the palace or divine building the appearance of *Binah* represents the unfolding of what was once hidden. The divine palace is a synonym for the world. The point which was Wisdom expands here through the nourishing & furthering agency of Understanding. The seven agencies which will flow out of her womb will become known as the seven days of Genesis. But this *Sefirah* along with the two which preceded it stand in a special relationship to the lower seven. This first triad of the *Sefiroth* represent the total manifestation of divine thought.

This triad of Crown, Wisdom & Understanding symbolize the three aspects of knowledge. The first *Sefirah*, The Crown, is 'knowledge;' the second, Wisdom, is the 'knower;' & the third, Understanding, is 'that which is known.' In effect, these three *Sefiroth* might be thought of as one thing, or rather the operation of one thing—knowledge. *Kether* is knowledge in that he contains all that may be known of *En-Sof*. He is, in the eyes of many Kabbalists, co-equal with *En-Sof*, the only difference being that *Kether* includes within himself a will to will. *Hokhmah* is the knower in that what originally resided in both *En-Sof* & *Kether* as an idea of the creation has by this time become a blueprint of the idea in all of its particulars. *Binah* is that which is known. She is the expression in full differentiated & substantial form of what *Hokhmah* knows. It is also of significance to note that the state of knowledge (*Kether*) is one in which the opposites reside in total union. This implies that the *Sefiroth*, if used as a meditational device in the process of spiritual transformation, has as its goal the reconciliation of the opposites which are distributed throughout the other *Sefiroth* in the mind of the devotee.

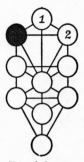

Binah bears wisdom in her womb.

Moses Cordovero warned against such meditation, citing Deuteronomy *xxii*, 6, 7:

'If a bird's nest chance to be before thee in the way in any tree, or on the ground, whether they be young ones, or eggs, & the mother sitting upon the young, or upon the eggs, thou shalt not take the mother with the young. But thou shalt in any wise let the mother go, & take the young to thee; that it may be well with thee, & that thou mayest prolong thy days.'

The reference to the mother here is taken to be *Binah,* (Intelligence or Understanding). The Kabbalist accepts this passage as a warning that he should not contemplate the mother, along with the two higher *Sefiroth*, but should withdraw his attention from this arena of divine thought & turn his attention to the 'young ones,' the lower seven *Sefiroth*, which belong to the class of divine emotions & actions. This is rooted in the idea that the triad of divine thought is so filled with the fire of numinosity, & so much a part of a world beyond our normal capabilities, that to contemplate it too long would be to call down the full fire of the Divine on oneself without the intervening protective shields of the 'younger' *Sefiroth*.

The danger here, it appears, is that of calling forth the pure archetype, which no man or woman can embrace without dying. You will recall from Part I of this work that the three *Sefiroth Kether*, *Hokhmah & Binah* reside in the first of the four worlds, *'atsiluth*, the world of emanation.[16] It is in this world that the divine *En-Sof* manifests himself in the form of pure energy. It is for protection from the rays of this world that the Jew wears his *kippah* (Yiddish, *yarmulka*), his skullcap in worship.

The second Triad, *Hesed*, *Gevurah* & *Tifereth*, is symbolic of God's moral power.

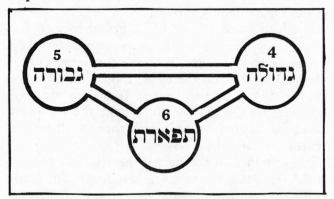

17 Levertoff, *The Zohar*, vol. 3, p. 20.

It is interesting to note here that Cordovero's citation of Deuteronomy *xxii*, 6, 7 also appears to shed some light on a passage in the *Zohar*.[17] There, in the *Zohar*, we are told that when the Messiah arrives he will come out of the Garden of Eden, from a place called 'The Bird's Nest.' Obviously, this is a reference to the two *Sefiroth Hokhmah* & *Binah*, the former identified with Eden in the system of the *Sefiroth*, the latter identified in the passage from Deuteronomy as the mother bird seated in her nest with her young ones, the lower seven *Sefiroth*.

With the appearance of the mother & father *Sefiroth*

the source of this androgyneity has its origin between his two arms, 'that part which is called *Tifereth,* which expands to form two breasts. It is here where we find the head of a woman, her hair covering the side of her head. We are also told that she has been extended 'from the heart,' the *Sefirah Tifereth* having the attribute of the heart.

This *Sefirah* symbolically represents the third day of Genesis when the waters under heaven gathered in one place & the dry land appeared. On this day also we are told God created the vegetable kingdom.

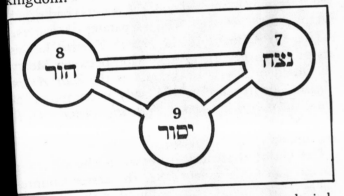

With the manifestation of *Tifereth* the second triad, that of God's moral power, is complete. The next & last triad is composed of *Netsah, Hod* & *Yesod.*

Netsah - Victory or Endurance §The seventh *Sefirah, Netsah,* is a masculine active principle & that which supports the *Sefirah* of Mercy.

This *Sefirah* symbolically represents the fourth day of Genesis, the day on which God created the sun & the moon.

Hod - Majesty or Glory §The eighth *Sefirah* is *Hod,* Majesty or Glory, feminine & passive in

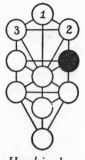

the differences between the sexes become established. From this point on all of the *Sefiroth* on the right side of the configuration are known as being masculine, while those on the left side are feminine. The *Sefiroth* located in the middle of the configuration, with the exception of the first & last *Sefiroth,* are thought of as composite figures made up of the values of the two *Sefiroth* preceding them.

This triadic formation of divine thought gives birth to the second triad composed of *Hesed, Din* & *Tifereth,* & which is representative of the *En-Sof's* moral power.

Hesed is the first day of creation.

Hesed - Mercy or Love §The fourth *Sefirah,* the 'Love or Mercy of God,' is produced by the union of Wisdom & Understanding & is considered a masculine force. *Hesed* is thought of as the productive & life-giving power which manifests itself not only in the universe but in man. This *Sefirah* symbolically represents the expansion of the will of the first triad. But as the Sefirothic system began with the principle of balance as may be seen in the attributes of *Kether,* so too must this triad & that to follow be in accord with that principle. Each *Sefirah* is so 'full,' so rich in the sense that the agencies contained within it are unrestricted by any deficiencies, there must be called forth a counterbalancing effect. Hence, in this instance we read that in order to set a limit for the powers contained in Mercy, the fifth *Sefirah, Gevurah* or *Din,* was created.

It is this *Sefirah* which symbolically represents the first day of creation when God created light & separated the darkness of the original chaos from that light to make the first day & night. According

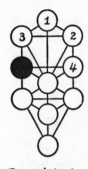

Gevurah is the power of God.

[18] Cf. *The Soncino Chumash*, A. Cohen ed., p.1, fn. 3.

to the Italian philosopher & Bible exegete, Obadiah ben Jacob Sforno (1475-1550) the light referred to in the first chapter of Genesis was a special light which existed only during the seven days of creation.[18] This idea was most probably put forth to explain how there could be light on the first day when the sun & moon were not created until the fourth day. A Kabbalist might find in Sforno's explanation further validation for belief that the *En-Sof* emanated Himself in the form of light.

Gevurah - Judgement or Power §*Gevurah*, the Power of God, is the *Sefirah* of Justice & Control, capable of also meting out punishment. Its nature is feminine, & it limits the abundance of Mercy. By the same token, the severities of Power are tempered by Mercy, so the two exist in a state of harmony. This *Sefirah* is representative of the contraction of the divine will. Because Mercy is a life-giving power, ever-productive in its activity, it would have been unwise to have let it express itself without setting some limit. It was for the reason that *Gevurah*, Judgment & Power, or Justice, holds things in check that it had to be created. Yet without the compassion & creativity of Mercy, Justice in its role of stern judge would cause things to contract to the point of non-existence. The fourth *Sefirah's* danger is to be found in its tendency to overexpand; the fifth, in contraction. The two together create a middle point. The marriage of these powers gives birth to Beauty, which is expressive of all that is harmoniously balanced.

This *Sefirah* symbolically represents the second day of Genesis when God separated the waters by causing a firmament to appear in the midst of them, thus bringing about 'above' (Heaven) or limitation

to the operation of the fourth *Sefira* is an outflowing expansion. This form of water is here checked b of Heaven (*shamayim*) which in H pound of 'there is water' (*sham may ing to note that it is also a com water' (*esh wamayim*). The Spanis Abraham ibn Ezra (1092-1167), mentary on the Bible[19] that the means the atmosphere which ha the fire of creation. This fire, strength after it & the wind (*ru* the spirit which hovered over the off the earth, is Heaven, which se

Tifereth - Beauty §The *Sefi* its primary role that of mediat & Judgment. It is also known (Lesser Countenance) whose bo the *Sefiroth* Hesed, Gevurah, Ti & *Yesod*—the body members we we discuss the *Sefirah* Yesod.

The major distinction bet Countenance (*Macroprosopus*) & nance (*Microprosopus*) is to be fo the former, while lending a p the *Sefirah* Kether, is thought o latter, *Microprosopus*, is referred est & manifest. Therefore we picture of him. In contrast t the *Microprosopus* has black h filled with dew, & my locks night.' Solomon v, 2), & has the most important differenc statement that the *Microproso* We are told in 'The Grea

Netsah, the endurance of the Sun & Moon.

The third Triad, *Netsah, Hod & Yesod*, is the material universe.

Hod, the Glory of God in His creation.

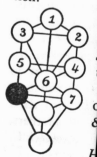

nature. It is the support of the fifth *Sefirah* Judgment or Power. It symbolically represents the fifth day of Genesis during which God created the creatures of the sea & air.

Yesod - Foundation §The ninth *Sefirah* is *Yesod*, Foundation, & is symbolic of both male & female genitals. This *Sefirah* completes the last triadic division of the *Sefiroth*, the triad representative of the result of God's reproductive or creative power, the material world. It symbolically represents the sixth day of Genesis when God created Adam & Eve.

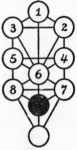

Yesod is the sexual organ of the Divine Hermaphrodite.

[21] Mathers, *Kabbalah Unveiled*, p.46.

This *Sefirah* is also the last of the six members of the *Microprosopus*. The 'Book of Concealed Mystery'[21] tells us that Mercy is his right arm, Judgment or Power is his left arm, Beauty is his trunk, Victory is his right leg, Majesty or Glory is his left leg, & Foundation are his reproductive organs.

To review the triadic arrangements of the *Sefiroth* up to this point:

The first triad, representative of the *En-Sof's* power of thought, is composed of the *Sefiroth Kether*, *Hokhmah* & *Binah*, the latter two also known as *Abba* (father) & *Imma* (mother) respectively. The union of the Father & Mother give birth to the configuration of the second triad composed of *Hesed*, *Gevurah* & *Tifereth*, which is representative of the *En-Sof's* moral power in the universe.

Malkuth, the exiled feminine.

The third triad symbolically represents the material universe in its multiplicity of forms, variety of change & all movement which may occur therein. This triad is composed of *Netsah*, *Hod* & *Yesod*. The latter *Sefirah Yesod* (Foundation) symbolizes the stabilization of the opposites.

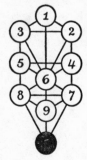

Malkuth - Kingdom §The tenth & last *Sefirah*, *Malkuth*, is a feminine & passive principle. This

Sefirah is also symbolically representative of God's feminine counterpart, the *Shekhinah* to whom we shall devote several pages shortly. It is through her that the divine grace of the *En-Sof* passes through into the lower world.

Malkuth is assigned to the seventh day of Genesis when God rested.

THE LAST few pages have concentrated on presenting the manner in which the *En-Sof* made Himself known through the agency of his emanations, the *Sefiroth*. The *Sefiroth* should always be thought of as different aspects of the *En-Sof*, different colors along a spectrum, & as intimate portions of His process. The greatest mistake would be to view them as aspects of His creation instead of the result of His divine *efflux*. Creation implies the establishing of something other than oneself, outside of oneself, wholly capable of existing as an independent unit or entity. Emanation on the other hand is an act of flowing (from the Latin, *emanare*, to flow), which implies not only the existence of a source, but that the activity of flowing is dependent on the source if it is to remain an activity. What flows through the *Sefiroth* is the light of the *En-Sof* which they need for their existence. They are composed of that light in much the same way as a bowl is composed of clay. The intimacy of the connection between the *Sefiroth* & the *En-Sof* extends to the relationships between the different *Sefiroth* themselves. Participating in a common reception of the *En-Sof's* emanations, they share also each other's qualities. The nature of their differences is marked only by the degree of predominance of the quality after which they are named. Apart from that they are equal in both power & value.

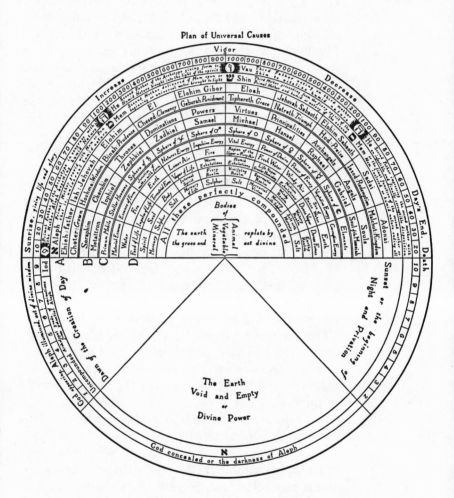

A table of Universal Causation or Sefirothic correspondences according to Robert Fludd in his *Collectio Operun*, Oppenheim, 1617.

The only exception to this equality is to be found in the theory of the *Partsufim*, the countenances, a theory foreign to the *Sefer Yetsirah* but fairly well-developed in 'The Greater Assembly' of the *Zohar*. Much of the theory of countenances as we have it now was worked out by Isaac Luria who took as his starting point the material in the *Zohar*. The *Partsufim*, as discussed in our section on the *Sefirah Kether*, are the *Macroprosopus (Kether)*, the Father (*Hokhmah*), the Mother (*Binah*), the *Microprosopus* (the six *Sefiroth* from *Hesed* to *Yesod*, inclusive) & the *Shekhinah*.

In this theory, I believe we are presented with a psychological 'overlay.' The *Partsufim* are a further differentiation of the powers of God as made manifest in reality. They are archetypal or mythological representations which have come to the fore out of the necessity to associate these values with more recognizable representations. The five figures given us are archetypal models peculiar to no single religion or mystical system of thought.

The Kabbalistic view that the manifestation & emanation of Godhead moves from an initial state of nothingness through *Kether* to the final state of *Malkuth*, the *Sefirah* symbolic of the created world, is fundamentally a psychological statement about the development of consciousness or ego from whatever stands before the *psyche*—the Self, the *Atman*, the *En-Sof* or the divine prime mover under any other appellation. If the Kabbalistic statements about the relationship between a God-principle standing before the world & His feminine counterpart in the world were an isolated instance in the history of either philosophy or religion, then this claim would be only a guess. But, as we shall now see, this is not the case.

The Hebrew word *ain* (nothing) & the Hebrew word *ani* (I) are composed of the same consonants. *Ani* is what God calls Himself at the precise moment that His *Shekhinah*, His feminine counterpart in the form of the *Sefirah Malkuth*, enters & completes the created world. That this is an archetypal statement about the mechanics of creation, a universal statement, may be supported by comparing it with another such moment as recorded in Tantric Buddhism.

In the *Kama-Kala-Vilasa*,[22] the manifestation of the created universe follows the entrance of the feminine principle, *Vimarsa*, into the space of creation. We are told that 'The Great Lord...is mere illumination. Merged in him is Vimarsa.' The appended commentary explains this verse by stating that in this stage, which precedes manifestation, the Lord, or masculine principle, is in a state of perfect 'infolded I-ness.' The feminine *Vimarsa* is reported to say of herself, 'I am the uncreated cause of the Creation, Preservation & dissolution of the Universe.' This state of infolded I-ness exists as long as the feminine principle is contained within the masculine. The moment this feminine principle becomes active, the masculine experiences itself as I. It is only at the time when the feminine becomes manifest as an emanation of the Lord, only when she begins the movement towards creative manifestation & substantial form—the cosmos as we know it—that the I state of divinity comes into being. The Kabbalistic statement that the last *Sefirah*, *Malkuth*, which is identified with the *Shekhinah*, represents the final development of the Godhead from *ain* (nothing) to *ani* (I or Being), is in perfect alignment

[22] Arthur Avalon, trans., *Kama-Kala-Vilasa*.

ment with the statements found in this Buddhist text.

Furthermore, inasmuch as the *Tattvas* (the subtle stuff out of which matter comes into being) become identified in Buddhism with aspects of mind, & inasmuch as the Sefirothic system in the form of Adam Kadmon (whom we shall discuss in the next section) becomes identified with man & his mind, we are forced again to consider the idea that the *Sefiroth*, in at least one aspect, may reveal the stages of development in a process which takes place in the human mind. It would be a great mistake for anyone to say at this stage that the postulation of an empirical relationship between the archetypal or divine manifestation of godhead & the findings of psychology amount to the reduction of mysticism to a psychological state of mind. The author of the *Zohar* understands this when he writes that any activity which takes place above stimulates a corresponding activity below. As above, so below. *We* are below & the process of mind inherent in each of us is patterned after an archetypal model, in this instance the system of the *Sefiroth*. In that fact the mystery lies.

ADAM KADMON - THE HEAVENLY OR PRIMORDIAL MAN

§ There are some Kabbalists of the opinion that the first form patterned by the ray of light emanated from the *En-Sof* were not the *Sefiroth* but the body of Adam Kadmon, from which the *Sefiroth* then flared out. Before we discuss the events leading up to the appearance of the *Sefiroth* within this context, let us first outline the *Sefiroth* considered as portions of the heavenly man's body.

Kether, the Crown, is the location of the head.

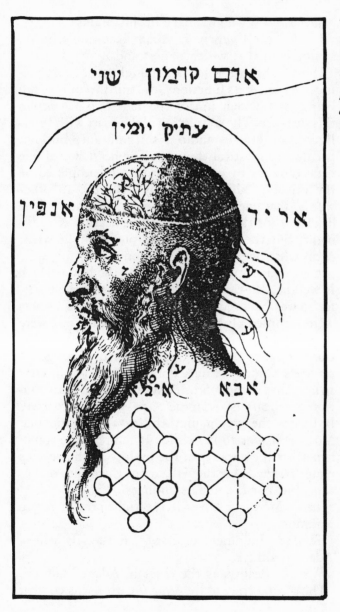

The head of Adam Kadmon, from Knorr von Rosenroth, *Kabbala Denudata*, Frankfurt, 1684.

Hokhmah, Wisdom, make up his brains.

Binah, Intelligence, is Adam Kadmon's heart, symbolic of that which understands.

These first three *Sefiroth* are thought of as constituting the head & its functions, the third *Sefirah*, *Binah* being that which unites the first two *Sefiroth* in this instance. The correlation of the heart with Intelligence or Understanding is significant, but not peculiar to mystical thought. The heart was at one time thought by a great majority of people to be the organ of thinking. Many believed, in other words, that one should think with one's heart. The head was for the process of rationalization & judgment, but the heart was what one thought with, & on what one based one's actions.

In Egyptian mythology it is not the brain which is weighed on the day of judgment, but the heart, for it was believed that in that organ a man's acts were recorded. In other words, one's actions were judged by the substance of one's *emotional* considerations, on the basis of one's understanding & not on one's rationalizations alone. It is also of interest to note that in the Sefirothic system under consideration the heart is feminine & passive or receptive. It listens the way a mother (*Imma*, the Supernal Mother) listens to her child. It tempers the sometimes harsh computer of the brain, which contains plans (*Hokhmah*) & the will to put them into operation, but not the understanding.

Hesed, Mercy or Love, is the right arm of Adam Kadmon.

Gevurah, Judgment or Power, is the left arm of Adam Kadmon.

Tifereth, Beauty, is the chest of Adam Kadmon. The second triad of the *Sefiroth* within this context

refers us to the activity of the right & the left
hand, of Mercy & Judgment when working harmoniously, to yield Beauty (the chest) which houses
Understanding (*Binah*, the heart). Understanding
is therefore the result of a harmonious relationship
between Mercy & Judgment, between the activity
of the right & the left hand.

Netsah, Victory or Endurance, is the right leg
of Adam Kadmon.

Hod, Majesty or Glory, is the left leg of Adam Kadmon.

Yesod, Foundation, are the genital organs.

Yesod, which symbolizes the source of all things
because of its association with the genital organs,
unites the seventh & eight *Sefiroth* to form the third
triad, the material world. For some mysterious
reason it is easier to describe the meaning of the
activity of those dimensions beyond or above the
material world than it is to describe the meaning
of those symbols which speak of the meaning of
those symbols which speak of the material world.
What is the symbolic meaning of legs if not locomotion? In some systems of symbolic thought they
represent the lower instincts. If we follow this last
suggestion then *Yesod* might be thought of as a
harmonizer only in the sense that it shuttles the
powers inherent in Victory & its ensuing Glory
into a creative & regenerative act. All of which
only suggests that we have yet another understanding of *Yesod*. The legs remain a mystery.

Malkuth, Kingdom, is symbolic of Adam Kadmon's harmony or completeness.

In passing, it should be mentioned that in the
configuration of Adam Kadmon traditionally given
we see him from the rear, facing in the same direction

The correct depiction of Adam Kadmon is one in which the right & left sides of the figure are aligned with the right & left sides of the viewer.

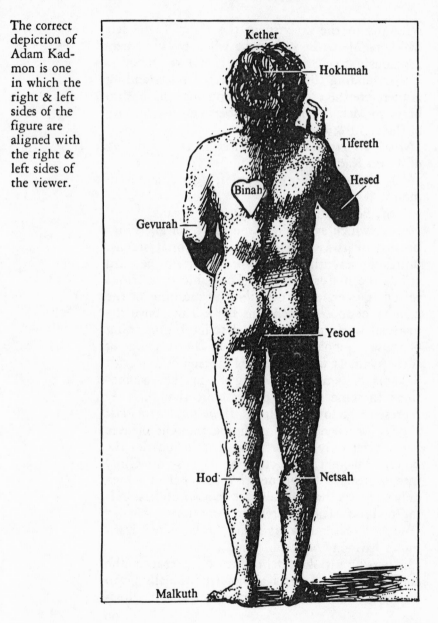

tion that we face. This depiction of Adam Kadmon
finds its source in Exodus *xxxiii,* 18-23, where Moses asks God to show him His Glory:

'And he said, I will make all my goodness pass
before thee, & I will proclaim the name of the
Lord before thee; & will be gracious to whom I
will be gracious, & will show mercy on whom I
will show mercy. And he said, Thou canst not
see my face: for there shall no man see me & live.
And the Lord said, Behold, there is a place by
me, & thou shalt stand upon a rock: And it shall
come to pass, while my glory passeth by, that I
will put thee in a cleft of the rock, & will cover
thee with my hand while I pass by: And I will
take away mine hand, & thou shalt see my back
parts: but my face shall not be seen.'

It is in Lurianic Kabbalism that we find the theory
of the *En-Sof's* original emanation resulting in the
body of Adam Kadmon. In many respects he might
therefore be thought of not only as the first of
the *Partsufim* (Countenances) but as their father.
In some Kabbalists' minds he is the first God who
can be comprehended by man by virtue of the fact
that man is made in his image.

En-Sof &
Adam Kad-
mon

From the first configuration, Adam Kadmon, there
burst forth lights from his ears, mouth & nose.
The lights streaming out of these sources produced
hidden configurations in the *pleroma* of the universe,
configurations so secret they have never until this
day been described. Then, from the eyes of Adam
Kadmon, burst forth the lights which were to play
the central part in the creation. But the vessels
which had been prepared to capture & hold this
light ruptured under their weight, causing the light
to burst into millions of particles which fell into

The fall of
Adam Kad-
mon

the darkest parts of the *pleroma*. This resulted in the birth of the evil shells discussed in part I in our outline of Lurianic Kabbalism.[23] The lights which afterwards proceeded from Adam Kadmon's forehead led to the configuration of the *Sefiroth* as they now stand.

However, the mishap which led to the breaking of the vessels was equated in some Kabbalists' minds with the fall of the Adam in the Garden. The original harmony which God sought to instill in His creation was marred by the bursting of the vessels & the establishment of evil. As above so below: the Fall of Adam in the Garden was understood as inevitable in that the archetypal drama of the Fall had already taken place in Adam Kadmon. The problem of restoring the original unity no longer lay in the arena of the Divine. Man was now equally responsible for the work of restoration. The Adam of the Garden was the anthropological counterpart of the ontological Adam Kadmon. Therefore, in much the same way that the body of the Adam Kadmon outlined the configuration of the *Sefiroth*, so too must that spiritual portion of man be thought of as containing the *Sefiroth*. Somewhere there is an Adam within each of us in need of restoration, in exile from the Garden. The aim of Kabbalism is the restoration of the divine man in the medium of mortal man. We are the laboratory & we are the workers who work in that space. All of this is to say that there is an intimate relationship between man & his spiritual counterpart. The mystery of this relationship is to be found in the *Sefiroth*. If one can learn how to connect the thread dangling free from the *Sefiroth* with the thread on one's own being, if one can discover the opening

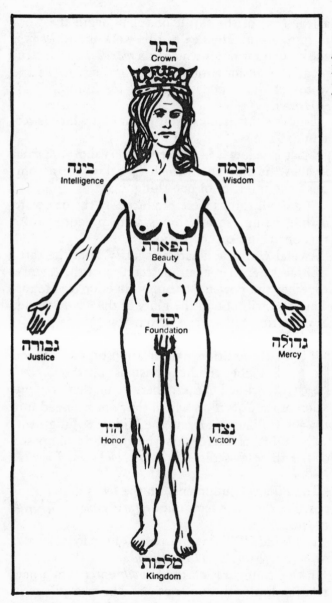

כתר
Crown

בינה
Intelligence

חכמה
Wisdom

תפארת
Beauty

יסוד
Foundation

גבורה
Justice

גדולה
Mercy

הוד
Honor

נצח
Victory

מלכות
Kingdom

Adam Kad-
mon as he is
generally de-
picted, fac-
ing the
wrong way.

The *Sefiroth* as a *mandala*

at the base of the skull, one may begin the work of restoration. The key to this work is the *Sefiroth,* the configuration of which is a *mandala,* an instrument of transformation, of the first order. In the words of the famous *Precepts of the Emerald Table of Hermes*:

'I speak not fictitious things, but that which is certain & True.

What is below is like that which is above, & what is above is like that which is below, to accomplish the miracles of one thing.

And as all things were produced by the one word of one Being, so all things were produced from this one thing by adaptation....

Ascend with the greatest sagacity from the earth to heaven, & then again descend to earth, & unite together the powers of things superior & inferior. Thus you will obtain the glory of the whole world, & obscurity will fly away from you.'[24]

[24] Quoted in *Alchemy,* E. J. Holmyard, pp. 97-8.

THE THREE PILLARS

§ In addition to the relationships to be found in the triadic divisions of the *Sefiroth* outlined earlier, there is another configuration of the *Sefiroth* in which they are arranged into the three pillars of Mercy, the Middle & Judgment.

The Pillar of Mercy, on the right, is composed of the three masculine *Sefiroth*, *Hokhmah*, *Hesed* & *Netsah.*

The Pillar of Judgment, on the left side, is composed of the three feminine *Sefiroth*, *Binah*, *Gevurah* & *Hod.*

The Middle Pillar is composed of the four *Sefiroth*, *Kether*, *Tifereth*, *Yesod* & *Malkuth.*

In this configuration the *Sefiroth* enter into a new relationship with one another. The two pillars of Judgment & Mercy are balanced by the pillar of the differences between the sexes become established. From this point on all of the *Sefiroth* on the right side of the configuration are known as being masculine, while those on the left side are feminine. The *Sefiroth* located in the middle of the configuration, with the exception of the first & last *Sefiroth*, are thought of as composite figures made up of the values of the two *Sefiroth* preceding them.

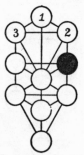

Hesed is the first day of creation.

This triadic formation of divine thought gives birth to the second triad composed of *Hesed, Din* & *Tifereth*, & which is representative of the *En-Sof's* moral power.

Hesed - Mercy or Love §The fourth *Sefirah*, the 'Love or Mercy of God,' is produced by the union of Wisdom & Understanding & is considered a masculine force. *Hesed* is thought of as the productive & life-giving power which manifests itself not only in the universe but in man. This *Sefirah* symbolically represents the expansion of the will of the first triad. But as the Sefirothic system began with the principle of balance as may be seen in the attributes of *Kether*, so too must this triad & that to follow be in accord with that principle. Each *Sefirah* is so 'full,' so rich in the sense that the agencies contained within it are unrestricted by any deficiencies, there must be called forth a counterbalancing effect. Hence, in this instance we read that in order to set a limit for the powers contained in Mercy, the fifth *Sefirah*, *Gevurah* or *Din*, was created.

It is this *Sefirah* which symbolically represents the first day of creation when God created light & separated the darkness of the original chaos from that light to make the first day & night. According

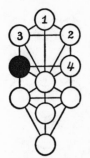

Gevurah is the power of God.

[18] Cf. *The Soncino Chumash*, A. Cohen ed., p.1, fn. 3.

to the Italian philosopher & Bible exegete, Obadiah ben Jacob Sforno (1475-1550) the light referred to in the first chapter of Genesis was a special light which existed only during the seven days of creation.[18] This idea was most probably put forth to explain how there could be light on the first day when the sun & moon were not created until the fourth day. A Kabbalist might find in Sforno's explanation further validation for belief that the *En-Sof* emanated Himself in the form of light.

Gevurah - Judgement or Power §*Gevurah*, the Power of God, is the *Sefirah* of Justice & Control, capable of also meting out punishment. Its nature is feminine, & it limits the abundance of Mercy. By the same token, the severities of Power are tempered by Mercy, so the two exist in a state of harmony. This *Sefirah* is representative of the contraction of the divine will. Because Mercy is a life-giving power, ever-productive in its activity, it would have been unwise to have let it express itself without setting some limit. It was for the reason that *Gevurah*, Judgment & Power, or Justice, holds things in check that it had to be created. Yet without the compassion & creativity of Mercy, Justice in its role of stern judge would cause things to contract to the point of non-existence. The fourth *Sefirah's* danger is to be found in its tendency to overexpand; the fifth, in contraction. The two together create a middle point. The marriage of these powers gives birth to Beauty, which is expressive of all that is harmoniously balanced.

This *Sefirah* symbolically represents the second day of Genesis when God separated the waters by causing a firmament to appear in the midst of them, thus bringing about 'above' (Heaven) or limitation

to the operation of the fourth *Sefirah* whose function is an outflowing expansion. This outflowing in the form of water is here checked by the firmament of Heaven (*shamayim*) which in Hebrew is a compound of 'there is water' (*sham mayim*). It is interesting to note that it is also a compound of 'fire & water' (*esh wamayim*). The Spanish poet & exegete, Abraham ibn Ezra (1092-1167), states in his commentary on the Bible[19] that the 'firmament' here means the atmosphere which has as its substance the fire of creation. This fire, gaining its full strength after it & the wind (*ruach*, the word for the spirit which hovered over the waters) had dried off the earth, is Heaven, which separates the waters.

Tifereth - Beauty §The *Sefirah Tifereth* has as its primary role that of mediation between Mercy & Judgment. It is also known as the *Zair Anpin* (Lesser Countenance) whose body is composed of the *Sefiroth Hesed, Gevurah, Tifereth, Netsah, Hod, & Yesod*—the body members we shall illustrate when we discuss the *Sefirah Yesod*.

The major distinction between the Greater Countenance (*Macroprosopus*) & the Lesser Countenance (*Microprosopus*) is to be found in the idea that the former, while lending a portion of himself to the *Sefirah Kether*, is thought of as unmanifest; the latter, *Microprosopus*, is referred to as both unmanifest & manifest. Therefore we are given a full-face picture of him. In contrast to the *Macroprosopus*, the *Microprosopus* has black hair ('For my head is filled with dew, & my locks with the drops of the night.' Solomon *v*, 2), & has eyes with lids. But the most important difference has to do with the statement that the *Microprosopus* is androgyne.

We are told in 'The Greater Assembly'[20] that

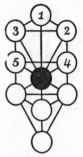

Tifereth, the *Microprosopus.*

[19] Cf. *The Soncino Chumash,* A. Cohen ed., p. 2, fn. 6.

[20] Mathers, *Kabbalah Unveiled,* p. 229.

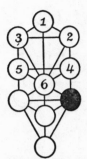

Netsah, the endurance of the Sun & Moon.

The third Triad, *Net-sah, Hod* & *Yesod*, is the material universe.

Hod, the Glory of God in His creation.

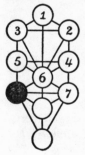

the source of this androgyneity has its origin between his two arms, 'that part which is called *Tifereth*, which expands to form two breasts. It is here where we find the head of a woman, her hair covering the side of her head. We are also told that she has been extended 'from the heart,' the *Sefirah Tifereth* having the attribute of the heart.

This *Sefirah* symbolically represents the third day of Genesis when the waters under heaven gathered in one place & the dry land appeared. On this day also we are told God created the vegetable kingdom.

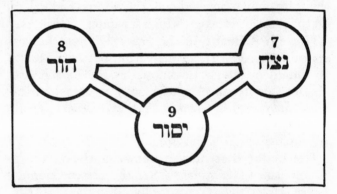

With the manifestation of *Tifereth* the second triad, that of God's moral power, is complete. The next & last triad is composed of *Netsah*, *Hod* & *Yesod*.

Netsah - Victory or Endurance §The seventh *Sefirah*, *Netsah*, is a masculine active principle & that which supports the *Sefirah* of Mercy.

This *Sefirah* symbolically represents the fourth day of Genesis, the day on which God created the sun & the moon.

Hod - Majesty or Glory §The eighth *Sefirah* is *Hod*, Majesty or Glory, feminine & passive in

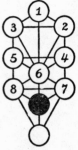

nature. It is the support of the fifth *Sefirah* Judgment or Power. It symbolically represents the fifth day of Genesis during which God created the creatures of the sea & air.

Yesod - Foundation § The ninth *Sefirah* is *Yesod*, Foundation, & is symbolic of both male & female genitals. This *Sefirah* completes the last triadic division of the *Sefiroth*, the triad representative of the result of God's reproductive or creative power, the material world. It symbolically represents the sixth day of Genesis when God created Adam & Eve.

This *Sefirah* is also the last of the six members of the *Microprosopus*. The 'Book of Concealed Mystery'[21] tells us that Mercy is his right arm, Judgment or Power is his left arm, Beauty is his trunk, Victory is his right leg, Majesty or Glory is his left leg, & Foundation are his reproductive organs.

Yesod is the sexual organ of the Divine Hermaphrodite.

[21] Mathers, *Kabbalah Unveiled*, p.46.

To review the triadic arrangements of the *Sefiroth* up to this point:

The first triad, representative of the *En-Sof's* power of thought, is composed of the *Sefiroth Kether*, *Hokhmah* & *Binah*, the latter two also known as *Abba* (father) & *Imma* (mother) respectively. The union of the Father & Mother give birth to the configuration of the second triad composed of *Hesed*, *Gevurah* & *Tifereth*, which is representative of the *En-Sof's* moral power in the universe.

Malkuth, the exiled feminine.

The third triad symbolically represents the material universe in its multiplicity of forms, variety of change & all movement which may occur therein. This triad is composed of *Netsah*, *Hod* & *Yesod*. The latter *Sefirah Yesod* (Foundation) symbolizes the stabilization of the opposites.

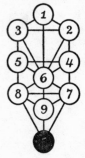

Malkuth - Kingdom § The tenth & last *Sefirah*, *Malkuth*, is a feminine & passive principle. This

Sefirah is also symbolically representative of God's feminine counterpart, the *Shekhinah* to whom we shall devote several pages shortly. It is through her that the divine grace of the *En-Sof* passes through into the lower world.

Malkuth is assigned to the seventh day of Genesis when God rested.

THE LAST few pages have concentrated on presenting the manner in which the *En-Sof* made Himself known through the agency of his emanations, the *Sefiroth*. The *Sefiroth* should always be thought of as different aspects of the *En-Sof*, different colors along a spectrum, & as intimate portions of His process. The greatest mistake would be to view them as aspects of His creation instead of the result of His divine *efflux*. Creation implies the establishing of something other than oneself, outside of oneself, wholly capable of existing as an independent unit or entity. Emanation on the other hand is an act of flowing (from the Latin, *emanare*, to flow), which implies not only the existence of a source, but that the activity of flowing is dependent on the source if it is to remain an activity. What flows through the *Sefiroth* is the light of the *En-Sof* which they need for their existence. They are composed of that light in much the same way as a bowl is composed of clay. The intimacy of the connection between the *Sefiroth* & the *En-Sof* extends to the relationships between the different *Sefiroth* themselves. Participating in a common reception of the *En-Sof's* emanations, they share also each other's qualities. The nature of their differences is marked only by the degree of predominance of the quality after which they are named. Apart from that they are equal in both power & value.

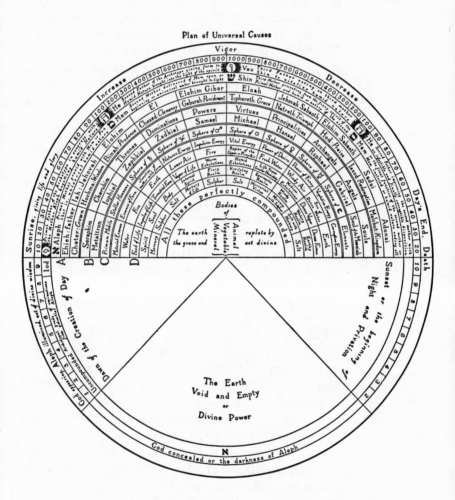

A table of Universal Causation or Sefirothic correspondences according to Robert Fludd in his *Collectio Operun,* Oppenheim, 1617.

The only exception to this equality is to be found in the theory of the *Partsufim*, the countenances, a theory foreign to the *Sefer Yetsirah* but fairly well-developed in 'The Greater Assembly' of the *Zohar*. Much of the theory of countenances as we have it now was worked out by Isaac Luria who took as his starting point the material in the *Zohar*. The *Partsufim*, as discussed in our section on the *Sefirah Kether*, are the *Macroprosopus (Kether)*, the Father (*Hokhmah*), the Mother (*Binah*), the *Microprosopus* (the six *Sefiroth* from *Hesed* to *Yesod*, inclusive) & the *Shekhinah*.

In this theory, I believe we are presented with a psychological 'overlay.' The *Partsufim* are a further differentiation of the powers of God as made manifest in reality. They are archetypal or mythological representations which have come to the fore out of the necessity to associate these values with more recognizable representations. The five figures given us are archetypal models peculiar to no single religion or mystical system of thought.

The Kabbalistic view that the manifestation & emanation of Godhead moves from an initial state of nothingness through *Kether* to the final state of *Malkuth*, the *Sefirah* symbolic of the created world, is fundamentally a psychological statement about the development of consciousness or ego from whatever stands before the *psyche*—the Self, the *Atman*, the *En-Sof* or the divine prime mover under any other appellation. If the Kabbalistic statements about the relationship between a God-principle standing before the world & His feminine counterpart in the world were an isolated instance in the history of either philosophy or religion, then this claim would be only a guess. But, as we shall now see, this is not the case.

The Hebrew word *ain* (nothing) & the Hebrew word *ani* (I) are composed of the same consonants. *Ani* is what God calls Himself at the precise moment that His *Shekhinah*, His feminine counterpart in the form of the *Sefirah Malkuth*, enters & completes the created world. That this is an archetypal statement about the mechanics of creation, a universal statement, may be supported by comparing it with another such moment as recorded in Tantric Buddhism.

In the *Kama-Kala-Vilasa*, [22] the manifestation of the created universe follows the entrance of the feminine principle, *Vimarsa*, into the space of creation. We are told that 'The Great Lord...is mere illumination. Merged in him is Vimarsa.' The appended commentary explains this verse by stating that in this stage, which precedes manifestation, the Lord, or masculine principle, is in a state of perfect 'infolded I-ness.' The feminine *Vimarsa* is reported to say of herself, 'I am the uncreated cause of the Creation, Preservation & dissolution of the Universe.' This state of infolded I-ness exists as long as the feminine principle is contained within the masculine. The moment this feminine principle becomes active, the masculine experiences itself as I. It is only at the time when the feminine becomes manifest as an emanation of the Lord, only when she begins the movement towards creative manifestation & substantial form—the cosmos as we know it—that the I state of divinity comes into being. The Kabbalistic statement that the last *Sefirah*, *Malkuth*, which is identified with the *Shekhinah*, represents the final development of the Godhead from *ain* (nothing) to *ani* (I or Being), is in perfect alignment

[22] Arthur Avalon, trans., *Kama-Kala-Vilasa*.

The *Tattvas*
& the *Sefiroth*

ment with the statements found in this Buddhist text.

Furthermore, inasmuch as the *Tattvas* (the subtle stuff out of which matter comes into being) become identified in Buddhism with aspects of mind, & inasmuch as the Sefirothic system in the form of Adam Kadmon (whom we shall discuss in the next section) becomes identified with man & his mind, we are forced again to consider the idea that the *Sefiroth*, in at least one aspect, may reveal the stages of development in a process which takes place in the human mind. It would be a great mistake for anyone to say at this stage that the postulation of an empirical relationship between the archetypal or divine manifestation of godhead & the findings of psychology amount to the reduction of mysticism

As above, so
below

to a psychological state of mind. The author of the *Zohar* understands this when he writes that any activity which takes place above stimulates a corresponding activity below. As above, so below. *We* are below & the process of mind inherent in each of us is patterned after an archetypal model, in this instance the system of the *Sefiroth*. In that fact the mystery lies.

The *Sefiroth*
as portions of
the body

ADAM KADMON - THE HEAVENLY OR PRIMORDIAL MAN

§There are some Kabbalists of the opinion that the first form patterned by the ray of light emanated from the *En-Sof* were not the *Sefiroth* but the body of Adam Kadmon, from which the *Sefiroth* then flared out. Before we discuss the events leading up to the appearance of the *Sefiroth* within this context, let us first outline the *Sefiroth* considered as portions of the heavenly man's body.

Kether, the Crown, is the location of the head.

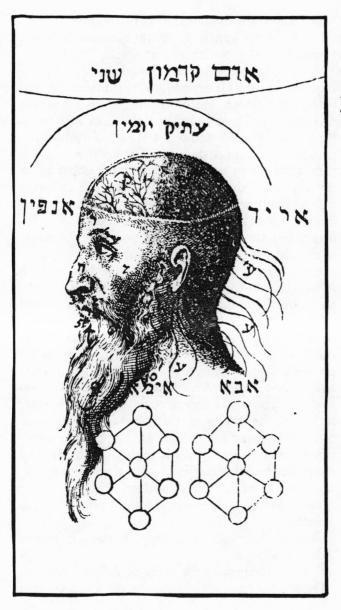

The head of Adam Kadmon, from Knorr von Rosenroth, *Kabbala Denudata,* Frankfurt, 1684.

Hokhmah, Wisdom, make up his brains.

Binah, Intelligence, is Adam Kadmon's heart, symbolic of that which understands.

These first three *Sefiroth* are thought of as constituting the head & its functions, the third *Sefirah*, *Binah* being that which unites the first two *Sefiroth* in this instance. The correlation of the heart with Intelligence or Understanding is significant, but not peculiar to mystical thought. The heart was at one time thought by a great majority of people to be the organ of thinking. Many believed, in other words, that one should think with one's heart. The head was for the process of rationalization & judgment, but the heart was what one thought with, & on what one based one's actions.

In Egyptian mythology it is not the brain which is weighed on the day of judgment, but the heart, for it was believed that in that organ a man's acts were recorded. In other words, one's actions were judged by the substance of one's *emotional* considerations, on the basis of one's understanding & not on one's rationalizations alone. It is also of interest to note that in the Sefirothic system under consideration the heart is feminine & passive or receptive. It listens the way a mother (*Imma*, the Supernal Mother) listens to her child. It tempers the sometimes harsh computer of the brain, which contains plans (*Hokhmah*) & the will to put them into operation, but not the understanding.

Hesed, Mercy or Love, is the right arm of Adam Kadmon.

Gevurah, Judgment or Power, is the left arm of Adam Kadmon.

Tifereth, Beauty, is the chest of Adam Kadmon.

The second triad of the *Sefiroth* within this context

refers us to the activity of the right & the left hand, of Mercy & Judgment when working harmoniously, to yield Beauty (the chest) which houses Understanding (*Binah*, the heart). Understanding is therefore the result of a harmonious relationship between Mercy & Judgment, between the activity of the right & the left hand.

Netsah, Victory or Endurance, is the right leg of Adam Kadmon.

Hod, Majesty or Glory, is the left leg of Adam Kadmon.

Yesod, Foundation, are the genital organs.

Yesod, which symbolizes the source of all things because of its association with the genital organs, unites the seventh & eight *Sefiroth* to form the third triad, the material world. For some mysterious reason it is easier to describe the meaning of the activity of those dimensions beyond or above the material world than it is to describe the meaning of those symbols which speak of the meaning of those symbols which speak of the material world. What is the symbolic meaning of legs if not locomotion? In some systems of symbolic thought they represent the lower instincts. If we follow this last suggestion then *Yesod* might be thought of as a harmonizer only in the sense that it shuttles the powers inherent in Victory & its ensuing Glory into a creative & regenerative act. All of which only suggests that we have yet another understanding of *Yesod*. The legs remain a mystery.

Malkuth, Kingdom, is symbolic of Adam Kadmon's harmony or completeness.

In passing, it should be mentioned that in the configuration of Adam Kadmon traditionally given we see him from the rear, facing in the same direction

The correct depiction of Adam Kadmon is one in which the right & left sides of the figure are aligned with the right & left sides of the viewer.

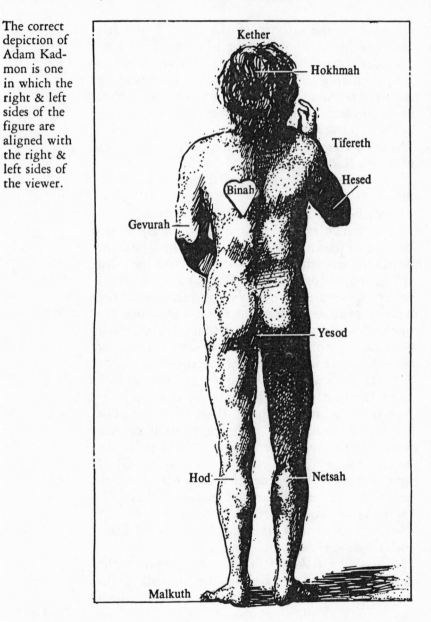

tion that we face. This depiction of Adam Kadmon
finds its source in Exodus *xxxiii,* 18-23, where Moses asks God to show him His Glory:

'And he said, I will make all my goodness pass
before thee, & I will proclaim the name of the
Lord before thee; & will be gracious to whom I
will be gracious, & will show mercy on whom I
will show mercy. And he said, Thou canst not
see my face: for there shall no man see me & live.
And the Lord said, Behold, there is a place by
me, & thou shalt stand upon a rock: And it shall
come to pass, while my glory passeth by, that I
will put thee in a cleft of the rock, & will cover
thee with my hand while I pass by: And I will
take away mine hand, & thou shalt see my back
parts: but my face shall not be seen.'

It is in Lurianic Kabbalism that we find the theory
of the *En-Sof's* original emanation resulting in the
body of Adam Kadmon. In many respects he might
therefore be thought of not only as the first of
the *Partsufim* (Countenances) but as their father.
In some Kabbalists' minds he is the first God who
can be comprehended by man by virtue of the fact
that man is made in his image.

En-Sof &
Adam Kad-
mon

From the first configuration, Adam Kadmon, there
burst forth lights from his ears, mouth & nose.
The lights streaming out of these sources produced
hidden configurations in the *pleroma* of the universe,
configurations so secret they have never until this
day been described. Then, from the eyes of Adam
Kadmon, burst forth the lights which were to play
the central part in the creation. But the vessels
which had been prepared to capture & hold this
light ruptured under their weight, causing the light
to burst into millions of particles which fell into

The fall of
Adam Kad-
mon

the darkest parts of the *pleroma*. This resulted in
the birth of the evil shells discussed in part I in
our outline of Lurianic Kabbalism.[23] The lights
which afterwards proceeded from Adam Kadmon's
forehead led to the configuration of the *Sefiroth* as
they now stand.

However, the mishap which led to the breaking
of the vessels was equated in some Kabbalists' minds
with the fall of the Adam in the Garden. The original harmony which God sought to instill in His
creation was marred by the bursting of the vessels
& the establishment of evil. As above so below:
the Fall of Adam in the Garden was understood
as inevitable in that the archetypal drama of the
Fall had already taken place in Adam Kadmon.
The problem of restoring the original unity no longer lay in the arena of the Divine. Man was now
equally responsible for the work of restoration. The
Adam of the Garden was the anthropological counterpart of the ontological Adam Kadmon. Therefore, in much the same way that the body of the
Adam Kadmon outlined the configuration of the
Sefiroth, so too must that spiritual portion of man
be thought of as containing the *Sefiroth*. Somewhere
there is an Adam within each of us in need of
restoration, in exile from the Garden. The aim of
Kabbalism is the restoration of the divine man in
the medium of mortal man. We are the laboratory
& we are the workers who work in that space.
All of this is to say that there is an intimate relationship between man & his spiritual counterpart. The
mystery of this relationship is to be found in the
Sefiroth. If one can learn how to connect the thread
dangling free from the *Sefiroth* with the thread on
one's own being, if one can discover the opening

the Middle. The *Sefiroth* contained within each pillar
or unit are connected only to the others contained
within the same pillar. The theme of polarity, the
distinction of the opposites as male/female,
positive/negative & dark/light is here emphasized.
In the triadic division of the *Sefiroth* the opposites
are present, but they are always seen within the

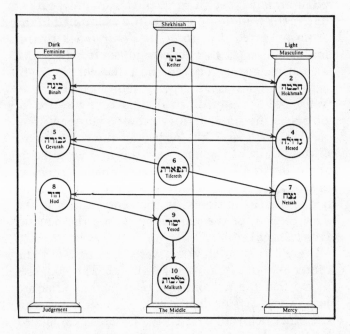

The *Sefiroth*
as the three
pillars of
Mercy, the
Middle &
Judgement.

context of relationship. In the first triad—*Kether,
Hokhmah & Binah*—the opposites are separated out
of the first *Sefirah* & are thought of as existing
in a permanent relationship with what gave birth
to them. In the second triad—*Hesed, Gevurah &
Tifereth*—the third *Sefirah*, *Tifereth*, is a composite
figure created by the amalgamation of the powers
of its parent *Sefiroth*. *Hesed & Gevurah* give birth

to *Tifereth* which then mediates between them. The third triad—*Netsah, Hod* & *Yesod*—follows the pattern of the preceding triad.

In the triadic division just outlined the *Sefiroth* running down the center of the configuration are in a way dependent on the *Sefiroth* to the left & right of them for their existence or value. In the pillar arrangement all three pillars are independent units, the middle pillar standing as a unit of pure & unsupported divinity. The *Zohar* refers to this middle pillar as the perfect pillar. It serves as a mediating factor between the pillars of the right & the left, but it is not dependent on their existence. What we are present to in this configuration of pillars is the idea of three powers: the powers of the left (darkness), the powers of the right (light) & the power of the soul, for the middle pillar is also called the *Shekhinah,* the feminine counterpart of God. There is also some Kabbalistic speculation about the suggestion that the center pillar is the Tree of Life, & the remaining pillars the Tree of Good & Evil.

The Pillar of Mercy receives its name from the center *Sefirah, Hesed* (Mercy or Love). This suggests to me that the remaining *Sefiroth* in this pillar are just two aspects of this *Sefirah*, one residing above, the other below. The quality of mercy symbolized by the pillar must therefore have, in order to be true mercy, the qualities of wisdom & endurance. Mercy must be wisely applied, & one has an enduring obligation to be merciful.

The Pillar of Judgment receives its name from the center *Sefirah, Gevurah* (Judgment or Power). Here too we find that the two *Sefiroth* on either side of it are integral components of the middle value. The proper judgment receives its essence from understanding & its application is glorious or majestic.

The center pillar is a direct line from the divine world of *Kether* to the material world of *Malkuth*, the two supreme opposites. Between them come the *Sefirah* Beauty & the *Sefirah* Foundation: the kingdom of the material world is founded on the creative principle, the generative principle of the opposites (*Yesod*), which in turn receives its beauty from the light of the central principle, *Kether*.

All of this is a very simplistic interpretation of some exceedingly profound & hidden relationships. They should not be taken as the unique & unambiguous meaning of these pillars. It is only a tear in a greater fabric.

THE SEFIROTH AS TREE
§ Another configuration to which the *Sefiroth* lend themselves is the Tree of the Garden of Paradise, & specifically the Tree of Life. In this form the *Sefiroth* in the center are thought of as the trunk, the *Sefiroth* on the left & right as its branches. In the *Zohar* it is said that the *Torah* is the sefirothic tree of Life & that all who occupy themselves with it are assured of life in the world to come.[25]

25 Levertoff, *The Zohar,* vol.2,p.25.

In discussing this analogy between the *Torah* & the Tree of Life symbolized by the configuration of the *Sefiroth*, some Kabbalists claim that at the beginning of His creative act God engraved all that was to come onto the *Sefirah Hesed*. The *Torah* contained in *Hesed* was referred to as *Torah Kelulah*, the unfolded *Torah*. It was in this *Sefirah*, the right hand of God, that the written & the oral *Torah* were contained in the form of fire. There they remained until activated by the *Sefiroth Hokhmah & Binah*. Then the written *Torah* became lodged in & expressed, through the *Sefirah Tifereth*, the oral Torah residing in the treasury of the *Sefirah Malkuth*.

The *Zohar* also refers to us the idea that the Tree of Life, extending over a 500-year journey, resided in the center of the garden, with a stream flowing from its base nourishing 'the beasts of the field' below. The *Zohar* explicitly states that the stream divides into a number of streams which led to the Tree of Good & Evil, so named because it acquired its sustenance from two opposing sides. This tree, which is not of the middle, is referred to as the six days of creation, & is accordingly composed of the *Sefiroth Hesed* to *Yesod* inclusive. It is the *Microprosopus*. The configuration of the *Sefiroth* therefore reveals a two-fold structure: the first three *Sefiroth*, the first triad, composes the Tree of Life, the second & third triads compose the Tree of Good & Evil. These two tree-configurations symbolize the Garden of Eden, the last *Sefirah*, *Malkuth*, representing the world which stands outside them. The fruit of the Tree of Knowledge of Good & Evil was made up of the composite values of the lower six *Sefiroth*. By eating this fruit borne by the sefirothic tree, man acquires knowledge of good & evil, & is in that regard considered equal with God:

'For God doth know that in the day ye eat thereof, then your eyes shall be opened, & ye shall be as gods, knowing good & evil.' (Genesis *xxx*, 5)

Another idea to be considered is that the Tree of Life, referred to as existing in the middle of the garden, is the central axis of the *Sefiroth* configura-

tion

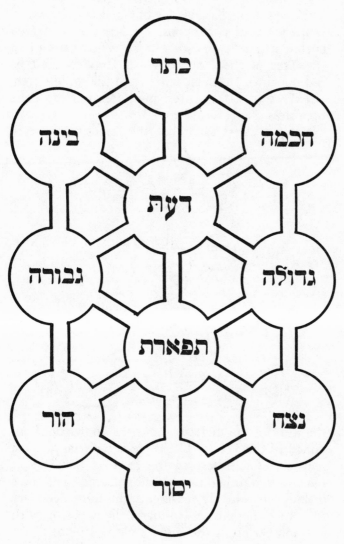

Tree of Life,
Tree of
Peace, Tree
of Perfec-
tion.

tion, made up of *Kether*, *Tifereth*, *Yesod* & *Malkuth*. The Tree of the Knowledge of Good & Evil, which is made up of two opposite sides, the six *Sefirah* encompassing it on either side. When man ate of the Tree of the Knowledge of Good & Evil he did not draw any sustenance from the middle tree, the Tree of Life, which mediates between the opposites.

It is for this reason that the opposites exist in

The *Shekhinah* & the human body, the Tree of Eternal Life.

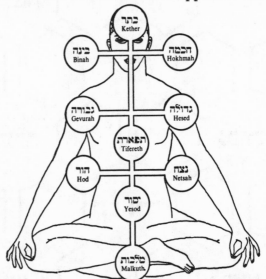

the world in conflict. Without the knowledge contained in the Tree of Life there is no balance. One may therefore interpret the fruit of the Tree of Life as containing a mediating factor. The Tree of Life symbolically represents the force necessary to unite the opposites, to marry the opposites with one another. It is the middle path, a place where the 'sound of one hand clapping' may be known. In light of the fact that the Tree of Life is often

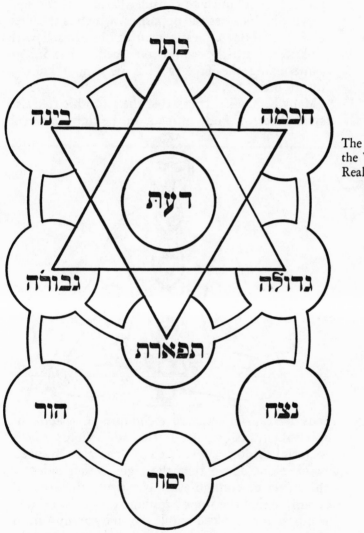

The Tree of
the Way of
Realization.

referred to by the Kabbalists as the *Shekhinah*, the soul, there is much to consider here. It is the soul alone which unites the opposites, which is the Tree of Eternal Life. Unless a man unites himself with this tree, with the values contained in the *Sefiroth* symbolizing the Tree of Life, he cannot know a future life.

Many Kabbalists think that the sefirothic tree also symbolizes the body of man. In the light of recent

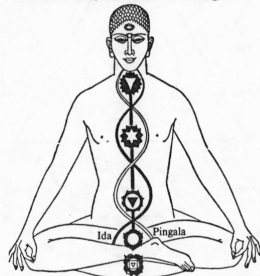

The *Chakras* & the paths of the Serpent Power.

consideration of Oriental techniques & systems of spiritual transformation, this idea yields much material seldom considered. It has already been pointed out above that the right & left sides of the sefirothic configuration constitute the arms of Adam, & that the *Sefiroth* running down the middle compose his trunk. I think the line running from *Kether* through *Tifereth* & *Yesod* to *Malkuth* should more correctly be thought of as the spine. In order

to develop this suggestion I will have to take a
detour & discuss briefly the Tantric discipline of
Kundalini Yoga.

The major premise of Kundalini Yoga is that the
residue of the feminine power, *Sakti*, which
fashioned the creation, settled at the base of man's
spine in the form of a coiled & slumbering serpent,
Kundalini. There she resides in a state of exile,
separated from her Lord who anxiously awaits her
return to his abode in the head of man. This cannot
be accomplished unless man rouses the slumbering
serpent & causes her to ascend in a straight line
upwards through his spinal cord. Thus in this discipline the human body is so illustrated.

The perpendicular channel believed to run through
the center of the spine, from the anus at the base
to the crown at the head, is called *Susumna*, the
void. The two intertwining channels to the left
& right of this primary channel are called *Ida* &
Pingala. The *Ida* channel commences on the left,
the *Pingala* on the right. The former is identified
with the moon, the latter with the sun. In other
words, they represent the opposites, dark & light,
good & evil. The five circles distributed over the
length of the middle channel, the *Susumna* passing
through their centers, are called *chakras* or subtle
centers. These subtle centers symbolize different
forms of consciousness, the grossest form symbolized by the bottom *chakra*, the purest at the
top. In the average man, the serpent awakens from
time to time & ascends one of the two channels
intertwining the middle channel. When this occurs
the forces residing in each center become activated.

The difficulty here is that the forces activated in
this manner, by the passage of Kundalini through

The Kunda-
lini rising
through the
different cen-
ters in the
Sushumna to
the thousand
petalled lotus
of the brain.

one of the two side-channels, influence the individual adversely because he is unconscious of their awakening. He is at the mercy of the emotions & desires released by each of these centers. At the same time the concentration of energies in only one of the side-channels causes an imbalance to occur. The imbalance is experienced as a state of conflict, the conflict between the potential energies of the unused channel & the exaggerated or over-

The energy force of Kundalini

The expansion of the Shekhinah, *the Tree of Perfection.*

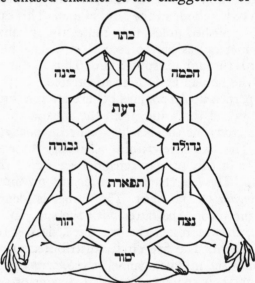

emphasized energies of the channel Kundalini ascends. Neither of these two paths lead to the Lord living in the head. They empty out into the nostrils, & whatever energy contained within the channels is dissipated. Union is unknown.

The only way by which Kundalini might come into a state of union with her Lord is by traveling through the subtle centers up the spine. This force, Kundalini, which moves from the base of the body to the top of the skull, is always visualized as feminine. The skull or brain where the Lord awaits her is identified with the supreme cosmic principle. In addition to all of the above, the spine in common yogic parlance is spoken of as the yoga tree & is feminine by virtue of the fact that it is a path used solely by the feminine principle in her ascent.

The reader may recall that the *Sefiroth* running down the center of the configuration, & thought

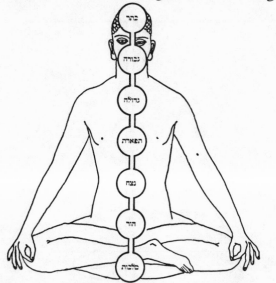

Tree of Life meditation, using the central column alone, using Head in place of Crown, placing Mercy & Power & Victory & Glory in the central column & removing Wisdom & Understanding & Foundation.

of as a unit separate from the other *Sefiroth*, has been called by the Kabbalists the *Shekhinah,* the feminine principle which unites the opposites as represented by the six *Sefiroth* distributed on either side of it. In addition, it is significant that the Kabbalists also refer to *Hokhmah* as the sun & *Binah* as the moon. These two *Sefiroth*, along with the *Sefiroth* lined up directly beneath them, coincide with the *Ida* & *Pingala* channels outlined in our description of Kundalini Yoga.

In addition to this, *Kether*, located at the head, is thought of in Kabbalism as longing for union with his bride, the exiled feminine principle residing in *Malkuth*, the slumbering world of our passions. It is significant that the location of these two *Sefiroth*, when the configuration of the *Sefiroth* in total is viewed as symbolic of the human body, is the same as the masculine & feminine principles

"Rabbi Schimeon spake unto his companions, and said: 'How long shall we abide in the condition of one column by itself?'"

of Kundalini.

Correspondences between the *Chakras* & the *Sefiroth*

It should also be obvious that the right & left portions of the sefirothic configuration point to two distinctively different types of action, based on two different ways of approaching the world & life: through either love & mercy or judgment & power.

There are numerous correspondences between the *chakras* & the *Sefiroth* ranging down the center of our diagram, too lengthy & technical to discuss here, but I might point out one of the more interesting & immediately recognizable correspondences. The *Sefirah Yesod*, symbolic of the genital region & all that it means, corresponds in both location & meaning with the first *chakra,* the *Muladhara,* which in the Kundalini system is identified with the sexual passions & energies. *Malkuth* would correspond with the slumbering Kundalini herself.

The yoga of
the Kabbalah

I would suggest at this point that the sefirothic & Kundalini configurations correspond in more ways than one. I would even suggest that the Tree of Life, the middle set of *Sefiroth*, are subtle centers in the same sense that the *chakras* are. In short, the sefirothic arrangement actually diagrams a yogic process for meditation & should be so used. The analogy which we are considering should become even more persuasive when one considers the fact that the great Kabbalist Abraham Abulafia not only laid down rules of body posture for the student to follow during his meditations on the *Sefiroth,* but a breathing discipline as well—a discipline found at the heart of every yogic system. Indeed, the student should turn his meditation directly to the *Sefiroth* & their relation to the *Shekhinah*. Perhaps something has been lost in the centuries. Perhaps a secret tradition existed in which the *Sefiroth* were viewed in much the same way that the *chakras* are in Kundalini yoga.

The goal of the student faced with the *Sefiroth* as tree should be to ascend it, following the central path after awakening the *Shekhinah,* & releasing her from exile. This is the yoga of the Kabbalah.

Before ending our discussion on the striking parallelism to be found between the *Sefiroth* & the *chakras* of Tantric Buddhism, I refer the reader to one final

The Tantric
creation of
the World.

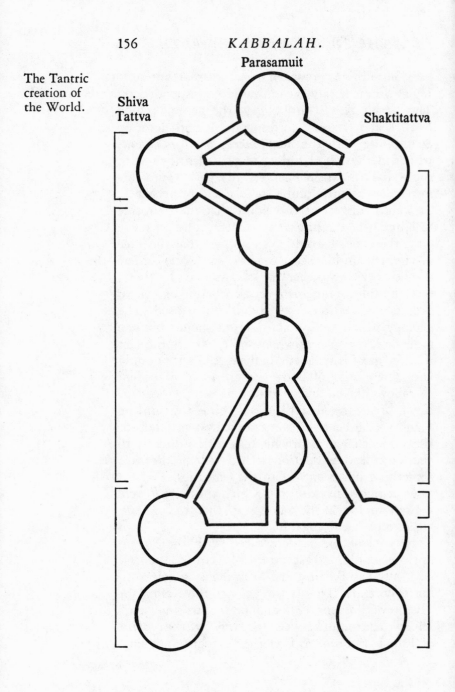

diagram, given on page 156.

The figure at the top of this diagram, *Parasamvit*, represents the changeless Brahman aspect—that God in which the plan of the universe & all of the opposites are contained. In every respect this answers the Kabbalistic description of *Kether*. The next two figures immediately following it, *Shiva Tattva* & *Shaktitattva*, are the supreme opposites, male & female, the mother & father from which issue the remaining portions of the diagram. These two principles correspond in every respect with *Hokhmah* & *Binah*. The brackets alongside the diagram refer us to the evolution of the *tattvas*, the various forms of the *Parasamvit's* manifestation through creation via his feminine counterpart. The *tattvas* become grosser & heavier in form the closer the creation comes to realization.

THE THIRTY-TWO PATHS OF WISDOM

Our next consideration of the *Sefiroth* will be with their paths, the connecting links between the *Sefiroth*. The thirty-two paths are designated in the same diagram.

This illustration sets out the number of each path together with the letter of the Hebrew alphabet assigned it. The nature of a path is determined not only by the letter assigned it, but by the two *Sefiroth* which it connects.

The best explanation of this diagram can be presented by citing the text of *The Thirty-Two Paths of Wisdom* itself.[26]

The assigning of astrological values to the paths is by no means a fixed matter. Kabbalists differ on this question. Rather than outlining the many different systems, I will give the astrological designations

nations

[26] The following text of the Thirty-Two Paths is a compilation of the translations of Westcott, Waite and Stenring. The author has taken this liberty because of the confusing and ambiguous phrasing each of the three translators were sometimes habit to.

nations of an established & respected Kabbalist, Knut Stenring, taken from his translation of the *Sefir Yetsirah*, the *Book of Formation*. (On page 173 of this book the reader will find the further connection of the thirty-two paths with the figures of the Tarot. I do not include this set of correspondences, because they did not become associated with the Kabbalah until after the eighteenth century & at that time mainly on the insistence of Christian Kabbalists.)

The Text of the Thirty-two Paths § 1. The title of the first path is 'Admirable' or Concealed Intelligence. It is the Light which communicates understanding of the Beginning which knows no beginning. It is the First Glory. No created being can attain to its essence.

2. The title of the second path is Illuminating Intelligence. It is *the* Crown of Creation & the splendour of Unity to which it is closest. Above every head is it exalted, & the Kabbalists call it the Second Glory.

3. The title of the third path is Sanctifying Intelligence, the foundation of Primordial Wisdom, otherwise called the Creation of Faith. Its roots are *Amen*. It is the mother of Faith, its emanation.

4. The title of the fourth path is That Intelligence Which Receives & Contains. It is given this title because it contains the spiritual emanations of the Higher Intelligences which have been sent down to it. It is from here that the emanations of the Supreme Crown again, in subtler fashion, emanate.

5. The title of the fifth path is Radical Intelligence. It is called this because it is closest to equality with the Supreme Crown, emanating from the depths of Wisdom.

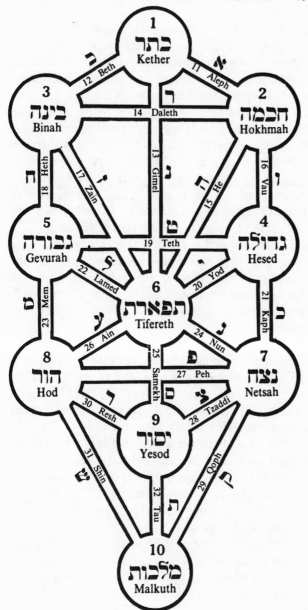

The titles of the thirty-two paths of wisdom of the *Sefiroth*.

The Tarot of
Paul Foster
Case for the
Builders of
the Adytum,
1947

6. The title of the sixth path is the Intelligence of the Mediating Influence, because *there* it is that the influx of the emanations are multiplied. It sends forth the resulting influence to those blessed men who have united themselves with it.

7. The title of the seventh path is the Concealed Intelligence, because from it the Intellectual virtues which are seen by the eyes of the spiritual through the ecstasy of faith receive its brilliant outpouring.

8. The title of the eighth path is the Perfect or Absolute Intelligence. It is from here that the ability to prepare principles emanates. It attaches itself to the roots hidden in the depths of *Hesed*.

9. The title of the ninth path is the Purifying Intelligence. It is called this because it purifies the numerations, qualifies & adjusts the manner in which they are represented, & unites them with itself so that they may not suffer division & destruction.

10. The title of the tenth path is the Resplendent Intelligence. It is called this because it is exalted above every head from where it sits on the throne of Binah. It illuminates the numinosity of all lights & causes to emanate the Power of the archetype of countenances or forms.

11. The title of the eleventh path is the Scintillating Intelligence. It is called this because it is the garment held up before the formations & the order of the superior & inferior causes. To possess this path is to enjoy great dignity & to come face to face with the Cause of Causes.

12. The title of the twelfth path is the Intelligence of Numinosity because it images Magnificence. It is the source of visions in those who see apparitions.

13. The title of the thirteenth path is the Uniting

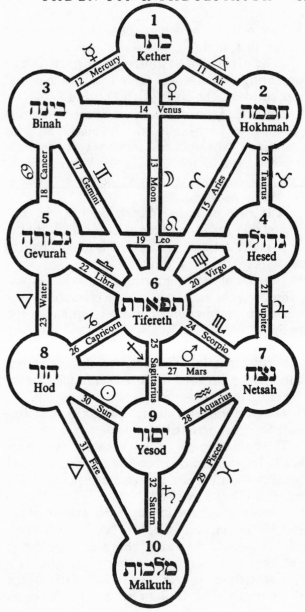

The thirty-two paths and their celestial correspondences.

Intelligence. It is the essence of Glory & it reveals Truth to all spirits.

14. The title of the fourteenth path is the Illuminating Intelligence. It is that which found concealed ideas, the basis of all holiness.

15. The title of the fifteenth path is the Constituting Intelligence. It is called this because it fashions the creation in the world's darkness. It is the darkness mentioned in Job *xxxviii,* 9; 'When I made the cloud the garment thereof, & thick darkness a swaddlingband for it.'

16. The title of the sixteenth path is the Triumphant & Eternal Intelligence. It is called this because it is the delight of Glory. It is also called the Paradise prepared for the just.

17. The title of the seventeenth path is the Disposing Intelligence. It provides perserverance to the righteous in preparation for their reception of the Holy Spirit.

18. The title of the eighteenth path is the Intelligence of the House of Wisdom, which it is. From within this are retrieved the arcana & hidden meanings hiding in its shadows.

19. The title of the nineteenth path is the Intelligence of Spiritual activities.

20. The title of the twentieth path is Intelligence of Will. It is called this because by it individual personalities are prepared for the reception of the Primoridal Glory's existence.

21. The title of the twenty-first path is the Intelligence of Mediation. It is called this because it receives the divine benediction from above & dispenses it below, thus influencing all in existence.

22. The title of the twenty-second path is the Intelligence of the Faithful, or Faithful Intelligence.

It is called this because in it are deposited spiritual virtues, which are increased until they flow unto those beneath its shadow.

23. The title of the twenty-third path is the Intelligence of Stability. It is called this because it is the source of that which is consistent in all of the numerations.

24. The title of the twenty-fourth path is Imaginative Intelligence. It is called this because it is that which is the model for the likeness of beings who are created in a manner which agrees with its aspects.

25. The title of the twenty-fifth path is the Intelligence of Temptation or Trial. It is called this because it represents the first temptation God tries His creatures by.

26. The title of the twenty-sixth path is the Intelligence of Renovation. It is called this because it is by this Intelligence that God renews all that is capable of Renovation in his creation.

27. The title of the twenty-seventh path is the Natural Intelligence. It is called this because by it everything in the orb of the sun is completed to perfection.

28. The title of the twenty-eighth path is called the Intelligence of the Active, or Active Intelligence. It is called this because it is here that the spirit of every being of the supreme orb is created. It is here too that the energy or activity which they display is created.

29. The title of the twenty-ninth path is Corporeal Intelligence. It is called this because it is that which forms the corporeal portion of all bodies existing beneath the orbs & also is the force behind their growth.

30. The title of the thirtieth path is the Intelligence of the Collective or the Collective Intelligence. It is called this because it is here that astrologers arrive at their speculations through judging the movements of the stars & heavenly signs. It is here where the perfection of that science is to be known.

31. The title of the thirty-first path is Perpetual Intelligence. It is called this because it governs the movements of the Sun & Moon, insuring that they follow the paths proper to them.

32. The title of the thirty-second path is the Administrating Intelligence. It is called this because it directs the movements of the seven planets.

Little commentary has been written on the practical usage of these paths. True, the suggestion that the paths might be likened to the stages of yoga has been made a number of times in recent years. How they were originally employed is another question. We can only assume that the paths outlined here are to be applied as vehicles for our own travels. A cursory examination of paths eleven to thirty-two in our illustration will reveal certain difficulties. How does one get from path twenty-nine to thirty, for instance?

Putting aside the topological difficulties, it will be noted that each path is a form of intelligence, a further differentiation of the original intelligence displayed in *Kether*. I would suggest that the term Intelligence used in the text might be better understood as a form of consciousness, & that what the text of *The Thirty-Two Paths of Wisdom* is putting forward is the observation that there are thirty-two specific forms of consciousness. Several psychologists from William James to Timothy Leary, not to mention the scholars of the East, have all made the observation that there are more than one form of consciousness. The paths outlined are spiritual stations for the individual pilgrim. How each path is to be traversed, is a secret each pilgrim must work out for himself or herself.

My suggestion is that the student consider the configuration of the paths in the way many other cultures have considered the elaborate designs of labyrinths. Labyrinths were originally constructed to safeguard the tombs of kings from the eyes of the uninitiated. Deep within these labyrinths rituals of spiritual renewal were performed which in time came to be associated with the design of the labyrinth alone, a talisman for regeneration. This configuration of the paths may be employed in the same way. All paths lead to the sanctuary of the king, *Kether.*

Another consideration to be discussed briefly appears in 'The Greater Assembly' section of the *Zohar*[27] where we are told of the existence of two Edens. The first Eden, 'Which shineth in Eden,' is called the superior Eden by virtue of the fact that it is hidden & totally self-contained. About this Eden it is said that no man has ever known it or shall ever know it. It is known only by *Macroprosopus*. In other words, it is the home of *Macroprosopus, Kether.*

[27] Mathers, *Kabbalah Unveiled,* p. 124.

The inferior Eden, on the other hand, is not self-contained. It is distributed into the thirty-two paths, even then only known by *Microprosopus*. All of which amounts to saying that the thirty-two paths of the sefirothic configuration are contained in man.

The inferior Eden is the Eden of the Bible. The superior Eden is the divine model after which the

inferior Eden was patterned. The one exists in a perfect state of unity, untainted by the Fall; the other, in need of redemption & regeneration. The two may not be united until the latter returns to its original state, a state which can only be achieved by the work of man.

No man, while alive, knows the superior Eden.

THE ALCHEMY OF THE SEFIROTH §In the early part of the eighteenth century there appeared the text entitled, *Aesch Mezareph*.[28] In this work the *Sefiroth* are referred to as alchemical qualities. This text almost certainly does not grow out of any alchemical tradition peculiar to Jewish mysticism. Alchemy was not a concern of the Kabbalists. Wherever we find mention of alchemy in Kabbalism today we may expect to find the roots of such speculation in eighteenth-century Europe. We may also expect to find the parents of such speculation to be the small band of Christian Kabbalists whose theories became prominent at that time. A cursory examination will reveal that the operations outlined in the *Aesch Mezareph* were never, and could never, be performed in a laboratory. At the most, we have in this text a precursor of what was to become spiritual alchemy—that branch of alchemy which no longer concerned itself with chemical, but solely with mental operations.

[28] See above, Part One, ch. 3, p.51.

WE HAVE GIVEN so much space to the *Sefiroth* because without even a rudimentary understanding of them, the theories of Kabbalism are lifeless. I am tempted to say that the *Sefiroth* represent varying gradations of psychic energy. But this would be a half-truth. It would be better to think of them as modals

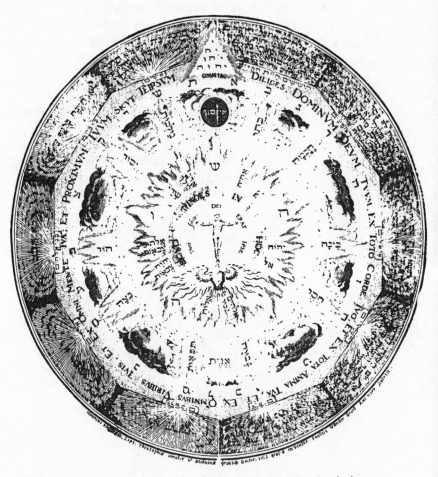

The ultimate goal as depicted in Heinrich Kuhnrath, *Amphitheatrum Aeternae Sapientiae*, Hanau, 1609.

of energy, configurations which not only penetrate Being & give orderly sense to its operations, but which also permeate the whole of nature. The operations of the *Sefiroth* extend themselves throughout the entire spectrum of the phenomenal world & man's psyche & soul make up only one of the many places where they manifest themselves.

In the *Sefiroth* one may find laws of both the material & psychic world. For this reason they may never be totally comprehended any more than may the *En-Sof*. One may come to appreciate the application of their values fully, but never learn the essence of their operation, for that essence is the same *En-Sof* which flows through & animates them.

One can pray for understanding.

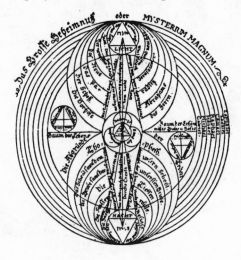

Chapter Two. The Numbers, Names, Letters & Computations of God

ABBALISTS BELIEVED that the written word of God was the result of God's inspiration & that Scripture contained within itself an essence of His being. By the same token they believed that because God is hidden, so too, beneath the divine words of Scripture, there was a hidden meaning, an essence to be ferreted out. To discover the hidden meaning they employed three methods of interpretation—*Gematria, Notarikon, & Temura*. The first made use of the fact that every Hebrew letter has a numerical value assigned it, & the second two employed intricate forms of abbreviation & substitution or permutation.

All three forms have been used from time to time by Kabbalists & Talmudic scholars, but this second group was divided on the legitimacy of such methods. As popular as these methods were with the majority of the Kabbalists, only one Kabbalist shaped a unified system of mystical thought & application around these methods: Abraham Abulafia, whom we have spoken of earlier. The system he devised has come to be known as Prophetic Kabbalism. His attempts to elucidate the meaning of these interpretative methods shed more light on their philosophical legitimacy than anything a commentator may have to say.

Gematria, Notorikon & Temura

In the first part of the chapter, I will outline
the three methods of interpretation; in the second,
I will give a brief account of what the Kabbalists
called 'the names of God', & the most famous example of these names, the *Tetragrammaton*. The last
two sections will be reserved for a discussion of
Abulafia's Prophetic Kabbalism & the language of
mysticism.

Gematria §*Gematria* is the science by which the
letters of a word are converted into their numerical
equivalent. Once one knows the numerical value
of the word, one may then find a correspondence
between the original word & another with the same
numerical value. In this way one number can
become representative of several ideas, all of which
are thought of as being interpretative of each other.

An example may be found by turning to Genesis
xlix, 10:

'The sceptre shall not depart from Judah, nor a
lawgiver from between his feet, until Shiloh; &
unto him shall the gathering of the people be.'

This passage was taken by the Kabbalists to be
a prophecy of the Messiah. By *gematria*, the phrase
IBA ShILH ('until Shiloh come') totals into 358:

י (10) plus ב (2) plus א (1) equals 13

ש (300) plus י (10) plus ל (30) plus ה (5) equals
345

345 plus 13 equals 358

משיח · The word for Messiah spelled *MShICh* also totals
358:

מ (40) plus ש (300) plus י (10) plus ח (8)
equals 358.

All of which leads to a rather curious 'gematriacal'
statement in Numbers *xxi*, 9:

'And Moses made a serpent of brass, & put it

upon a pole, & it came to pass, that if a serpent
had bitten any man, when he beheld the serpent
of brass, he lived.'

The Serpent of Moses, *Nachash* (*NChSh*), also
yields the number of the Messiah:

ל (50) plus ח (8) plus ש (300) equals 358.

The last example offered encouraged many Christian Kabbalists to state that the image of the brazen
serpent was a prefiguration of the Christ on the
cross. There are many instances from Mediaeval
Christian iconography where the Christ is represented by a serpent draped across the crossbar
of a crucifix.

It should be apparent to the reader that there
is no obvious limit to what can be yielded by
employing such a method as *gematria*. Twentieth-
century Kabbalists think of it as the central core
of Kabbalism, which is probably what prompts so
many of them to say that if you do not read Hebrew
you cannot know the Kabbalah.

Notarikon §*Notarikon* is employed in two ways,
both aimed at abbreviation.

The principle
of *Notorikon*

The first way involves the forming of one word
by taking the initial & final letters of another word
or words. The second way involves taking the letters
of one name as being the initial or final letters
of each word in a sentence.

Employing the first form & taking the question
Moses asks in Deuteronomy *xxx* 12, 'Who shall
go up for us to heaven?', *MI IOLH LNV HShMILH*,
we find that the initial letters of the question yield
מילה, *mylah*, the Hebrew word for circumcision.
Then, taking the final letters of the question, we
receive *IHVH*, the name of God, *Tetragrammaton*.
The answer, by means of *notarikon*, is contained

in the question & is that the circumcised shall reach God.

The well-known prayer-ending, *Amen* (אמן) also comes to us through *notarikon* from the phrase 'The Lord & faithful king ' (אל מלך נאמן).

The Christians were quick to use this method of permutation in identifying, or rather in finding further justification for the fish as symbolic of Christ. The Greek word for fish is *ichthus*. Employing *notarikon* they then arrived at the sentence *Iesous CHristos THeou Uios Soter* ('Jesus Christ, the son of God, the Saviour').

Temura § The third type of permutation is called *temura* & is a much more complicated procedure involving the interchanging of upwards of twenty-five letters according to certain rules. Even the simpler rules yield interesting possibilities.

Writing one half of the Hebrew alphabet in a reverse order & placing it on top of the remaining half, we arrive at the following figure:

k	I	th		ch	z	v	h	d	g	b	a
l	m	n		s	o	p	th	q	r	sh	t

Turning now to Jeremiah *xxv* 26, we find the statement: '. . .and the king of Sheshak shall drink after them.' Turning to chapter 51, verse 41, we discover that Sheshak (ששך) is none other than Babel (בבל). How did the writer of this Biblical passage arrive at *Sheshak* as another name for Babel? Through the method of *temura*. Taking the word *ShShk* (ששך) & substituting each letter for one either above or below it on the above arrangement of the alphabet, we receive:

Sh Sh k	*Sh (e) sh (a) k*
b b l	*b (a) b (e) l*

Figure.		Names.	Corresponding Letters.	Numerical Power.
א	0	Aleph	- - -	1
בּ	1	Baith	B	2
ב		Vaith	V	- -
ג	2	Gimmel	G	3
ד	3	Daleth	D	4
ה	4	Hay	H	5
ו	5	Wav	W	6
ז	6	Zayin	Z	7
ח	7	Cheth	Ch	8
ט	8	Teth	T	9
י	9	Yood	Y	10
כּ	10	Caph	C	20
כ		Chaph	Ch	- -
ל	11	Lamed	L	30
מ	12	Mem	M	40
נ	13	Noon	N	50
ס	14	Samech	S	60
ע	15	Ayin	- - -	70
פּ	16	Pay	P	80
פ		Phay	Ph	- -
צ	17	Tzadė	Tz	90
ק	18	Koof	K	100
ר	19	Raish	R	200
שׁ	20	Sheen	Sh	300
שׂ		Seen	S	- -
תּ	21	Tav	T	400
ת		Thav	Th	- -

19   THE SUN

20   JUDGEMENT

21   THE WORLD

All of which would seem to indicate that at least one of the writers of the Bible employed the methods outlined above, if not several.

Those readers desiring a full description of the other forms of permutation belonging to this system should refer to C.D. Ginsburg's *The Kabbalah*.[29]

As we shall see in the next section some of the names of God were arrived at by *temura*.

[29] Christian D. Ginsburg, *The Kabbalah, its Doctrines, Development and Literature.*

TETRAGRAMMATON & GOD'S OTHER NAMES.

§ Any four letter word is a *Tetragrammaton*, but the Kabbalists only apply this term to the unspeakable name of God, IHVH, the name translated by biblical translators as Jehovah. When *Tetragrammaton* is vocalized it is given the pronunciation of *adonai,* the Lord. In early times, when the correct pronunciation of the name was known, it was pronounced only once a year by the high priest on the Day of Atonement. Tradition tells us that once every seven years the sages were allowed to verbally pass on the secret pronunciation to their disciples.

"I am that I am"

The *Tetragrammaton* appears to have its origin in the phrase found in Exodus *iii*, 14, 'I am that I am,' אהיה אשר אהיה. Before this it was known as the *Shem ha-meforash,* the seventy-two syllabled name of God, made up of 216 letters. The source of the *Shem ha-meforash*, according to tradition, are verses 19-21 of Exodus *xiv*, each of the three verses containing seventy-two Hebrew letters. The letters of verse 19 were written down in separated form & in correct order; the letters of verse 20, also in separated form, were written down in reverse order, & the letters of verse 21 were written down in correct order. Reading from above down, one obtains seventy-two three-letter names, all of which combine to make one. To these three-lettered names were then added either *AL* or *IH* to form the names of the seventy-two angels of Jacob's ladder.

יה אל

Because the Hebrew language does not employ vowels in its written form, the correct pronunciation of this ineffable name of God was lost & not rediscovered until about 300 c.e. by the Kabbalists who gave it the title *Tetragrammaton*, 'the word of four letters,' & 'the square name,' or more simply, 'the square.' At that time the *Shem ha-meforash* became represented by the simpler form *YHVH*.

The correspondence between the *Shem ha-meforash*

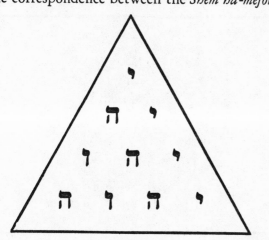

The *Tetragrammaton.* By arranging the four letters of the Great Name, (IHVH), in the form of the Pythagorean tetractys, the seventy-two names of God are manifested.

& the *Tetragrammaton (IHVH)* is revealed when we apply another rule of *gematria* to the four-letter word.

The number equivalents of the letters of the *Tetragrammaton* are as follows: י (10) ה (5) ו (6) ה (5) totaling 26. Then, adding the values of the letters in the following manner: י equals 10; יה equals 15; יהו equals 21.

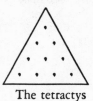

The tetractys

The seven dots of the tetractys (the *Elohim*) form the star of David, the seventh day is in the center.

The *Tetragrammaton* as the tetractys within the inverted human heart. Underneath the interpolation of *Shin,* the name of Jehovah is transformed to Jehoshua. From Jakob Bohme, *Libri Apologetici,* London, 1764.

10†15†21†26=72, *Shem ha-meforash.*

Therefore, the correct pronunciation of the four-letter name of God is thought of as being just as effective as the correct pronunciation of the *Shem ha-meforash* because *gematria* shows that the latter is contained within it. The inherent power of the name is revealed in the traditional belief that it was with its aid that Moses caused the Red Sea to part.

But so far we have only dealt with the *Tetragrammaton* as a vocable which, if properly pronounced, brings to the fore the power of God. In such a manner was the four-letter word used in later Euro-

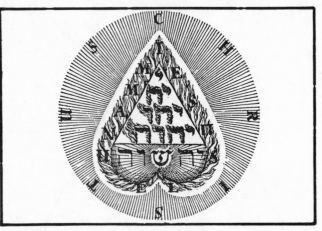

pean magic. It is difficult to find a magical text of that period which does not invoke the power of God through the use of *Tetragrammaton.* As a vocable it appears to be the property of magicians & others who worry themselves over its pronunciation, some audacious enough to report that they *knew* the correct pronunciation but were honor-bound to keep it secret. (S.L. MacGregor Mathers,

the translator of the *Kabbala Denudata*, is one example.) From this avenue of mystery we may expect
to gain nothing. When we consider the *Tetragram-*

The seventy-
two names of
God in-
scribed on
the petals of
the symbolic
sunflower.
Above the
circle they
are written
according
to the He-
brew Kab-
balah, below
are two trees
bearing the
symbols of
the planets
(left), the
zodiac signs
with the
names of the
tribes of
Israel (right).
From Atha-
nasius Kir-
cher, *Oedipus
Aegyptiacus*,
Rome, 1652.

maton in its written form, however, a much deeper
significance can be found, & it is with that aspect
of the *Tetragrammaton* that all true Kabbalists

primarily concern themselves.

The *Zohar* tells us that before God created the
world His name was contained within Him. But
because it was contained within Him, He & His
name were not considered a unity. The reasoning
here was that a unity refers us to the merging of
two or more distinct parts. In order that His name
could be known to Him, the *Zohar* tells us, the
world He created was a part distinct from him.
As we already know, this creation is brought about
by the manifestation of the *Sefiroth*, the development
of which in this instance not only corresponds with
the emergence of the universe, but with the birth
of the *Tetragrammaton* which we shall see unites
the *Sefiroth*.

When the *Sefirah Hokhmah* became manifested,
so too was the letter י *(Yod)*. The manifestation
of the *Sefirah Binah* brought along the letter ה
(Hé) usually referred to as the first or upper *Hé*.
The third letter, ו *(Vau)*, is symbolic of the heavens
& was made manifest along with the *Sefiroth Hesed*
through *Yesod* inclusive. The second or lower
Hé symbolically represents the earth & came into existence along with the *Sefirah Malkuth*.

The *Tetragrammaton* therefore contains the whole
of the sefirothic configuration: the point of the *Yod*
(י) is the *Sefirah Kether*, the Crown; the *Yod* itself
is *Hokhmah*, Wisdom; the first *Hé* (ה) is the *Sefirah
Binah*; the *Vau* (ו) the next six Sefiroth & the
second *Hé*, *Malkuth*.

This outline of the *Tetragrammaton*, as pointed
out earlier, symbolizes the body of man. Yet it
suggests also the existence of a process of creation
within man which becomes mythologized in terms
of a family. The *Yod*, in that it is identified with

the *Sefirah Hokhmah*, is thought of as masculine & is the father; the first *Hé*, in that it is identified with *Binah*, is thought of as feminine & is the mother; the *Vau,* in that its numerical value is six, & is composed of the six *Sefiroth* which constitute the body of the *Microprosopus*, is the son born of their union. The final *Hé* is *Malkuth*, the *Microprosopus's* bride or *Nakba*. The bride which emerges from him is his Eve, the so-called Inferior Mother.

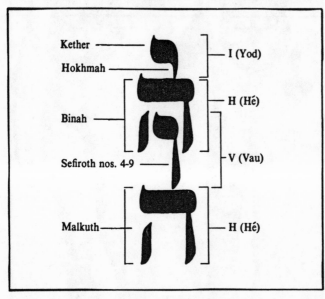

The *Tetragrammaton* symbolizing the body of man & the process of creation within him.

Technically speaking, the *Sefirah Tifereth*, Beauty, standing at the center of the *Sefiroth* composing the body of the *Microprosopus*, is called the Son.

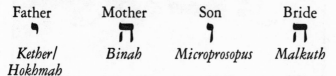

Father	Mother	Son	Bride
׳	ה	׳	ה
Kether/ Hokhmah	*Binah*	*Microprosopus*	*Malkuth*

The Divine
Tree in man,
front & back.
The roots &
trunk on the
front of the
figure repre-
sent his
spirituality,
the branches
are the sep-
arate parts of
his individu-
ality & the
leaves corres-
pond to his
personality.
On the re-
verse figure
the "night"
or inferior
condition is
shown: The
top sphere of
the Astral
mind & the
bottom
sphere of the
Senses are
filled with
the "noctur-
nal" stars;
The middle
sphere of
Reason cor-
responds with
the illumi-
nated Under-
standing in
spiritual man
—the "day" side.

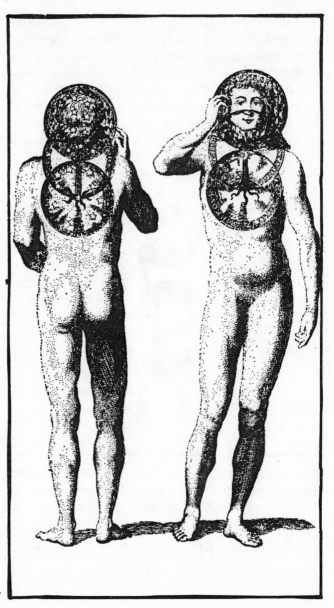

From what has been said about the written *Tetragrammaton* it should be obvious to the reader that the vocalized *Tetragrammaton* has greater possibilities than the mere calling forth of magical powers. The *Tetragrammaton* is a mantra of the first order. In her book *Initiations & Initiates in Tibet*, Alexandra David-Neel[30] speaks briefly of the mystical use of the mantra, *Aum mani padme hum!* ('The Jewel is in the Lotus!'). Each of the six syllables refers us to a specific world or universe. As the practitioner breathes in while repeating the mantra, the worlds come into being within his body, an event which he is to visualize. As he breathes out, they dissolve into nothingness.

The *Tetragrammaton* has to be employed in the same way. The initiate must imagine the first lightning flash which caused the *Sefiroth* to come into being & trace its effect when finally released from the womb of *Binah*. Then he must follow the pattern of creation contained within the six *Sefiroth* which constitute the body of *Microprosopus*, ending with *Malkuth*, & then begin the ascent back to *Kether*.

It must be emphasized that certain requirements have to be met before such a program may begin. According to a passage on the holy name cited by M. Gaster in *The Sword of Moses: an ancient book of magic*, it is only to be used by one in middle life, who is pious & modest, & who never gives way either to anger or drink. In consideration of the more stringent requirements asked of many Occidentals who follow the disciplines of Oriental techniques such as yoga, these are simple prerequisites.

The *Tetragrammaton* & the *Shem ha-meforash* were the most popular amongst the Kabbalists. There

[30] Alexandra David-Neel, *Initiations and Initiates in Tibet*, p.87.

Om Mani Padme Hum

were other names as well, the most common being those made up of fourteen, twenty-two & forty-two letters.

The name of God made up of fourteen letters was arrived at by taking the *Shema* (the declaration of Deuteronomy *vi*, 4, 'Hear, O Israel, the Lord is our God, the Lord is One.'), & applying the

Hear, O
Israel, the
Lord is our
God, the
Lord is One

method of *temura* to it. Rarely used by the mystics, this name of God was inscribed on the back of the *mezuzah*, the small doorpost symbol attached to the right side of doors by pious Jews & in which is to be found the first two paragraphs of the *Shema* (Deuteronomy *vi*, 4-9; *xi*, 13-21).

The name of God composed of twenty-two letters was in much greater demand by the Kabbalists. It first appears in the *Sefer Raziel* or *Book of the Angel Raziel* which is traditionally attributed to Eleazar of Worms of the thirteenth century. We assume today that the vocalization, the choice of vowels, looks like this: *Anaktam Pastam Paspasin Dionsim (ANQTM PSTM PSPSYM DYVNSYM)*. The name has no meaning since it contains no words which may be found in the Hebrew language.

אנקתם
פסתם
פספסים
דיונסים

It was traditionally believed that the name of twenty-two letters was a Kabbalistic permutation of The Blessing of the Priests in the *Authorized Daily Prayer Book*:[31]

31 Singer, *Authorized Daily Prayer Book*, p. 325.

'The Lord bless thee & keep thee:
The Lord make his face to shine upon thee & be gracious unto thee:
The Lord turn his face unto thee & give thee peace.'

This name was so popular that in the seventeenth century it was actually introduced into the reading of the above prayer in the synagogue. Much of its power was attributed to the fact that like the Hebrew alphabet, it too contained twenty-two letters.

The name with forty-two letters, *ABG YTS QRA STV NGO YCS BTR STG CQB TNA YGL PZQ SQVSYT,* was believed to be composed of the first forty-two letters in the Bible, an ascription which many Kabbalists firmly held to. Each term of this holy name was believed to hold as much magical potency as the entire name.

אבנ יתץ
קרע שטן
נגד יכש
בטר צתג
חקב טנע
יגל פזק
שקרצית

The Kabbalists warned that the employment of the names of God was a serious task which demanded one be firmly grounded in Kabbalistic theory. Because it was believed that by such names the powers of God in various forms could be made manifest, one who employed them had an enormous responsibility before him. Those who borrowed heavily from this tradition of magic names were the mediaeval magicians, to whom theory was not only bothersome, but of little use from their pragmatic viewpoint. All that was necessary, in their estimation, was a thorough knowledge of the names & nothing more.

"The Center as God & the manifestation of his circumference."

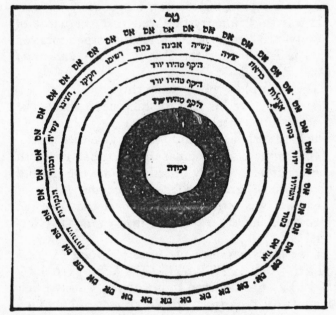

Much in twentieth-century Kabbalism is the result of this attitude, & many who practice magic alone mistakenly call themselves Kabbalists. None could be further from the heart of Kabbalism. I say this because the true Kabbalist employed these names, invoked these powers, either in his quest for divine aid in his attempt to establish a meaningful relationship between the Above & the Below, or in his striving to organize & vitalize the powers of the

Microprosopus with whom he shared a common destiny.

The magician, on the other hand, sought these agencies of power for other than altruistic reasons, & always for purposes of control. Nature, which may be thought of as the wife of *Kether* insofar as the spirit of the *Shekhinah* composes its body, was not to be aided in its attempts at unity; nature was to be overcome & controlled, its dynamism coupled with demonic agencies for such singularly selfish purposes as the winning of a woman's heart or the downfall of an enemy. This was not the path that the Kabbalist followed. The names of God to them were potencies to be employed only for union & creation.

ABULAFIA & PROPHETIC KABBALISM §Of the twenty-two prophetic treatises & at least twenty-six grammatical, kabbalistic & mystical works of Abulafia, it appears that only three have been published & made available to the twentieth-century public.[32] From one such work, his *Epistle*, written in answer to rabbi Solomon ben Abraham ben Adereth's public attacks, I quote those sections which in many ways best encapsulate Abulafia's doctrine. The reader will find in them, I am sure, as well reasoned & finely balanced a presentation of philosophical speculation as can be found anywhere in the corpus of kabbalistic or mystical thought.[33]

'The Kabbalistic tradition may be traced back to Moses & can be divided into two parts, the first part of greater value to the second, but in the order of study subordinate. This first part occupies itself with knowledge of the Deity through the system of the Sefiroth as set forth in the book Yetsira.

[32] Adolph Jellinek, ed., *Auswahl Kabbalistischer Mystik;* Jellinek, ed., *Philosophie und Kabbala, Erstes Heft, Enthaelt Abraham Abulafia's Sendschreiben ueber Philosophie und Kabbala;* Jellinek ed. and comment, "*Sefer Ha-Oth, Apokalypse des Psuedo-Propheten und Psuedo-Messias Abraham Abulafia.*" In *Jubelschrift Zum Siebzigsten Geburtstage des Prof. Dr. H. Graetz.*

[33] Jellinek, *Auswahl,* Pt. I, p.13.

Those who follow this part are as those philosophers who attempt to know God through his works & He stands before them as a ray of light in their understanding, objectively. They also give the Sefiroth many names by which they may be recognized. Some of them are little different than Christians, for what they do is substitute a decade for a triad . . . The second & more important part of this Kabbalistic tradition attempts to learn of God through the twenty-two letters of the alphabet . . .The many & divine names are brought together in combination by means of the mingling of the letters with their vowel points & accents. This raises the Kabbalist to the level of prophecy by drawing out his spirit so that it might become one with God. This is done gradually in the following way. The ten Sefiroth slowly sublimate into the Sephira Kether, known as thought, the Crown, & primordial air. It is the root of all the other Sefiroth & rests in the En-Sof. In much the same way the numbers can all be reduced to one & all trees, their roots & branches included, are changed back into the primordial earth no sooner than they are cast into the fire. The ten Sefiroth...have as correspondences the letters of the alphabet divided into three rows containing ten letters each...These ten Sefiroth...compose a triad in which we find the letters Aleph, Beth, & Gimel. This correspondence also includes the three principles found in man: the vital principle in the heart, the vegetable in the liver, & that which may be deemed pleasurable in the brain. All of these combined form a unity. The Kabbalist initiated into Prophetic Kabbalism slowly concentrates & directs all of his concentrated powers towards one point in God & unites himself with him...the permutation of numbers & letters are stepping-stones upon which one ascends to God.'

A carefully planned program of meditation

What Abulafia presents us with in this passage is an outline of a method by which one may become united in God. It is not a shamanistic flowering in trance that he refers us to when he speaks of ascension & union, nor the soul-flinging of the *Merkabah* mystics. It is a purposeful & carefully planned program of meditation equal to any found in Oriental systems of spiritual discipline. His emphasis is on a gradual & orderly ascension, not an upward or downward flinging of a soul whose success depends on the efficacy of magical talismans & the protection of faith. It is the kernel of a finely developed discipline whose goal is integration, union & transformation. The ecstatic aspect of the experience of the Divine is most certainly still present, but it is the sort one wins through mental preparations rather than through the chanting of magical formulae & fasting.

Abulafia believed that the soul exists in all men in a state of bondage & that it is literally tied up by the seals which have been stamped upon it. The purpose of these seals is to protect the soul from coming into immediate & constant contact with the Divine which would otherwise annihilate it. The purpose of his system, therefore, was to teach the initiate how to untie the knots sealing the soul so that the Divine might be experienced in its original unity.

The theory of the seals, it appears, was rooted in the idea that in perceiving the world of sensible form the mind fills itself with the images of these forms & no others. The form & experience of the transpersonal is slowly replaced & sealed by the images of sensible forms. The life of the soul, in this process, becomes totally caught up in the apprehension of these forms & forgets the divine forms.

The mind involves itself with the natural world in exact proportion to the degree by which the soul forgets the nature of the divine forms. Abulafia believed that the mind had to achieve a new position, a different mode of consciousness which would include the forgotten divine forms. The reasoning behind the method he developed is simple: if the phenomena of the natural world are the cause of the soul's entombment, & if it is the mind which perceives these forms, then it is the mind which must divorce itself from these forms for the soul to be able to return to its natural state.

What underlies this view is the conviction that the mind must be called into the service of the soul & should not act solely on its own behalf. Obviously the mind, or ego, must be thought of as possessing a power of its own for otherwise it would not be capable of interfering with both a natural & a divine process. If the mind is so powerful that it can act as a barrier between the divine, & that portion of the divine locked up in man, his exiled soul, then it must also be possible for the mind to act as an instrument for freeing the soul. If it has the power to obstruct, it must also have the power to mediate.

The problem arose in the first place because it is in the nature of the mind to perceive. *What* it perceives is the multiplicity of forms to be found in the world, & it is this which constitutes the substance of the seals. Inasmuch as the world is a multiplicity, the mind in perceiving it will operate most naturally within a framework of multiple forms. But where, Abulafia must have asked, can one find multiple forms with which the mind could concentrate on the Divine & not the mundane? If one is caught up in contemplating the multiple forms of nature, or even a single form of nature—a stone, for instance—then one's mind cannot be thinking of the divine, for divinity is not to be found in the stone.

If the basic tenets of Judaism were pantheistic, then such meditation would be fruitful. But they are not. God is God, & nothing more. He is, if you will recall our statements on the *En-Sof*, the negatively existent one. One must therefore find forms which are pure in that they make no reference to natural objects. Abulafia decided that the letters of the alphabet answered such a description & set about to devise his *Hokmath ha-Tserur*, the Science of the Combination of Letters.

Here it must be emphasized that Abulafia was a student of the *Sefer Yetsirah*, the *Book of Creation*. What makes the letters of the alphabet divine in Abulafia's & other Kabbalists' eyes can be found in a statement from that work:

'Twenty-two letters: He drew them, hewed them, combined them, weighed them, interchanged them, & through them produced the whole creation & everything that is destined to come into being.'[34]

It was not enough for Abulafia to have the mind meditate on the Divine itself. By doing so it would only have replaced the objects of the mundane world with an object of the Divine. The object of one's meditation had not only to be divine in nature, but abstract as well. Because the letters of the

God is God, & nothing more

[34] Abelson, *Jewish Mysticism*, p.101.

alphabet had no meaning in themselves one would be allowed the free play of pure abstraction, the free play in nothingness which is essentially the *En-Sof.*

The sacredness of the letters of the alphabet, the pure abstraction of divinity, is also to be found in the Hindu & Tibetan use of *mantras* & seed-syllables. A *mantra* may be a complete sentence such as *Om Mani Padme Hum* ('The Jewel is in the Lotus,') or it might simply be a seed-syllable such as *krim*, which has no meaning other than the power of time & death which is believed to be contained within it.

[35] Lama Anagarika Govinda, *The Foundations of Tibetan Mysticism.*

Again, as reported by Lama Anagarika Govinda,[35] the last seed-syllable of this phrase, *hum*, pictorially represents the five states of wisdom, or the five *Dhyani-Buddhas.*

This personification of the form of a letter is most beautifully employed in the Kabbalistic equation of *IHVH* with man:

IHVH as we said earlier is called *Tetragrammaton* & is the name of God Himself. Because Scripture

The mantras *IHVH* & *Hum.*

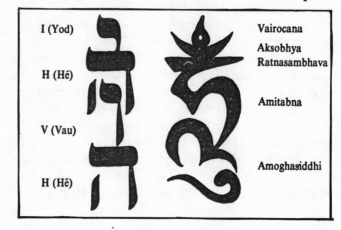

tells us that man was created in God's image, the body of man should correspond with the name of God.

. In much the same way the Tantric seed-syllable *hum* contains within it unspoken powers, so too does the *Tetragrammaton* refer us silently to the four worlds & their hierarchy.

THE LANGUAGE OF MYSTICISM

§It should now be easy for the reader to imagine the power of the meditational science with which Abulafia suggested one should help release the soul from its bondage. He asks nothing less of the initiate than a turning away from the world of natural objects & a contemplation of the divine name to be found hidden in the letters of the alphabet. He calls for the extension of consciousness through a willed directing of one's mind. The methods he prescribes constitute a yoga as difficult & as rewarding as any to be found in the Orient.

The objective of Abulafia's Prophetic Kabbalism is not just ecstasy & union. The goal of his system is the union of the devotee with his spiritual master, or his *guru* as twentieth-century man now knows him. The idea of a spiritual teacher, a teacher of pure spirit & not a living man, is unusual in Western mysticism. The Western mystic as a rule receives instruction from a flesh & blood master with whose aid he himself, in time, arrives at wisdom. Even in the most developed forms of Buddhism the guru & guide is a living being. The only distinction between the guide & the devotee is that the former has already made contact with the Divine & is therefore aware of the paths necessary for another to take in order to arrive at his goal. The only Occiden-

tal

A teacher, or *guru,* of pure spirit

36 C. G. Jung, *Memories, Dreams and Reflections*, p. 182.

tal I have come across in my readings besides Abulafia who had taken a spiritual teacher in the full sense was C.G. Jung.

In his autobiography, Jung relates that during his initial encounters with the deep unconscious a figure manifested itself to him called Philemon.[36] He was a winged being with a lame foot & the horns of a bull. Jung states that in his fantasies he had many conversations with Philemon which in time led him to the conclusion that this figure was a force which in no way represented himself. He learned from Philemon. Still, he felt somewhat wary of the situation. It was not until fifteen years later, while conversing with a learned & elderly Indian, a friend of Gandhi's, that he discovered the true nature of Philemon. The two had been discussing the relationship between a guru & his student when Jung, with some hesitation, asked his visitor what his guru had been like. His visitor calmly replied that his guru had been Shankaracharya. Jung was stunned, for Shankaracharya was the famous commentator on the *Vedas* who had been dead for several centuries. It was then he had it explained to him that there are some who have flesh & blood gurus, but others may have a spirit for a teacher.

It is by now a commonly accepted fact that the mystic's experience of the Divine is not expressible with logical consistency. The experience is one in which all opposites & contraries are reconciled & exist in an indivisible state of unity. The experience of the reality of the world involves distinctions which arise from the activity of the opposites. It cannot be possible, therefore, for language, which depends for its effect on the distinction between subject & object (the opposites), wholly to capture mystical experiences. In the mystic's experience of the Divine, the relationships existing between subject & object, the field of language, do not exist. What the mystic must do, if he wishes to communicate his experience to others somehow, is dissect the unity of his experience. This in itself limits the adequacy of any account he gives. When he has to express himself in language, the task seems impossible.

First, he must find those words & phrases which come closest to defining the emotional intensity of his experience. Failing to find exact correlates, he must then modify or amplify those he has employed by further explanation & definition, being careful all of the time to remind the reader that what he is speaking about is indefinable & that the examples he is forced to use are illusory & insubstantial. They were originally created by man to describe the phenomena of an immediately discernible reality dependent on the interplay of the opposites.

Once the mystic has set down what he feels are the statements explaining his experience, no matter how pale they may be when held up to the experience itself, then he must go about the business of initiating the reader to the deeper meaning of what he has written. Sometimes he may dedicate a lifetime to this, always knowing in the back of his mind that he is trying to accomplish the impossible. This, too, he constantly tells the reader, reminding him that true understanding can only be had by immediate experience & that this might be said of the understanding of anything, & not just of the experience of the Divine.

The mystic in history has invariably chosen the

existing framework of the religious tradition in which he lives as the vehicle for the expression of his experience. If he is a Hindu he will employ the images, symbols & pantheon of the Vedic religion; a Buddhist, those of Buddhism; a Christian, those of Christianity, & so on. If the mystic is to succeed in using traditional scripture as the language for recording his experience of the Divine, he must instill in his reader the idea that the traditional scripture or system contains a dimension of meaning distinct from the usual one & that it is this other dimension which he is trying to explain. Because traditional scripture is understood as the definitive statement of the Divine, any further interpretation or amplification must be presented as contained in them from the beginning. For the mystic to claim otherwise would be to place his life in danger. As history bears out, however, the mystic genuinely believes that he is expounding hidden meanings & not revising scripture. The mystic sees himself as an interpreter or revealer of something which already exists but is concealed.

This, of course, gives to scriptural language a numinosity or spiritual dimension beyond the scope of everyday language. The scriptural words remain the same, but their meaning becomes altered & enhanced. In practically every religion, the thought of altering Scripture in any way is unheard of. If the mystic's experience is to be understood & accepted as genuine the unexpressible unity of the moment of revelation must somehow be linked with the unity of the original words of God, the untouchable & definitive writings of a religion. The unity of the traditional scripture, for the mystic, is merely confirmed by his ability to reveal a hidden dimen-

sion

sion in its pages, which coincides essentially with the conventional meaning.

The transformation of the ego

Yet, the experience of the mystic cannot be conveyed adequately unless the reader tastes something of the experience himself. Mystical traditions therefore often append to their canonical literature mechanical devices which they hope will shuttle the common reader up through the corridor of the Divine for his own experience. If the unity experienced by the mystic is the same as that hidden in traditional scripture, then the experience of the Divine might be had by walking through the open door of Scripture alone. What the mystic does, then, on this account, is to clear the way for the initiated by imposing on language a mystical system or grammar of numerations & signs.

The purpose behind such systems is to let the initiate experience for himself, by mechanical means, the unity which the mystic finds impossible to explain fully by using the language of the mundane world. Of course, I do not mean to imply that this is a conscious manipulation on the part of the mystic or mystical tradition which give rise to such methods, but that this is essentially the function & goal of all such devices. The mystic believes such devices are themselves hidden in Scripture, & that they are but the lost key to the understanding of the Word. Of course, for such systems to be effective in introducing the initiate to the Divine, they must be taken wholly to heart & practice.

The essence of faith is the suspension of critical & logical judgment. Because judgment is normally understood as being one of the functions of the ego, many see this as a call to get rid of the ego.

It is argued that since it is the function of the ego to make distinctions between subject & object, how can one experience the unity of all things while the ego is still in control? 'Away with it!' they say. But with systems as complicated as the three described above, what else except the ego could possibly apply them? How can they be put to use if there is no ego present?

What is required is not the destruction of the ego, but the transformation of its attitude that its major function is to serve itself & nothing else. How to win the ego away from this attitude was the problem which Abulafia tried to solve.

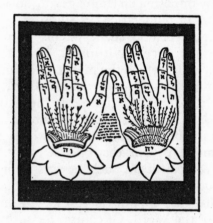

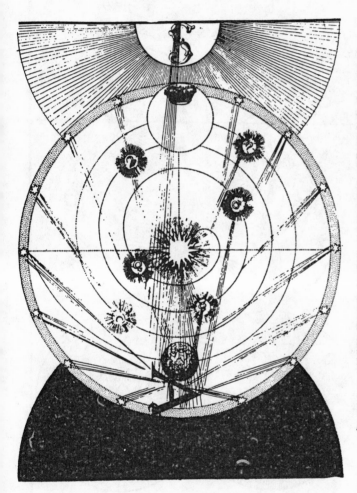

"Here now is poor Adam actually fallen away from all his former Happiness & Glory, and has lost whatsoever was good & desirable both in himself & round about him: He lies as dead, on the outmost Borders of the Spirit of this World. Sophia has forsaken him . . ." Number nine in a series, from *The Works of Jacob Behmen.*

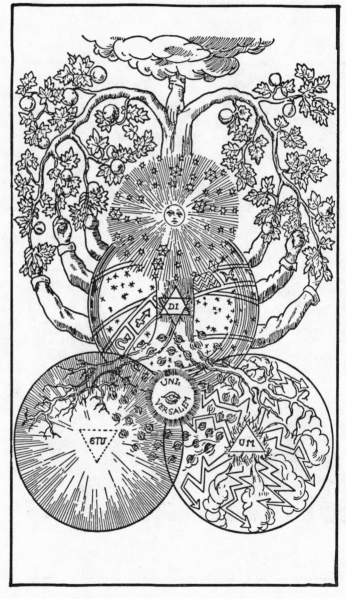

The Tree of
Good & Evil
Knowledge,
from *Geheime
Figuren der
Rosenkreut-
zer,* Altona,
1785.

Chapter Three. The Essence of Man

 HE THEORY of the existence of the soul was not the invention of the Kabbalists. One of the most striking examples from the Bible of belief in the soul occurs in I Samuel 28 when King Saul, after banishing 'those that had familiar spirits, & the wizards, out of the land,' finds it necessary to speak with the dead Samuel. Arriving in disguise at the house of a woman reported to have a familiar spirit, he becomes witness to the soul of Samuel returned from the dead.

'And the king said unto her, Be not afraid: for what sawest thou? And the woman said unto Saul, I saw gods ascending out of the earth. And he said unto her, What form is he of? And she said, An old man cometh up; and he is covered with a mantle. And Saul perceived that it was Samuel, and he stooped with his face to the ground, and bowed himself.'

What is important to note here is the idea that souls are contained in the earth. At the time this passage was written the soul was considered a singular entity. Its home outside the body, once the body has been removed from it, is the earth & while still in the body, its home is the blood. It was this belief which lay behind the rite of 'kashe-

ring,'

ring,' or making meat Kosher. The restriction
placed on the eating of blood, or meat with blood
in it, first occurs in Genesis *ix*, 3, 4 where God
says,

'Every moving thing that liveth shall be meat
for you...But flesh with the life thereof, which is
the blood thereof, shall ye not eat.'

And again in Deuteronomy *xii*, 23:

'Only be sure that thou eat not the blood: for
the blood is the life; & thou mayest not eat the
life with the flesh.'

Both these notions—the idea that the soul after
death lived below in the earth & that while present
in man resided in the blood—were in time to become associated with the lowest aspect of a triune-
soul, the *Nefesh*.

During the latter part of the Second Temple-period
we already find in the Babylonian Talmud the statement that,

'Just as the soul fills the body, so God fills the
world. Just as the soul bears the body, so God
endures the world. Just as the soul sees but is not
seen, so God sees but is not seen. Just as the soul
feeds the body, so God gives food to the world.'[37]

Here an intimate connection appears between God
& the soul. The soul's activities mirror a divine
activity, an activity occuring above, somewhere in
the heavens & not just in the earth. In addition,
the rabbis, prompted by the Platonic doctrines of
the soul, also believed that all souls exist prior
to the existence of the body. The soul was of
heavenly origin, given to man by God.

'O my God, the soul which thou gavest me is
pure; thou didst create it, thou didst form it, thou
didst breathe it into me; thou preservest it within

[37] I. Epstein,
ed., *The Babylo-
nian Talmud,*
vol. 9, p.392.

me; & thou wilt take it from me, but wilt restore it unto me hereafter. So long as the soul is within me, I will give thanks unto thee, O Lord my God & God of my fathers, Sovereign of all works, Lord of all souls! Blessed art thou, O Lord, who restorest souls unto the dead.'[38]

The Kabbalists were to quickly take up the idea of pre-existence & include it in their theory of transmigration or reincarnation, *gilgul*, which also had roots in Platonic & Neo-Platonic theory. It is this juncture, this point where the Kabbalists begin fully to develop their theories of the soul, on which the first sections of this chapter will concentrate.

The *Shekhinah*, the feminine aspect of God, apart from being His promised bride, is also referred to as the *Neshamah*, the third & highest portion of the soul. The last section of this chapter will therefore be dedicated to her & her significance in Kabbalistic thought.

THE SOUL & ITS DIVISIONS
§Because of the multiplicity of relationships inherent in the Kabbalistic theory of the soul, it will be necessary for our discussion to proceed slowly. The complexity of the theory may only be understood if each of its aspects is discussed separately. For this reason we will discuss the nature of the soul in five parts.

The first part will concern itself with the three divisions of the soul. The second, with the heavenly origins of the soul. The third, the masculine & feminine distinctions. The fourth, with the individual's relationship to the soul. The fifth, with the soul after death during which time we shall discuss the theory of reincarnation developed by the Kabbalists.

[38] Singer, *Authorized Daily Prayer Book*, p.6.

The three grades of the Soul

The three
grades of the
Soul

The soul is comprised of three grades: the *Nefesh*, the gross element which bears all the instincts & bodily cravings; the *Ruah*, the grade which contains the moral virtues & the ability to distinguish between good & evil; & the *Neshamah*, the sublimest grade of the trinity which may be properly called the soul. (All three Hebrew terms mean, literally, 'soul'.)

These three elements or grades of the human soul are thought of as pre-existing in the first of the Four Worlds, the World of Emanation. During an individual's lifetime they act in some unity with each other. In order to understand the nature of the balance struck we must first look at each element separately.

Nefesh §The *Nefesh* grade of the soul is in total rapport with the body &, according to the *Zohar*, is the only element of the three capable of committing sin. It is rightly called the animal soul for it represents the entire range of instinctuality which, when expressed in certain forms, is spoken of as bestial. When the Kabbalists speak of man's vital principle, they refer to the *Nefesh*. It is the grossest & lowest of the three elements composing the soul.

According to the *Zohar* a man is first given the stage or grade of *Nefesh*, the raw vital energy necessary for maintaining the engine of the body & insuring the propagation of the species. The other two grades, the *Neshamah* & *Ruah*, cannot be proffered until the individual has purified the grade of *Nefesh*. Until that time he is not thought of as fit for the next grade, the *Ruah*. All of this implies, to the author of the *Zohar*, that the *Ruah* & *Neshamah* grades are latently present in the first grade; that

each of the upper two grades are essentially refine-
ments of the first. The power & validity of this
suggestion is brought out even further when we
consider the fact that each of the three grades of
the soul correspond with three of the *Sefiroth*.

The *Nefesh* grade corresponds with the third triad
of the *Sefiroth* (*Netsah, Hod & Yesod*), which represents the material world. The *Ruah* grade corre-

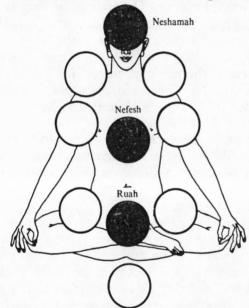

Neshamah

Nefesh

Ruah

The grades
of the Soul
distributed
among the
Sefiroth.

sponds with the second triad of the *Sefiroth* (*Hesed, Gevurah & Tifereth*), which represents the moral world.
The *Neshamah* grade corresponds with the first
triad (*Kether, Hokhmah & Binah*), which represents the
intellectual world. In turn, each grade is localized
in one of the three center *Sefiroth*: *Nefesh* in the
Sefirah Yesod (genitals); *Ruah* in the *Sefirah Tifereth*
(heart) & *Neshamah* in the *Sefirah Kether* (head).

(Isaac Luria was to later amend this outline & locate *Nefesh* in *Malkuth*, *Ruah* in *Tifereth* & *Neshamah* in *Binah*.)

One of the symbolic meanings of this arrangement of the soul suggests a progressive development of a different form of consciousness. The *Sefirah Yesod* might be said to symbolize the stage at which all conscious energies are concentrated in the sexual & instinctual sphere. The individual here is conscious only of his own needs.

The *Sefirah Tifereth*, the place of the heart, would then be the place where the individual would be conscious of the needs of others. He would attain a position where he could see others not in the light of his own needs, but in the light of their own.

The *Sefirah Kether*, the place of the head in which we are told resides the ultimate divine principle knowable to man while he is alive, would be the place where the individual perceives the 'plan' or meaning of being.

In yet another passage from the *Zohar*, however, we are presented with a different picture, one which almost appears to contradict the order just discussed. There[39] we are told that the *Nefesh* does not possess any light of its own, & that it is tightly meshed with the sinews of the body. It is the *Ruah*, which is directly above it & which imposes laws upon it. And above the *Ruah* stands the *Neshamah* which in turn rules it & sheds life on its life. What we are presented with here is the picture of the three in an unfolded state. If the *Nefesh* is not worked on by the individual the *Ruah* grade does not manifest & no light of any type is shed. Once the *Nefesh* has refined itself of its own volition, then it receives

[39] Quoted in Abelson, *Jewish Mysticism*, p.160.

aid from the evolved *Ruah* & not before.

Ruah §The *Ruah* grade is the seat of moral qualities & is sometimes referred to as the Intellectual
Spirit.

The mediator
between man
& the Divine

The *Neshamah* is the soul proper & the *Nefesh*
a dynamism best described as vital or instinctual.
The *Ruah* is the spirit proper. One may call the
Nefesh the animal soul, the *Neshamah* the divine
or over-soul & the *Ruah* the spirit which in certain
ways mediates between the two polarities of soul.
Its mediation is slight however because the *Ruah*
is thought of an intertwined with the *Nefesh*.[40]
For this reason it is sometimes said of these two
grades that they are not separate entities, but one
grade with two aspects. Whichever the case, once
the *Nefesh* has qualified itself, it becomes a throne
for the *Ruah*.

[40] Simon
and Sperling,
The Zohar,
vol.1, p.203.

Because of the intimacy of these two grades the
Kabbalists warn us that if man does not continue
striving for purity & righteousness once the *Ruah*
has become enthroned, he will remain animated
by these two grades alone, & never come to know
the *Neshamah*. Because the emergence of the *Ruah*,
as understood by the Kabbalists, is an experience
of 'the spirit...poured on us from on high' (Isaiah
xxxii, 15) the numinosity of the moment may easily
mislead one into believing that the task of spiritual
development has been completed.

Neshamah §The *Neshamah* grade is the highest
of all grades & even when it is not consciously
realized it rules the course of a man's life. In one
place the Kabbalists say that a man may not know
the *Neshamah* until he dies, & yet in another they
say that the perfect devotee may come to know
her. This apparent contradiction seems to mean

that the perfect devotee is one who dies in a spiritual sense only, both for himself & the world. For those who do not know this spiritual death, only the natural & common death may bring the *Neshamah* before their eyes.

The *Neshamah*, the highest phase of existence, is in no way bound to the two lower grades. It is beyond sin & judgment & is often identified with the divine *Shekhinah*.

ORIGIN OF THE SOUL

§ According to Kabbalistic tradition the soul was formed in the Garden by the coming together of four winds issuing from the North, South, East & West. But it is the West wind which is regarded as the breath which forms the soul out of the conjunction of the winds. This activity takes place at the exact moment that the first man is being fashioned below out of the four elements gathered from the four corners of the earth. It is when the two operations are completed that the form created by the conjunction of the four winds & the form created by the conjunction of the four elements are bound together. It is for this reason that the Kabbalists say that man is composed of the substances of two worlds.

The *Zohar* [41] adds that the four elements, fire, air, earth & water are the roots & sources of all things both below & above. It qualifies this statement by stating that the four winds which were gathered in the Garden for the creation of the soul contained the elements in them as well: fire was in the North wind, air in the East wind, water in the South wind & earth in the West. Man's body was composed of the dust contained in the lower world, his soul from the dust of the upper.

The coming together of the four winds

[41] Levertoff, *The Zohar,* vol. 3, pp. 79-81.

This soul was then poured forth from the upper waters in the form of God's breath ('And He breathed into his nostrils the breath of life.' Genesis *xxi*, 7). When this first soul rose up in the body of Adam, it was realized that, because each man to come was to be patterned after this first creation, all men by nature would be united with the Divine.

At the time of the creation of this first soul which was given to Adam, other souls were created as well. According to the 'Greater Holy Assembly'[42] the souls of all to be born are contained within Adam. This one mention of this idea is a qualified statement, however. The NShMH (*Neshamah*) souls alone are contained within him. We must therefore assume that the souls created by God were composed of only the *Nefesh* & *Ruah* grades, the *Neshamah* grade being awarded accordingly.

The *Zohar* tells us that when God desired to create the universe He formed all the souls which were destined for the bodies of man & caused all to pass before Him in preliminary judgment. Each soul, arriving in the form in which its body would eventually be cast, stood before Him & begged to remain in the upper heavens. In each instance God directed them to the place on Earth where their newly formed bodies awaited them.

Before the soul descends to this world we are told[43] that it must ascend from the earthly paradise which is its home to the throne. The throne referred to here is clearly the *Merkabah*, the Throne Chariot of God. Once there, it draws its being from the throne. As the text reads, it 'takes its spirit from the four pillars upon which the Throne sits.' This, I believe, alludes to the drawing forth of the *Neshamah* grade which in another instance is referred

[42] Mathers, *Kabbalah Unveiled*, p. 242.

[43] Levertoff, *The Zohar*, vol. 3, p. 40.

to as hewn from the four sides of the throne. One can only assume that the four sides of the throne, or the four pillars, refer us to the four elements upon which everything is based, & from which Adam receives his spiritual & corporeal form. It is here that the created soul is prepared for entry into the world. Even then there is yet another operation to be performed, almost at the last second, before life as we know it may occur.

MAN/WOMAN: THE ORIGINAL SEPARATION

§'In what world did we meet?...There are moments when I think I can feel, through the ages & all the darkness of appearances, our secret connection. Scenes that happened before men appeared on the earth come back into my memory, & I see myself under the golden boughs of Eden, sitting beside her.'—Gerard de Nerval[44]

All the souls created by the activity of God were originally one, the male & female portions of them not yet separated, existing in conjugal bliss. When they first begin their journey to the Below on this earth they do so as male & female together. Once arrived, they become separated, & only God knows where the two halves of the original soul reside. A man, according to the *Zohar*, may only find his other half by walking in the way of truth. Only then may he have a chance at completion.

When they leave the sanctuary of their original wholeness they are placed in the hands of the night, which has charge of conception, & which ultimately decides which of the two shall be born first. When & if these two souls meet again in this life they answer the scriptural statement that 'there is nothing new under the sun,' for their union was pre-or-
dained

[44] Gerard de Nerval quoted in *Aspects of Love*, Suzanne Lilar, p.119.

dained by virtue of the fact that they were originally one.

But there are no guarantees in this regard[45] for
a man may become 'perverted in his ways,' & if
he does his true mate is transferred to another.
He may never know her in this life unless he, by
his own efforts, rectifies his ways. If not, then he
will not be joined to her until he dies, at which
time the other who has been mated to her is
removed. All of which, the *Zohar* contends, is a
grievous event in the eyes of God, but one which
was ordained by Him nonetheless.

All women are in the shelter of the *Shekhinah*,
the feminine counterpart of God of which the
Neshamah is a portion. We are also told that a
man of good character should be willing to give
up all of his property & earthly goods to obtain
the marriage of a woman who is the daughter of
a man learned in the *Torah*.[46] The implication here
is that wisdom & perfection is genetically transmitted, & may only be transmitted through those who
are intimately united with God. It also appears
that it is put upon the male to *find* the missing
half of his soul. The woman wins her half as a
matter of course, as painful as the course may be.

The Kabbalists add one further admonition on
this matter: whoever has not begotten children in
this world, whether it be with his true soul-mate
or with another, will not have a place set aside
for him in the future world. His soul will be
banished & never find rest.

THE SOUL IN MAN

§ The manner in which a man may become
acquainted with his soul, according to the
Kabbalists, is in Psalm *xxiv*, 7:

[45] Lever-
toff, *The Zo-
har*, vol. 2,
p. 333.

[46] Simon
and Sperling,
The Zohar,
vol. 1, p. 301.

'Lift up your heads, O ye gates; & be ye lift up, ye everlasting doors; & the King of glory shall come in.'

Knowledge of God cannot be had without his passing through the gates of the *Sefiroth*, & the *Sefiroth* are the 'members of the body' through which the soul may be known. One must first pass through the gates of the soul in order to reach the Divine King. That the soul is a mediator & messenger between man & the Divine is emphasized in the Kabbalistic statements made concerning the soul's activity during the time that man sleeps.

The common belief is that while a man sleeps his soul, in the *Neshamah* specifically, departs from his body. Midway between earth & heaven reside 128,000 winged creatures whose sole function it is to report the words of voices below for judgment. The voices they hear are those of men's souls reporting the activities of man so that he might be judged.

The soul of a man who has not lived righteously is met with throngs of unclean spirits the moment it leaves the body. These take her up in their arms & cling to her, all the while disclosing events which they foresee will shortly occur in the world, a great part of the information being fabrications. The soul of a man who is just passes through this stratum of evil spirits & ascends to the area of holy angels. These souls receive true information concerning future events. On their descent, for this reason, the band of evil spirits are all the more anxious to halt the soul so that they might receive the news of heaven for their own ends.

The information received by such souls during their stay with the angels is relayed by them to man in the form of dreams. The source of dreams

is therefore seen by the Kabbalists to be of a divine
nature & thought of by them as a sixtieth part
of prophecy. They cite the scriptural passage:

'And he said, Hear now my words: If there be
a prophet among you, I the Lord will make myself
known unto him in a vision, & will speak unto
him in a dream.' (Numbers *xii*, 6)

Prophecy is the highest grade of prophetic wisdom
given to man by God. The second highest is vision,
with the grade of dream at the bottom of the scale.
In each instance, the information contained in each
grade is communicated to the recipient by an angel.

It was also believed that when the *Neshamah*
nightly departed from man his body was open to
attack by unclean spirits. The only way in which
a man could protect himself from being assailed
by these demons was to follow in the way of the
Torah during his waking hours, for when he slept
unclean spirits hovered over his bed. The *Neshama*,
as long as it remained with the body, actually pro-
tected it from the ever-present spirits. At night,
man was on his own & the actions of his day were
visited upon him.

According to the *Zohar*[47] a man whose soul finds
favor in God's eye immediately becomes afflicted
so that the soul may gain immediate freedom from
earthly bondage. Only in that way may the soul
come to realize its full power, only when the body
is 'broken & crushed'.

[47] Lever-
toff, *The Zo-
har*, vol. 2,
p. 48.

The announcement that a man is soon to die occurs
when he no longer dreams. That is, when the soul
no longer brings back pronouncements of the future.
Thirty days prior to his leave-taking his soul nightly
ascends to that place in the world above which
has been set aside for it.

DEATH & THE SOUL

§ For thirty days prior to a man's death he is without the *Neshamah* grade of the soul, & during this time he casts no shadow. This is to say that it is the *Neshamah* which gives man his substance. During the time of his final illness the *Neshamah* is brought to trial above where she confesses the thoughts & deeds of the man in whom she has resided. The pain of death in the

The judgment

man's body is greater at this time than at any other. If the judgment given above should turn out to be favorable, a sweat breaks out over the man's body, he is relieved of his pain, & the *Neshamah* returns to illumine him.

At the moment of a man's death the four elements which were at one time joined in him begin fighting with one another, & a herald comes forth who proclaims to all the worlds that the man is on the brink of death. The moment the proclamation is made a flame shoots out of the North & rushes to the four quarters of the earth where it burns the souls of sinners. That done, the flame rests between the wings of a black cock. The black cock—black because this is the color of judgment—then crows three times, a sound audible only to the dying man. At the last cry all of a man's dead relatives & friends come & stand before him. If he has been judged virtuous, they all rejoice at his coming & his soul is immediately raised to the place set aside for it. If not, only those companions who are sinners recognize him & a great cry of woe shatters the silence as the figures turn into columns of flame shooting up to heaven. This man brings about the imprisonment of his soul

The interment

on the earth for a certain period of time.

At the moment of death the *Neshamah* & the *Nefesh* separate themselves out of the body, the *Ruah* grade remaining permanently with the body. During the first seven days of the body's interment the *Nefesh* goes to & fro, weeping, from the deceased's grave to his house & back again. Once the body begins to decay on the seventh day the *Nefesh* gains release from the world. At least this is one of two views held. The tradition is obscured on several aspects of this event because the term 'soul' was used interchangeably for all three grades. The alternative view states that the *Nefesh* remains with the body for the period of twelve months before gaining release from the world. I would like to think that what was originally meant was that the *Neshamah* had to remain for seven days before release, since the *Nefesh* was the grade which remained behind for twelve months. But this is only conjecture.

The ascent of *Nefesh*

Whichever of the two grades was referred to here, once the period of either seven days or a year is reached, the *Torah*, which has been standing over the body's grave protecting the *Nefesh* until its departure, then rises with the *Nefesh* for the ascent. Clearing the way for the *Nefesh*, the *Torah* plunges ahead until it reaches the cave of *Machpelah*, the resting place of the three Patriarchs. The *Torah* then returns to the grave where it will stand guard until the day of the general resurrection of the dead.

The *Nefesh* in the meantime reaches the gates of the Garden of Eden where it is confronted by the Cherubim with swords of fire. If the *Nefesh* grade is deemed worthy of entering, it is allowed into the Garden where it finds four angels holding the form of a body in their hands. This the *Nefesh* joyfully dons & awaits its appointed time when

it will be allowed to ascend even higher, possibly
to be joined to the body of the King if it is judged
worthy enough.

The soul of a man who has not been judged to
be righteous is grabbed up & flung down into Hell,
Gehinnom. Here too tradition is obscure. We know
with certainty that the *Neshamah* grade is not referred to, for at death it immediately flies upwards
to its source. The *Ruah* grade, as already mentioned,

The descent   remains with the body. We can only assume that
of *Gehinnom*   the grade imprisoned in *Gehinnom* is the *Nefesh*.

The *Nefesh* is handed over to the Prince or Angel
of *Gehinnom*, Dumah. There he is led through the
seven gates to the heart of Hell where he is bound
in on all sides by fire. On the Sabbath it is believed
that all the gates are temporarily opened & that
the *Nefesh* grades may wander as far as the outer
gates to commune with the souls living there. There
in *Gehinnom* they remain until the general resurrection.

The ascension   Those souls which have reached the degree of ascension commensurate with their achievements in the
world are stored up by God until the time they
are joined with their bodies at the end of time.
At that time God will cause to exude from His
head a dew which will flow through the *Sefiroth*
& fall on the bodies contained in the earth. This
dew is contained in the Tree of Life & would have
caused Adam & Eve to have become immortal if
they had eaten the Tree's fruits. It flows constantly
out of the Tree of Life in the form of a celestial
river, but its life-giving effects are curtailed by
the evil serpent symbolized in the darkened moon.
It is not until God causes the 'unclean spirit to
pass out of the land' (Zachariah *xiii*, 2) that the

boon of the celestial river will be given to all, & then, according to Isaiah *xxx*, 26:

'...the light of the moon shall be as the light of the sun, & the light of the sun shall be sevenfold, as the light of seven days, in the day that the Lord bindeth up the breach of his people, & healeth the stroke of their wound.'

Then the *Nefesh* will be rejoined with the body, the *Ruah* which has been made to remain with the body in the earth will be released & oned with the *Nefesh* & the *Neshamah* will again descend to illuminate the body, fusing the three soul-grades together once & for all. But this general resurrection refers only to those souls who have not won release through the natural course of *Gilgul*, metempsychosis or reincarnation.

The resurrection

The *Zohar*[48] tells us that all souls must undergo transmigration & that the souls of men revolve like a stone which is thrown from a sling, so many turns before the final release. Those souls which have fulfilled & worked out their spiritual restoration by adhering to the commandments are set aside in their holy places to await their remerging with the soul of Adam. They are not subjected to *Gilgul*. Only those who have not completed their perfection must suffer the wheel of rebirth by being reborn into another human body. In rare cases, those instances where the soul has sinned beyond reason & with full knowledge of what it was doing, the soul enters into the forms of plants, wild beasts or even stones.

[48] Quoted in Abelson, *Jewish Mysticism*, p.164.

The theory of *Gilgul* (revolving) first appears in the twelfth century *Book Bahir*.[49] It was immediately understood as both a blessing & a punishment. On the one hand, one had to return to the lower

[49] See above, Part One, ch. 2, p.52.

world & live through the difficulty of being all
over again; on the other, it was a chance for the
soul to work out its salvation & aid in the great
work of restitution. Because all souls were originally
contained in Adam, or actually made up the soul
of Adam, the objective of each individual soul was
to win its place back in the soul of Adam, & by
so doing restore him to his original form before
the Fall. In this way each man shared in Adam's
exile, & each man was a partner in the process
of restoration, *tikkun*.

The state of
dybbuk

In time, the theory of *Gilgul* became modified.
Instead of an endless cycle of rebirths, each soul
was only allowed to be reborn three times. If by
the third time the soul had not achieved the min-
imum form of attainment, which would at least allow it entry into the lower sanctuary of *Machpelah*,
it was forced to roam the earth. In this state it
took on the form of a *dybbuk*, a spirit which possesses
another man's body.

The saddest note in the whole fabric of the Kabbalistic theory of the soul is struck by the idea
that a man who is not aware of the precepts of
righteousness may never see the *Neshamah* until
he has left this world. Only then may he understand
that the *Shekhinah*, God's bride, is the *Neshamah*
& that he had for a brief time shared her presence
in him.

THE SHEKHINAH

§In terms of the *Sefiroth*, the *Shekhinah*
represents the middle pillar of the three
pillars. She is also known as the Superior
Supernal Mother & the Inferior or Infernal Mother,
the mother & the daughter, the upper *Shekhinah*
& the lower *Shekhinah*—all appellations referring

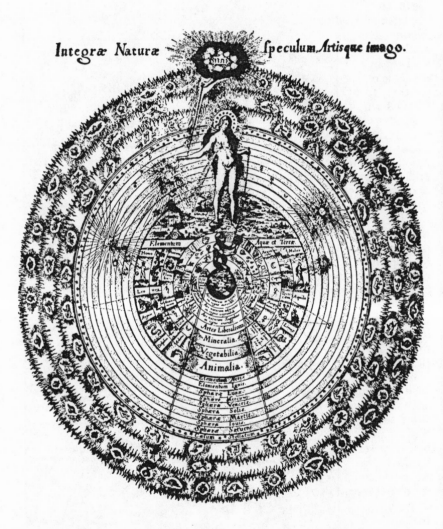

The Mirror of nature & the image as Art: Nature standing upon the elements, the link between God (right hand) & the lower world (left hand).

Around the ape of animal-creation are the various industries, followed by the circle of minerals, then plants & animals. Around these is the circle of earth, followed by air & the elements & planets, then the stars. Circling it all is the triple fire of the Supreme Creator in the outer ring of which is the sacred name *IHVH* surrounded by clouds containing the hand & chain of the higher world shackling nature by her wrist. By de Bry for Robert Fludd, *Collectio Operum,* Oppenheim, 1617.

to the *Sefiroth Binah & Malkuth* respectively. She therefore also figures in the figure of the *Tetragrammaton*, the upper (first) & lower (last) *Hé*. In short, she is the *anima mundi*, the world soul who gives a portion of herself to each man in the form of the *Neshamah*.

We mentioned in Part I of this book that the Şhekhinah was originally thought of as God's indwelling or presence.[50] We also mentioned that the Kabbalists later took up this idea of a presence & made of it a *part* of God, a feminine part, pointing out that when the Biblical statement was made to the effect that God's *Shekhinah* went into exile with Israel, a portion of God Himself went into exile. The redemption of this feminine helpmate of God is actually the redemption of a portion of God Himself.

[50] See above, Part One, ch. 3, p.72.

What the Kabbalists are stating is that God in His whole state is androgynous & that in His present condition He is incomplete. The Kabbalists assign the statement 'Let us make man,' to the lips of the *Shekhinah*, & go on to further stipulate that because man was made in God's image he too is androgynous—as may be easily attested by referring to the manner in which Eve was created. It is for this reason that one constantly finds statements to the effect that a man must always be male & female. That is, in order for a man's faith to be firm he must always remain in contact with the feminine portion of himself.

Man as an androgyne

In a simple sociological sense this means that a man should not be without a wife. This, assuredly, has much to do with the idea that a man's soul may not be redeemed unless he has brought children into the world. But behind this stands the idea that the *Shekhinah* is represented by every woman alive. This is the reason why we are told in the *Zohar*[51] that when a man is about to travel on the road away from home & his wife, he must first pray to God that He allow the *Shekhinah* to come & rest on him so that he 'may remain male & female.'

In addition to this he is warned that when he is finally upon the road, with the *Shekhinah* resting upon him, he should not do anything which would offend her. If he should in any way do so, the *Shekhinah* will abandon him & 'leave him defective.' Once returned from his journey it is his obligation to 'give pleasue' to his wife because it is *through her* that the *Shekhinah* came to him. It is for this reason that students of the *Torah* who dedicate themselves to their studies for six days of the week, & are therefore in constant presence of the *Shekhinah* because of their righteousness, are obliged to 'gladden their wives for the sake of honoring the *Shekhinah.*'

The honoring of the *Shekhinah*

Kabbalistic tradition tells us that a student of the *Torah* is well on his way to becoming 'a bridegroom of the *Torah*,' or of the *Shekhinah*, for she & the literal *Torah* are one, it is the outer garment of the *Shekhinah*. One who diligently studies the *Torah* clothes the *Shekhinah*, for in her exile she is naked. If the Fall had not occurred, if man had not given in to sin, she would have had no need of a covering. Every sinner is therefore thought of as one who disrobes the *Shekhinah*, & in so doing prolongs her exile. This is the interpretation given to Isaiah *i*, 1: 'Thou shalt not uncover thy mother's nakedness.'

In an exceedingly beautiful passage in the *Zohar*

the *Torah* is likened to a lovely woman courting her lover:

'Truly, the *Torah* releases a word & emerges a bit from her sheath, & then quickly hides herself again. This she does only for those who know her...The *Torah* is like a beautiful & stately woman, hidden in a secreted chamber in her palace with a secret lover...This lover constantly passes the gate of her house, searching for her...She opens her chamber door & reveals her face to him but for an instant...He alone sees it.'[52]

[52] Gershom G. Scholem, *On the Kabbalah and Its Symbolism,* p. 55.

The passage continues to relate how the mystic is the one who haunts her house & that he had been drawn to her when she once beckoned to him, revealing a portion of her face to him, & he came at the first sign without hesitation. Then she begins to speak to him, simply, within the range of his understanding, from behind a curtain until insight comes to him. This insight is called *derashah*, a form of interpretation popular with the Talmudists by which exoteric oral doctrine was created from the written words of Scripture.

Then she takes up a veil through which she speaks allegorical words, or *haggadah*. Only by the latter may he become familiar with her, & only then does she reveal her face. She tells him of all the hidden secrets contained in her, & only then for the first time does he understand the true meaning of the *Torah*.

According to this passage, therefore, it is not impossible for a man to meet his *Neshamah* face to face before his death, if he is a Kabbalist. The union of the mystic with his soul, & therefore the restitution of the original divine order, may be known through the *Shekhinah* who is the *Neshamah*.

The union of the Mystic & his Soul

The *Torah* is in essence what clothes her & conceals her nakedness from the world.

Ultimately, the whole of Kabbalistic speculation is only a key to the chamber of the *Torah* in which each of us may find the *Shekhinah*.

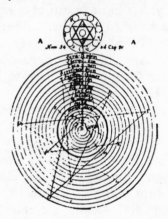

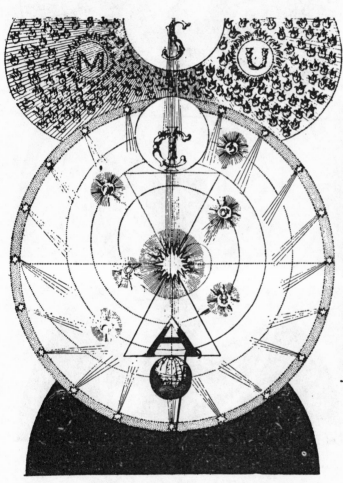

"Here Adam, by that Word of Grace treasured up in his heart . . . is raised again so far, that he can stand above the earthly globe upon the basis of the fiery triangle which is in excellent Emblem of his own Soul."
Number ten in a series from the *Works of Jakob Behme*.

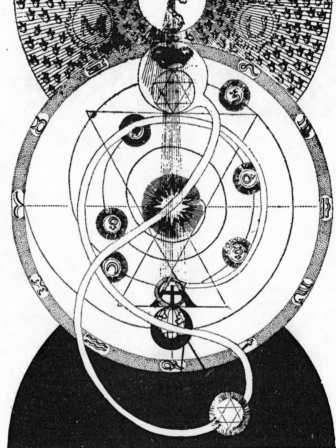

"Here Adam, in the same Place as before, appears again. . .the second Adam in our Humanity upon Earth . . ." Number eleven in a series, from *The Works of Jacob Behmen*.

Part Three
The Kabbalah Today

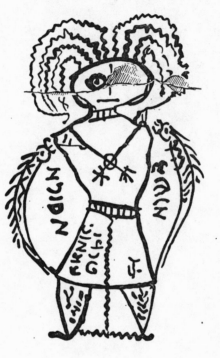

Inside of a Jewish incantation bowl, a magical charm to ward off "ghosts", represented as a manacled demon. From James Montgomery, *Aramaic Incantation Texts from Nippur*, Philadelphia, 1913.

The Kabbalah Today

T SHOULD BE apparent to the reader by now that the Kabbalistic tradition is not a unified system of thought or a fixed theology with hard & fast theorems. There are certain basic ideas to be found in Kabbalistic speculation, but on the whole each mystic approached the material at hand from a different avenue, adding something here, subtracting something there. The six themes or principles which are found in all Kabbalistic thought are:

Six common principles

The true transcendent God is not the creator of the universe. Referred to as the *En-Sof*, the Illimitable, He is without will, intention or plan & may only be described by what He *is not*.

The true creator of this universe is the *Sefirah Kether*, the first of the ten *Sefiroth* which emanated out of the *En-Sof*.

The creator had a feminine helpmate, an aspect of Himself which is presently in a state of exile in the world.

The basic law governing the operations of the universe & the world is that of the opposites.

The desired assimilation of the created universe by the Divine, the reconstitution of the original unity, is dependent on the redemption of all souls, which is in turn dependent on the union of the opposites.

The work of redemption is the sole responsibility of man. To achieve it he must not only accept the reality of evil, but must penetrate it for meaning. This he must do in direct opposition to the traditional attitude which causes Rabbinical Judaism to shrug its shoulders at the mere mention of the problem.

MYSTICISM, RATIONALISM AND TRANSFORMATION

§In the harsh light of the twentieth century, it may seem that such principles deserve the rationalist accusation of being no more than occult gibberish. Considering the great number of works which purport to explain the Kabbalah, one can sometimes sympathize with this attitude.

Fairy-tale scholasticism

Much of the material available consists of fairy-tale scholasticism & embarrassing attempts to convince the general public that the Kabbalah is important because the Christian doctrine of the Holy Trinity may be found 'hidden' in its writings.

There are also voluminous tomes which discuss the enlightened speculations of Jewish mystics within the context of black & white magic. This just adds weight to the general consensus that mysticism, if not religion in general, is both the child & parent of mental aberration. Much of the misunderstanding over the true nature of the Kabbalah has grown out of such works. The commonly accepted picture of the mystic—or anyone for that matter who consciously seeks to find meaning in life—as a self-indulgent escapist has also contributed much to the misunderstanding of mysticism in general. The acid-laced posturing of the many week-end mystics & ascetics which this generation has spawned with such Messianic fervor has not helped change this caricature.

Others argue that a mystical attitude, a concern with the inner world & the problems of redemption & transformation are ultimately selfish because the individual concerned with such ideas often retreats from the stage of social involvement. Wherever such a retirement from the visible activities of the world results in an attitude of reticence & unconcern, then the withdrawal is most certainly selfish. It is only when the individual replaces the value of active social participation in his group with another value that he can assume the privilege of withdrawing from the active scene. His retreat must yield a result which is at least equal in quality, if not in quantity, with the value of his continual participation in the group.

Throughout his illuminating work on the Kabbalah, Gershom Scholem[1] has stressed that a ritual form which no longer allows or contains the experience of the orgiastic or ecstatic dimension will always fall short of its goals. Because the goal of ritual is transformation & rejuvenation in sacred time & space, ritual forms without this dimension produce no effect & can therefore be thought of as a flailing of arms in empty air. It was precisely because the rituals of Rabbinical Judaism no longer contained the elements of ecstasy & orgy that Kabbalism arose originally.

[1] Scholem, *Major Trends in Jewish Mysticism.*

The rituals of Rabbinical Judaism are primarily rites of remembrance & conjurations which bring into being nothing but memories of the historical reality of the Jews. Such rituals only divorce the Jew from the immediacy of reality, from the here

& now. They transform nothing. As rituals they are ineffective precisely because they lack the intensity of the ecstatic dimension which invariably accompanies rituals of transformation. It was the Kabbalists' acceptance of *Aggadah* (legend), the mystical dimension of Judaism,

which made of Kabbalism a transformative element in Jewish history. The philosophical nature of the *Halakhah* (law), lacking the emotion necessary for ecstasy, could not inaugurate the process of transformation which spiritual & religious fulfillment requires. Only the mythical ritual of the Kabbalists could achieve that. Yet the two questions which then immediately come to mind are, what is there that should be transformed & how does a mythical ritual effect such transformation?

The idea of transformation in our time is difficult for many to accept. What it speaks of is the alteration of an ephemeral substance, & this is a metaphysical concept lying beyond the reach of quantitative analysis or deductive reasoning. Whatever we decide to call it—soul, Self, Adam Kadmon—it is indescribable & inaccessible to conscious manipulation. It is a substance mystics tell us is contained within man, trapped within man, & in need of redemption & transformation. By virtue of the fact, or the idea, that this substance is in a fallen or unborn state, one's humanity must be regarded as incomplete as long as redemption is not known. The thing to be transformed is man himself. What is to be achieved by this act is the raising & illumination of the aboriginal & instinctual sphere of his nature, a solidification of his emotional & instinctual range into a diamond-body formed by the marriage of all opposites contained within him. The orgiastic sphere is not only the thing to be transformed, but the very thing which transforms. The mythical dimension is an emotional dimension. To refuse this dimension active participation in one's life is to shut the door on passion, for it is emotional intensity, the heat of passion, which welds the opposites together. Here I do not necessarily refer to the passion of carnality, the splintering & indiscriminate scattering of one's energy. Instead, I refer to the emotion itself, the ecstasy, not the many forms in which it may become personified.

If, in experiencing an emotion—any emotion—a person consciously refrains from acting on it while at the same time keeping the event alive within

Ecstasy & the transformation of man

himself, he will discover that the emotion leads
him to another dimension of experience. He will discover that the energy of the emotion does not die
because of his refusal to give it a space outside
of himself. If he holds on to the tail of this tiger
as it rebounds inward, he will discover its source.
He will then learn why the Mediaeval alchemists
& Kabbalists insisted that man contains within him
a sun, a center of pure energy. It should be stressed
that the method I am talking about here is nothing
new. The idea is implicit in all Oriental yogas.

The mythical dimension is that 'other place' where
the pantheons of gods, angels, powers reside for
endless time. It is the place from which *this* place,
this reality which we experience as the world, originally received its substance & structure. At least,
this is the view presented to us by every religious
or spiritual scripture in history & substantiated by
those mystics who from time to time have claimed
to have entered for a moment the eternity of that
dimension. Mircea Eliade, one of the leading historians of religion in our century, has time & again
throughout his works emphasized the idea that
because a myth speaks of the events which take
place in the dimension of the Divine, ritually to
reenact a myth is to suspend temporal time for
a moment & enter into sacred time.[2]

[2] Mircea Eli-
ade, *The
Sacred and
the Profane*.

Myth not only teaches & regulates, it heals &
transforms. To enter into the mythical dimension
is to enter into the time of the primordial unity,
a time when all things were & are in order. If
there is a substance or aspect in man needful of
redemption, healing & transformation, then contact
with this other reality rejunevates that part. The
passion we refer to in talking of the need for mythical

ritual arises when the two dimensions—the transpersonal & the mundane—are brought into contact
with one another through the mediating act of the
ritual. It is the spark which flies when two stones
are struck together, the *mysterium tremendum* accom-
panying every truly religous experience, & the cure
for spiritual sterility.

The rationalistic tendencies of Mediaeval Rabbinical Judaism led to the rejection of the pantheistic
unity of God, cosmos & man in favor of a rational
explanation of the sphere of the Divine. The concept
of God diminished & eventually became empty of
meaning. The Jewish rituals which served to incor-
porate man in the drama of birth, death & regeneration displayed in the flux of nature, became de-
mythologized. It was through these rituals which
concerned themselves with the reenactment of the
powers of life & death present at harvest & planting
time that man could be transformed. In Rabbinical
Judaism the 'time' of the nature ritual became
relegated to the historical sphere. It no longer
reflected the natural year's cycle & so no longer
reminded man that the spirit contained in him
could be known through its effect in nature, &
that the two were of the same pulse.

The Kabbalists alone fully understood the need
for myth, & it is in this that their importance
lies. Their tradition grew out of an attempt to
retain & contain the sacred dimension, the significance of which, they thought, was being continually
diminished by the laborious rationalistic efforts of
rabbinical Judaism. The ethical monotheism of
Judaism had from the beginning excluded anything
which hinted of pantheism or mythology. Metaphor
was made of mythology. Mythology was no longer

The need for
mythology

viewed as a depiction of sacred events but, instead, as a veiled but nonetheless rationally explicable code.

The fundamental problem with which the philosophers & theologians of rabbinical Judaism were faced was the divestment of the concept of God of all anthropomorphic & mythical elements. This purification was an attempt to make God a palpable unity & involved stripping the concept of divinity of everything which was not immediately analyzable & comprehensible. Anything which spoke in symbols had to be discarded so that the flawless logic of theological argument could be uniformly applied, practiced & understood by the common man.

The attempt to purify God

The outcome of this was the establishment of a God without logical defects, a God whose actions were within the scope of *human* understanding. The inevitable failure of this revision is not hard to explain since the substance of divinity is not analyzable, & to do away with the mystery contained in the core which can never be totally comprehended is to do away with the living presence of the divine. Where does the mystery lie if not in the symbolic dimension of mythology? The best way to divest a symbol of its mystery is to speak of it as if it were nothing but an allegory. Once the allegorical statement has been deciphered, the next step is a rationalist explanation of the moral & sociological meaning of this symbol-turned-allegory. In this way everything is neatly explained away.

This type of discourse & analysis is not the bread of men whose religious feelings are fed by songs of the heart. Sooner or later those whose nature would not allow them to follow the dialectics of

rabbinical Judaism had to separate themselves &
form a group of their own. These men of intense
feelings were the Kabbalists. Eventually they came
to view their religion through the eyes of a mystical
philosophy. The result was a broader, more sustain-
ing & ecstatic awareness of further truths hidden
beneath the existing ones.

But what is twentieth-century western man to
make of all of this? To the Kabbalists, religion
needed a totally new perspective, but it was
nonetheless real to them. The self-imposed task
of the Kabbalists was a re-evaluation of a spiritual
tradition, a tradition which was still very much
within reach. To twentieth-century man, religion,
along with God, is all but dead. Our era has been
recognized as the first in the history of mankind
to have exiled the sacred from the field of activity
called the world & Mircea Eliade[3] stresses that the
totally despiritualized cosmos is a very recent event
in the history of mankind.

Modern man, in his attempt to find the 'scientific
basis of reality,' has sealed himself off in an intellectual vacuum. Religion no longer permeates the
structure of either society or the individual. True,
many rituals are still performed in the name of
religion, but they are viewed as social obligations,
gestures that any respectable man or woman is
expected to perform. From such gestures, all emotion & all intimacy with the Divine is absent. We
too seldom question ourselves &, too seldom therefore, find cause to question the meaning of our
existence. To find meaning it is necessary for one
to immerse oneself constantly in the problem of
Being.

But this is an enormous task, an undertaking

Modern
man's intel-
lectual vac-
uum

[3] Mircea
Eliade, *The
Sacred and the
Profane*.

which demands guidelines. When it comes to integrating the message of mystical scripture, contemporary man is at first sight without a method. Both ancient & mediaeval man found himself living in the certainty of the existence of a Godhead. The concept of Godhead in the West became identified much too easily not only with the Good, but also with the Purposeful & Rational. In a world marred by war, poverty & by ignorance of both greed & prejudice, such a view is no longer tenable. If, instead, evil had been given its rightful place in the pantheon of Western religion & ethics, then perhaps we would not now find ourselves faced with the contradiction of the apparent absence of God. If instead we had accepted the Kabbalist & gnostic statement that the light also contained within it a darkness, perhaps we would not have fallen prey to that very darkness in our own century. But this is material for a different dialogue, beyond the scope & purpose of this book.

The revivication of myth & religion

It is enough to say that the revivification of both myth & religion, especially the former, where the darkness is always a part of the whole, demands a system which pours new wine into old bottles. The new bottles have proven to be too plastic, too open to manipulation of their shape, without spirit, constructed more for show than for use. In suggesting that old bottles be brought back into use I only suggest employing the method which the Kabbalists themselves employed. In seeking to revitalize their spiritual heritage they did not reject the old religion, but, by uncovering the meaning of the mythical dimension contained within it, actually made of the old, dead form a new young spirit which refurbished & rejuvenated the beaten

& exiled soul of the Mediaeval Jew. This revivification of religion was made possible only by a re-entry into the mythical dimension, out of which religion emerged in the first place. As C. G. Jung argued,[4] the validity of a human's experience is to be found in the mythical dimension of his life, a life lived in the awareness that myth is not fiction. Religion without myth not only fails to work, it also fails to offer man the promise of unity with the transpersonal & eternal.

We have suggested that the key to understanding the difference between the rabbinical tradition & the Kabbalism is to be found in the latter's attitude towards mythology. We have also touched lightly on the idea of the importance of mythology to twentieth-century man. Before we discuss the methods by which mythology has become, or may become, an active principle in the world again, we will have to take a short look at mythology, lifting it up out of the nursery & looking at its metaphysical underside.

[4] C. G. Jung, *Answer to Job,* p. 96.

The cosmos entwined by the creative spirit, from Jacob Bryant, *An Analysis of Ancient Mythology,* London, 1774.

KABBALIST METAPHYSICS AND MYTHOLOGY
§There are four major themes to be found in mythology: 1. The Illimitable; 2. The Original Unity; 3. The Separation of the Opposites; 4. The Union of the Opposites.

The Illimitable §There is nothing that can be said about the central concept of Kabbalism. The *En-Sof*, the Illimitable or the Infinite, is unknowable. That it does exist can only be proven by proving its non-existence. The Kabbalah tells us that the only way this concept of Godhead might be explained is by telling you what it is not. God, the ultimate God which stands above & beyond

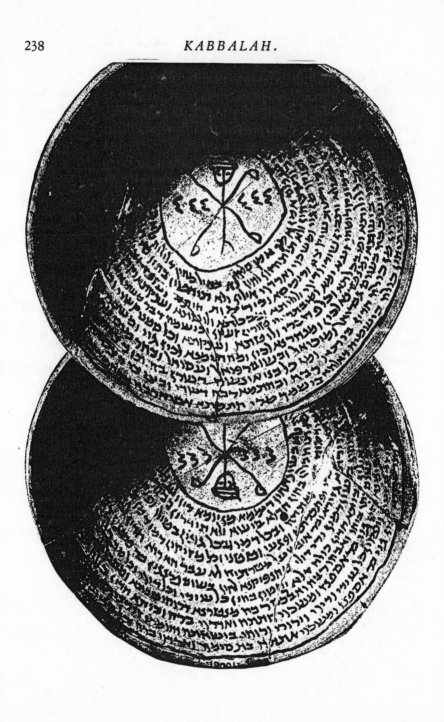

all process, can only be understood by what He is not.

This *En-Sof* is the Hidden God of the Kabbalah which at one time was a plenum, a fullness, that became a nothingness through the act of expressing itself, by making itself known, by producing something which is real in the commonly accepted sense of the term. But this expression of the *En-Sof*, this externalization of itself into what was to become the cosmos, did not exhaust it. Its becoming a nothingness did not mean it became an emptiness, a vacuum in which nothing exists. Its state of being nothing has nothing to do with being empty. It has more to do with its being nothing knowable, indescribable & without structural qualities which may be diagrammed or logically explained. The *Zohar* tells us that of it, 'no trace may be found, nor can thought by any means or method reach it.'[5]

The *En-Sof* cannot be defined, is without form, may only be known by what it is not & is in a state of perpetual concealment. The theme is not peculiar to Kabbalist thought.

The *Tao Te Ching* tells us,

'The Tao that can be talked about is not the unchanging Tao. Names may be known, but not the Eternal Name...We may look at it with our eyes but yet not see it. It is without form. Listen to it with your ears & you will not hear it. It bears no sound. Try to take hold of it with your hand & you cannot. It is incorporeal.'[6]

The *Kena Upanishad* defines the location of the Limitless, known to the Hindu as *Brahman*, as a place where,

'...sight cannot go, speech cannot go, nor the

Opposite: Incantation bowl with a long & repetitious charm for a man & his family. From James Montgomery, *Aramaic Incantation Texts from Nippur*.

[5] Simon and Sperling, *The Zohar*, vol. 1, p. 89.

[6] *Tao Te Ching*, vss. 1 & 14 (Author's trans.).

[7] Quoted in
*Hindu Poly-
theism,* Alain
Danielou,
p. 20.

[8] *Bhagavad-
gita,* XIII,15,x.

mind. We cannot know, we cannot understand. How can one explain it? It is other than all that is known. It is above the Unknown.'[7]

Again, we are in the presence of that which may only be defined by what is not known, & even then 'one cannot say that it exists nor that it does not exist.'[8]

This theme of inaccessibility, limitlessness, invisibility &, at times, indifference on the part of the ultimate Godhead, is also to be found in the more primitive but nonetheless metaphysical statements made about sky gods. They too are invisible, beyond reach & expressly defined as everything which man is not. On the whole, however, this concept of non-being & even non-nonbeing is a sophistication to be found in the early phases of religious metaphysical speculation, rather than at the heart of mythology. It is to be found specifically in religious or metaphysical systems which have sought to include or retain the mythical dimension in them. This limitless, eternal principle, this *En-Sof* stands before the business of mythology. Mythology speaks of things. The *En-Sof*, the *Tao* & the God, Brahman, cannot be spoken of. All one may do is remain blissfully mystified by this reality which can only be known by that which it is not, was not & can never be.

The Original Unity §The concept of the Illimitable or the Indefinable does not contain within it the concept of duality or multiplicity. It is beyond even these things. It is all things without category or definition.

Yet you will recall that the first *Sefirah*, *Kether*, is definable by concepts acceptable to the reasoning intellect. In personified form, *Kether* is always represented

resented in profile to comply with the Kabbalistic statement that this *Sefirah* is only partially concealed. Inasmuch as this *Sefirah* is the first emanation or representation of the *En-Sof*, it shares some of its qualities. In direct contrast to the *En-Sof*, on the other hand, *Kether* is referred to as the creator spoken of in Genesis. Because the *En-Sof* has neither will, desire, intention nor thought—all acts which

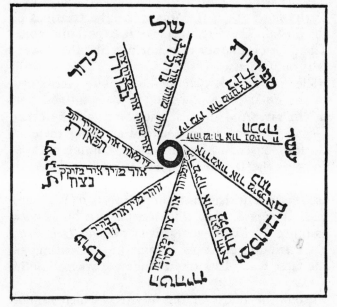

"The circulation of the Ten Sefiroth in the form of the Wheel of Life."

by their very nature imply limitation—& because the act of creation calls for limit & measure, the Illimitable could not create even if it should desire to do so. In order to create it would have to extend its own illimitableness as the substance of creation, thereby instilling all things with properties & states as boundless as itself.

The *En-Sof* could have only produced something

perfect & eternal. The only manner in which the *En-Sof* could make His unmanifest & invisible non-existence known was by expressing Himself in emanations or qualities which, as intangible as we may find them, are nonetheless tangible limits by which we can say, '*En-Sof* is not this, not that.' The *Sefiroth* are in no way the creations of the *En-Sof* but its emanations. The odor, leaf, petal & stem formation of a flower are no more the creations of the flower than the *Sefiroth* are the creations of the *En-Sof*. They are aspects of it & nothing more. The odor of a flower does not describe the flower. It is only an essence.

The first *Sefirah*, *Kether*, was a power contained in the *En-Sof*, the power of its own fullness one might say. And in this first *Sefirah* all the other *Sefiroth* to come are understood as being there in the form of seeds. Much misunderstanding has arisen over the fact that later Kabbalism tended to take the Lurianic view that *Kether* was not the highest *Sefirah*, but that the second, *Hohkmah* (Wisdom) was. It appears that when certain attributes once assigned to *Kether* were given over to *Hohkmah*, the attributes of *En-Sof* became in the writings of the later Kabbalists interchangeable with those of *Kether*:

'From the midst of this mystery which cannot be penetrated, this *En-Sof*, there one might have seen the faint glimmer of a light no larger than the point of a needle. [9]

'When the King wished to make his effect known, he engraved signs into the supernal sphere about him. From the impenetrable depths of the En-Sof a vapour-like fog issued.'[10]

This activity continues until a small spark emerges

[9] Simon and Sperling, *The Zohar*, vol. 1, p.89.

[10] Simon and Sperling, *The Zohar*, vol. 1, p.63.

in what is now understood to have been the *Sefirah Hokhmah*. What is important for us to note here is that the king spoken of is *Kether*. The term king is one of many attributes assigned to this *Sefirah*. The first *Sefirah* is the creator spoken of in Genesis, & not the *En-Sof*. He is the one who initiates creation. The manner in which he goes about the initial movements towards creation is not unlike that to be found in other creation myths. The *Zohar*[11] tells us that the single point which he created was transformed into a thought & that it was in that thought where he engraved the signs which were to become the remaining *Sefiroth* or archetypes. From the midst of this thought he went on to construct an edifice.

[11] Simon and Sperling, *The Zohar*, vol. 1, p. 6.

This beginning was unknowable by name, existent & non-existent at one & the same time, & was called *Mi* (Who?). Once this was achieved it then wished to become fully manifest & be known by a name. It created *ELeH* (these), & was known by that name. The two words *MI* & *ELeH* then intermingled to form the name *ELoHIM* (God). All of this is a Zoharic exegesis on the scriptural question, 'Who hath created these?' (Isaiah *xl*, 26), aimed at proving that the Ancient One, another name for *Kether*, applied also to the creator.

Another point to be discussed here is that this original unity, *Kether*, contains all which will eventually flow forth from it. Here again we find a distinction between this first *Sefirah* & the *En-Sof*. The *En-Sof* contains no distinctions or qualities be they of sex, value or quantity. The *En-Sof* is pure no-thing. We find much the same said about the Hindu God, Brahman.

'This Immutable Brahman is that. It is neither gross nor minute, neither short nor long, neither

[12] Madhav-
ananda, *Brha-
daranyaka Up-
anishad*, p.
517.

red colour nor oiliness, neither shade nor darkness, neither air nor ether, unattached, neither savour nor odour, without eyes & ears, without the vocal organ of mind…not a measure, & without interior or exterior.'[12]

The similarities to be found between the Kabbalist's *En-Sof* & the Hindu's Brahman are sufficient for us to say that we are in the presence of a universal model—an archetype. The universality of these metaphysical statements might be questioned if they were found to correspond only on this one point. But there are further similarities. The deity directly beneath Brahman corresponds with *Kether*. This deity is called Brahma, the immense-being.

[13] See above,
Part Two,
ch. 1, pp.113
-15.

In the chapter on the *Sefiroth* we pointed out that *Kether* is also called *Macroposopus*.[13] Because *Kether* contains the point through which the Divine manifests itself, he also contains the potential of time & space, height & depth, male & female, & so on. In fact, as the 'Book of Concealed Mystery'[14]

[14] & [15].
Mathers,
*Kabbalah Un-
veiled*, p.44.

tells us, it is in *Kether* where the 'equilibrium hangeth'; that is, the equilibrium of the yet unmanifest opposites, the remaining *Sefiroth*: 'Thus were those powers (the remaining *Sefiroth*) equiponderated which were not yet in perceptible existence.' And again: 'In His form (*Kether*) existeth the equilibrium: it is incomprehensible, it is unseen.'[15]

Brahma in the Hindu system is understood as the creator, as distinct from the gods Vishnu & Shiva, the preserver & the destroyer. His relationship to Brahman is the same as *Kether's* to *En-Sof*. He also contains within him, is composed of & *is* the balance of the forces which will in time extend themselves beyond the interior of his being. He too, like *Kether*, is masculine in essence. When he creates he does so by expounding the four sacred books of the Hindus, the *Vedas*. This corresponds with the idea that the sacred *Torah* of the Jews is the vehicle of all creation, & that it is made manifest through the activity of the primordial point hidden in *Kether*. In both Hindu & Kabbalistic creation stories we are told that there is an inactive, undefinable principle standing above & beyond that principle which is the active & true creator of the universe.

In bringing these comparisons into view I do not in any way mean to imply that there exists some secret traditional avenue connecting the two cultures. What I do suggest is that the ground of religious experience is common to all mankind & that the energies arising from that ground take on the garb of the psychological and spiritual peculiarities of the culture in which they are manifested. In both the Kabbalistic and Hindu examples offered we find the mythical ideas of a creator God standing beneath the heights of an infinite and immeasurable God. It is difficult at first to discern which is the product of highly speculative & metaphysical construction, & which is the pure product of that stratum we call myth. I therefore close this section with an example of the skeleton shorn of its metaphysic.

In Frank Waters' *The Book of the Hopi* [16] we are given the Hopi Indian tale of the creation in which it is stated that the first created world was one of endless space without time, shape, life, beginning or end, existing in the mind of the creator. After He created the finite world in his mind, the creator, Taiowa, realized that it would have to be made manifest. To this end He created another God,

The universality of religious experience

[16] Frank Waters, *The Book of the Hopi*, pp.3-4.

Sotuknang, & instructed him to fashion the universe & the world after the plan Taiowa had constructed in His own mind. In such a manner this world came into being. As simple as this creation tale is, it bears all the markings of the relationship found between the Kabbalistic Gods *En-Sof* & *Kether*. The plan for the creation also exists in *En-Sof* as a potential which must become finite & fixed but which, because of the *En-Sof's* illimitable nature & his inability to create that which is not Himself, infinite, the task of the creation falls to a second God. In this case *Kether*. What is surprising about the Hopi tale of the creation is that it is not the product of philosophical speculation but rather a spontaneous & magical expression of that mythical dimension in man. If one reduces and analyzes the elements of the tale one is left with a piece of Gnostic speculation. Speculation of the type which has always been thought of as being the result of highly imaginative but nonetheless *philosophical* considerations. And there we find the value of myth. Myth is to philosophy what the *En-Sof* is to *Kether*.

The Separation of the Opposites §The point located in space, quoted in the passage from the *Zohar*, refers us to the universal monad which appears in many mystical & religious texts under an assortment of names. It speaks of the moment of contact between the macrocosm & what is to be the microcosm. It is from this point that the known universe manifests itself. Eliade has pointed out that religious man does not experience space as something homogeneous.[17] The sacredness of certain areas in space—a church, altar, or a memorial—are thought of as places where the Divine has broken through the shell of this reality

[17] Eliade, *The Sacred and the Profane*, p.21.

& established itself as a center. In the creation myth of the *Zohar* this breakthrough is imagined as a point, a dot of concentrated energy which establishes the center of all future activity. From this point, or monad as it may also be called, all things will eventually take their orientation. The sacredness of this primordial point is to be found in all religious traditions & even finds expression in the Kabbalistic speculations of the sixteenth-century alchemist John Dee:

'The first & most simple manifestations & representation of things, non-existent as well as latent in the folds of Nature, happened by means of straight line & circle.

Yet the circle cannot be artificially produced without the straight line, or the straight line without the point. Hence, things first began to be the way of a point and a monad. And things related to the periphery (however big they may be) can in no way exist without the aid of the central point.'[18]

Wherever the point at which creation takes place is found, *that* is the center, fixed and eternal. The point where the first man was created, Adam, became identified as the center of the world. At this center was Adam buried. Upon this center the cornerstone of the Temple was placed. Around this center Mount Golgotha took form. On Mount Golgotha, the crucifixion took place. This center, this universal monad is contained within man as well as in space.

But the theme we are to discuss in this section is that of the manifestation of the opposites. Of all themes to be found in creation mythologies, of all variations which may be found on the theme of creator and any other particular of creation, this

Creation— the separation of opposites

[18] C. H. Josten, trans., "A Translation of John Dee's '*Monas Hieroglyphica*' (Antwerp, 1564). With an Introduction and Annotations" *Ambix*, p. 55.

one theme does not vary. The names & locales, the attributes & anthropomorphisms might differ from country to country, from century to century, but the dynamic structure of the theme has been found to be constant. Their existence is the one inescapable reality against which all arguments must shatter. Because the point is invariably referred to as a seed-point, a golden germ of the Divine in which is contained all that is to become the world, the universe, & man, there we must discern the first manifestation of the opposites. The *Zohar* tells us that this point is called *Reshith* (beginning), & that it is the starting-point of all things. But there is a further mystery to be found here.

When the *En-Sof* produced from the midst of its infinitude the Point, it did so through the expansion of itself, its body, vaguely described as an ether. This ether *(AWIR)* was then exhausted by the expansion of the point to become light *(AWR)*. This point we are told is the Hebrew letter *Yod* ( ), which is also associated by the Kabbalists with the first *Sefirah, Kether*. The *Zohar*[19] then goes on to tell us that this light extended itself & in so doing caused to shine forth from within itself, in fluid form, seven letters of the alphabet. Then darkness manifested itself, in which another seven fluid letters appeared. And finally, the firmament came into being bringing yet another eight letters. The presence of the firmament prevented the darkness & the light from coming into conflict with one another. Then, 'seven letters leapt from the side of the Light, & seven leapt from the side of the darkness & became engraved in the firmament, where they all yet remained in fluid form. When the firmament itself solidified, the letters assumed

[19] Simon and Sperling, *The Zohar,* vol.1, p.70.

material shape.' We are then told that the darkness
is the left, & the light the right—our first pair
of antinomies.

Let us for a moment turn to a Tantric Buddhist
text which outlines the creation of the universe
(*Kama-Kala-Vilasa*).[20] There we are told that the
first thing to have been made manifest was the
point, the *bindu*. This point, red in color, slowly
began to expand as if it were pregnant. The swelling
is explained as the preparation for the birth of sound,.

'From that sound came Ether, Air, Fire, Water,
Earth, & the letters of the alphabet.'[21]

Here, too, the creation of the universe is synonymous with the creation of the alphabet.

Because the twenty-two letters of the Hebrew
alphabet include masculine & feminine values, in
the *Zohar* passages just paraphrased we are in the
presence of not only the delineations of dark &
light, right & left, but male & female. Once the
primordial point becomes manifest all opposites
must be understood as potentially present. The
primordial point, as John Dee suggested, is the
beginning of all distinctions. By the center the
circumference may be known.

The first act of Creation is separation:§'And God
said, Let there be a firmament in the midst of
the waters, & let it divide the waters from the
waters.

And God made the firmament, & divided the waters
which were under the firmament from the waters
which were above the firmament. And God called
the Firmament Heaven.

. . .Let the waters under heaven be gathered unto
one place, & let the dry land appear . . . And God
called the dry land earth.' (Genesis *i*, 6-10).

20 & 21
Avalon,
*Kama-Kala-
Vilasa*, p.69.

First we have the separation of the waters which represent the chaos existing prior to the time of creation; then, the separation of Heaven and Earth. Kabbalistic tradition tells us that the waters above are masculine, the waters below, feminine. Until the time of the separation of the upper waters from the lower waters, nothing could be produced in the world. The creation myth tells us that the union

The *T'ai Chi* or Primal Unity of the Chinese.

of the masculine & the feminine as they exist in the initial state is an unproductive one. In order for creation, creation in general, to begin the opposites must be separated. As long as they exist in an undivided state they indulge themselves the pleasure of each other's company without creating.

Here we have the first distinction of the opposites as they exist within the primal unity. Within the context of the Kabbalah, this primal unity would be thought of as *Kether*, the first of the *Sefiroth*. Another familiar symbol representing the idea of the opposites as contained within a unified field, but not yet separated, is the *T'ai Chi* of the Chinese. In the Chinese system it is not until the opposites are separated that the universe can come into existence.

The first step in creation, therefore, is the making of qualitative distinctions. This is brought about by a separation of the essences of the original unity *while they are contained in the original unity*, in potential. This is the separation which concerns itself with distinguishing the parts of the whole, the moment when the whole is thought of as a composite figure.

The next step of separation is the one which one normally thinks of when the word 'separation' is used: the imparting of a *distance* between the qualities already described as distinct from one another. The waters referred to in Genesis are already thought of, in the *Zohar*, as male & female prior to their separation. That they are distinctly different from each other in a unified state means absolutely nothing in terms of productivity, creation & transformation. Their distinction is always emphasized in mythology by their total separation from one another. This comes to pass by the application of the further distinction of above & below. Until that time an oppressiveness might be experienced by mere virtue of the fact that light, & all it might symbolically imply, cannot be produced. In Genesis it is not until after the separation of the waters & the distinctions of Heaven & Earth are made that light comes into existence. This idea is dynamically

The cosmic
drama

cally expressed in the Maori creation myth:
"Rangi & Papa, the heaven & the earth, were
regarded as the source from which all things, gods,
& men originated. There was darkness, for these
two still clung together, not yet having been rent
apart; & the children begotten by them were ever
thinking what the difference between darkness &
light might be . . . At last, worn out with the oppression of darkness, the beings begotten by Rangi
& Papa consulted among themselves . . . Tane-
mahuta, the god & father of the forests, of birds,
& of insects, . . . planted his head on his mother
Papa, the earth, & his feet he raised up against
his father Rangi, the sky; he strained his back &
his limbs in mighty effort . . . he regarded not their
cries & their groans; far, far beneath him he pressed
down Papa, the earth; far, far above him he thrust
up Rangi, the sky. Hence the saying of old time:
'It was the fiercest thrusting . . . which tore the
heaven from the earth, so that they were rent apart,
& darkness was made manifest also." [22]

[22] Johannes
C. Anderson,
*Myths and
Legends of the
Polynesians,*
pp. 367-68.

The refinement of the mythological theme of separation in mysticism & most major religions leads
to a cosmic drama of magnificent & sometimes ter-
rifying proportions. I say this because we find in
time that the theme of separation comes to deal
with the separation of a complementary & necessary
portion of God himself. Furthermore, this portion
of God invariably becomes identified with a force
located either in man or in the world. In either
case, it becomes man's task to redeem this split-off
portion of the Divine. In the following section,
therefore, we shall make a small leap forward. From
the idea of the mythology of the world, we will
now discuss the mythology of the soul, the

individual's portion of the cosmos.

  The Union of the Opposites§ In Talmudic literature we are presented with the idea of an aspect of God which dwells in the world—the *Shekhinah*. In this form the *Shekhinah* is understood as nothing

" 'It is below as it is in Heaven.' That there is a correspondence between the activity of the heavens & the affairs of man was a principle the Kabbalists never lost sight of."

more than the active presence of God in the daily affairs of a nation, specifically Israel. This aspect of God is not to be thought of in this context as an entity unto itself, separate from the Divine,

A system of
Gnostic
speculation

but rather the mode of his being in the world, his face as some Talmudists express it. Nor does this mode of being have any particular quality attributed to it. The *Shekhinah* is God, & nothing more. In the Kabbalah, things change. The *Shekhinah* becomes his feminine counterpart, an intrinsic component of God rather than a mere aspect. On the one hand she is identified with the exiled Israel, & on the other with the soul with which man, along with God, yearns for union. It is at this juncture that we begin to speak of the Kabbalah as a system of Gnostic speculation.

Gnostic has come to be generally accepted as a term for that conglomerate body of sects which grew up alongside the Early Christians, & which were essentially Christian in nature. There is now good reason to believe that Christian Gnosticism was preceded by a form of Jewish Gnosticism.[23] The definition of the term Gnostic & Gnosticism is difficult because many of the sects which historians of religion now label under the generic Gnosticism differed in mythological dogma & terminology. What was common to all, however, was the idea that the inner spiritual man could be redeemed through self-knowledge. By means of the divine revelation of the nature of man's origins, the Gnostic knew the cause of his fall from grace, the means necessary to achieve redemption, & the nature of birth & rebirth. His knowledge was the direct result of the revelation won by his concern with this mystical anthropology. His position in regard to other religious men was unique in that his relationship with the Divine was based on *knowing* rather than on faith alone. The concept of a transmundane source, such as the *En-Sof*, was central

23 Scholem, *Jewish Gnosticism*, p. 2.

to the Gnostic system of speculation. The aim of
knowledge was the revelation of the Godhead itself,
not the knowledge won through rational discourse
& argument.

Another special feature of Gnosticism, & the feature we are most concerned with here, was the
idea that an aspect of God, a valuable counterpart
without which he must be considered incomplete,
had at one time either fallen from his immediate
vicinity or been exiled. This fallen Being was God's
feminine companion. In the Kabbalah we find the
Jewish mystics redefining the concept of the
Shekhinah within the scope of this mythology. Like
the whole of Israel, she is in exile, & the place
of her exile is this lower world.

*Redefining
the feminine
principle*

The Kabbalists go one step further: man's soul
finds his home in her, & therefore shares her fate.
All of this is nothing less than saying that a portion
of God himself is in exile, trapped down here with
us & in us. The *Zohar*, in commenting on Isaiah
xlv, 12, clearly points to man's position & function
in the world. The scripture reads, 'I have made
the earth for the sole purpose of creating man upon
it.' To this, the *Zohar* explains that in order for
the cosmos to regain its organic wholeness & unity
man had to be present.[24] The purpose behind creating man was so that he could work on the problem
of redemption & in that way reconstitute the divine
order. If God is ever to become whole again it
will only be because of man's efforts to redeem
the fallen *Shekhinah*, for in her, 'All worlds are
formed & sealed within.'[25]

[24] Lever-
toff, *The Zo-
har*, vol. 2,
p.279.

[25] From the
Friday eve-
ning Sabbath
meal hymn.

The idea of a God with a feminine helpmate is
not unusual in Buddhism & other related Near
Eastern systems. More often than not it is for this

reason many of us in the West today turn to Eastern religions. The idea is psychologically 'right.' One can sympathize immediately with a divine couple. Here, the reader might really feel that the invention of a female counterpart for God by the Jewish mystics was a truly daring innovation, a stretch of the imagination overstepping the bounds of Scripture. However, the Kabbalists did not have to go very far to invent this idea of a female *creatrix*. They had only to go as far as Scripture itself. There, in Proverbs *viii*, 22-3, they found Wisdom, the feminine principle we have met many times in our discourse, saying,

'The Lord possessed me in the beginning of his way, before his works of old. I was set up from everlasting, from the beginning, or ever the earth was.'

God & the sacred union

The very first line should make it apparent that the statement is not extolling the virtues of a platonic relationship. Some Kabbalists even go as far as to say that when God enters paradise every midnight to converse with the righteous, he also performs a sacred union with his *Shekhinah*. Wisdom frankly speaks of her existence before that of the earth, even before God began the creation in general. She was present from the 'beginning of his way,' which we can only assume means from the time of his decision to become manifest.

'When there were no depths, I was brought forth, when there were no fountains abounding with water. Before the mountains were settled, before the hills was I brought forth: While as yet he had not made the earth, nor the fields, not the highest part of the dust of the world.

When he prepared the heavens, I was there: when

he set a compass upon the face of the depth:
When he established the clouds above: when he
strengthened the fountains of the deep: When he
gave to the sea his decree, that the waters should
not pass his commandment: when he appointed
the foundations of the earth: Then was I by him,
as one brought up with him: and I was daily his
delight, rejoicing always before him.' (Proverbs *viii*,
24-30)

In other words, even before the distinctions accomplished by the act of separation of which we spoke
earlier, before the idea of the opposites, this
feminine *creatrix* was with the Lord as his daily
companion.

The reader must excuse my quoting from a book
so close at hand, a best-seller so common it might
be found in eight out of ten homes, in the night-
drawers of every hotel. I have done so not only
because these remarkable statements appear to have
eluded the eyes of the West for so long a time
& therefore deserve some repetition, but also because
of the emotional intensity with which they were
obviously written. It is almost as if the feminine
principle had a premonition that her voice & her
role would be lost, & that she had therefore almost
found it necessary to shout her case. The Kabbalists
heard her voice and granted her her dominion.

The similar structures of all mystical, religious & mythical systems

It has been a long journey from our opening
statements on the problem of transformation. In
its course we have glimpsed at the lineaments of
the mythical dimension where it is supposed to
take place. The theme we have been pursuing is
that practically all mystical, religious or mythical
systems speak from within a distinctively similar
framework & that a number of themes have a striking

ing resemblance with those found in Kabbalism. They all appear to imply that there is a divine plane or dimension which may only be defined by that which it is not. Out of this unnameable & illimitable source emerges a field of unity in which the opposites are contained as potential forms; the creation of the universe & the world ensues with the emergence of or distinction between these opposites whose sole desire is to remain in eternal union; their separation usually entails the idea of a fall from divine stasis, & therefore demands the eventual redemption of one portion of the original unity; the reunion or marriage of these opposites can only be accomplished with the aid of man. The language, the personifications & terms used in all of the systems mentioned were created to explain the above set of circumstances, the pattern of folding & unfolding. The language employed in each instance is that of mythology.

The findings of modern researchers imply that if a mythology can no longer be experienced by the individual at the collective level, within the context of a societal or communal myth, & if this type of thinking & experiencing is essential to being, then one can usually expect to find the impetus or spirit behind these old systems of transformation manifesting itself in new forms. The purpose, therefore, in studying such systems as the Kabbalah is to reacquaint modern man with the nature & structure of the mythical dimension.

The construction of mythology

It is now the task of the individual to construct mythology. The form of the mythology has to be dynamically personal & subjective in nature. Each of us must become a hero for ourselves & experience the tension of the mythical drama of fall & redemption

tion in ourselves. In order mythically to reconstruct the universe, we must reconstruct or rediscover the original unity within us by calling forth & constellating the total man, the whole man, the new Adam who each of us has the potential to become.

The potential of the new Adam

This, then, is the unity of the opposites: the marriage of all the contradictions one might find between what one would like to do & what one is, & what one does & pretends to be. To this end must we reawaken the heart of the hero in

Jacob Bohme, the teutonic theosopher, by J. B. Bruhl, Leipzig, c. 1650.

our daily encounter with the dragon of the world, the beast that mythology tells us demands fresh flesh daily, if not the spirit of our generation.

To many of us the Kabbalah is dead. In order to revive it we must bring to it a new mythology. In much the same way as the first Kabbalists brought to their sacred scriptures a new life & greater depth by the application of mythical structures, so too must we now approach the Kabbalah with a new mythical language. That has been the goal of this introductory work: not only to introduce the general public to the basic ideas of the Kabbalah, but to the most recent method of interpretation with which Jewish mysticism may be understood. Here I refer to the latest development in the Jewish mystical tradition, Hasidism. It is a new way of looking at things, a twentieth-century method which is in essence a new mythological structure.

A system of self-knowledge

Mysticism and Psychology §For Scholem Kabbalism is quite simply a mystical psychology. He points out that it's only by descending into one's own depths that one can come to know not only the world but God Himself.[26] Kabbalism, he adds, is a psychological tool by which self-knowledge may be attained to a degree which would astound the scientific mind. This may be said of the many spiritual disciplines which have come to the attention of modern man. This statement from the definitive work on Jewish mysticism is most certainly not a scholarly or rationalistic attempt to reduce all spiritual or mystical phenomena down to being nothing more than the metaphorical operations of the sympathetic nervous system or its malfunctioning. On the contrary, by finding parallel structures of development between the macrocosm & the microcosm, & by showing such parallelisms to have substance in fact, the only statement one may arrive at is that there is more to being human, & more to mysticism, than many of us would have thought.

[26] Scholem, *Major Trends in Jewish Mysticism*, p.341.

Again, by finding such correspondences between the reported operations of divinity in the cosmos at the macrocosmic level, the scientifically defined & limited sphere of human consciousness becomes enhanced, extended & furthered in its move towards wholeness. That the operations of the human psyche are reflective of the operations of the Divine is to say that there *is* a relationship between man &

the cosmos, & that this relationship is expressive of a unity. But these ideas are nothing new to psychology. They have unfortunately been clouded over & forgotten in the course of much scientific debate, leaving the layman with the false impression that psychology & psychoanalysis˙have only to do with psychic disorders.

Unity of man
& the cosmos

At the end of William James' Gifford lectures which were given in 1902, & which later became the text for his book *The Varieties of Religious Experience*, he says that the whole of his experience persuaded him that what we normally refer to as consciousness is but one of many worlds of consciousness existing beyond our range of immediate comprehension.[27] Even so, he added, these other worlds have a meaning in our life, a meaning which at times does become discernible when the energies contained within them filter into this world. The other worlds James refers us to are the worlds experienced by the mystic, & of which the Kabbalists possibly refer us to when they speak of the four worlds. That point or monad where the energies from these other worlds filter through into this world is that juncture in space & time where the opposites are united. The objective of mysticism & some psychologies is the union of those worlds with this one.

[27] William James, *The Varieties of Religious Experience*, p.519.

Martin Buber[28] is even more specific when he states that modern psychoanalysis has revived an old Hasidic view that psychic energies may be diverted & channeled into spiritual realms, & that such events take place in man in himself. Buber does emphasize the idea that psychoanalysis (& here I am certain he addresses himself to earlier forms, when neither Jung nor Laing were in the forefront)

[28] Buber, *Hasidism*, p.54.

deals with these energies as they exist in man *al o n e*
& not as the Hasidic method of raising the sparks
in man & in the world.

With all due respect to the scholarship of Buber
& Scholem, I would advance their statements a
step further by stating that this recent development
or understanding is merely the crystallization of
intuitions about the true ground of the Creator's
divine operations by Kabbalists writing long before
the emergence of the Hasidic movement. What
has happened is that the seed planted by these early
mystics has now blossomed to the point where we
may all clearly see what it was they attempted to
express.

That the early Kabbalists might not themselves
have understood their formulations & mystical statements as the rudiments of a psychology is beside
the point. The value of their statements for us today
lies in the fact that they spoke of realities which
could in no way have been arrived at through the
opacity of labored deduction. These were men who
through an intense consideration of both themselves
& the nature of man in general plumbed the depths
of Being.

The goal of twentieth-century psychology would
have been the science of the soul, the instruction
of individuals in the method of the Dantean plunge
through hell to heaven. But with the advent of
the physical sciences the methods of cause & effect
experimentation were universally adopted. What
could not be duplicated in the laboratories on any
one day of the week & be explained by scientific
analysis the next day was construed as non existent.
Western man could no longer tolerate anything
that was not exclusively physical, measurable, &

open to planned repetition. And in the meantime in India, China, Tibet, in monasteries in Europe & America, in synagogues in New York City & the Middle East men continued to experience the immeasurable without question, & with human benefit to all who experienced the power of their voices.

We should rid ourselves of the term psychology & leave it to those who insist it is a science dealing only with the organization & malfunctioning of neural pathways & chemical reactions, with pathological behavior & brain disorders. Mind & brain are not interchangeable terms. There have been only a handful of psychologists & psychiatrists who have insisted that what is under investigation & analysis is not just the mechanical process, but the dynamic operations of the soul itself.

What has been revealed is the idea that the human psyche contains within it a process, a dynamic of transformation which has from the beginnings of time tried to make itself available to man. It appears that for the first time in history this century has been admitted to the inner sanctum of that process in the discovery of the unconscious. That the lineaments of this theory are to be found in the writings of men themselves not aware of the implications of what they wrote, I repeat, only punctuates the idea that there is a dimension of experience in man which is & has been trying to manifest itself & make itself known to *all* men through the medium of religion & mysticism. Even if we were to discover that the present-day theories of depth psychology are indeed nothing more than another mythological formulation, we would still be left with the singular fact that myth transforms, no matter what garb

Science &
psychology—
new mystical
languages

it assumes or what tongue it speaks in. Whatever one would then choose to call or define the dynamics of transformation, its function would remain the same.

In any event, in much the same way as medieval man used his science, unashamedly, without excuse or apology, to explain the nature of himself & the universe, we should put this science to the test. If it is nothing more than another myth, then at least we are working in an ancient mainstream. If it is truly a science, that is if it is truly representative of the way things work objectively, then there is all the more reason why we should make use of it if we are to get to the heart of things. If nothing else, psychology is a new language which defines otherwise incomprehensible events in a form palpable to the rational intelligence of twentieth-century man.

No matter how profound or inspiring mystical treatises may be, it is essential that we do not lose sight of the fact that they are written by men living in the world. The profundity of an inner experience does not absolve one from the responsibility of living, nor does it make of one an instant saint. If, in experiencing that other dimension, one should come away with the certainty one can do no wrong & is therefore absolved from the turmoil inherent in Being, then that person may be certain that he has missed the message of the experience.

For each individual, it is certain the message will be different, but the setting will be the same. What is undeniably experienced by all in such moments is the reality of the Other. Experiences of the transcendent realm lead one to the conclusion that there are at least three aspects of reality &

not just one. There is the mundane reality of the rational, causal & banally explicable world of events. The reality which everyone at one time or another wishes could be enhanced or relieved by something or someone, by meaning or by anything at all. The intensity, the thickness & heaviness of this mundane reality at times seems to be so unbearable, so meaningless, that one is almost forced into a defensive & atheistic position.

Then there is the transpersonal & so-called mystical reality standing over the mundane, shimmering with mystery. It is the other extreme, the pole opposite that of the mundane. For many centuries experience of this realm was allowed to only those deeply ensconced within religious institutions. For the others, those of the secular community, public ostracism or the stigma of madness was their reward. Even though this century finds itself with more & more personalities experiencing this realm, this transcendent sphere of the Divine, still there are many who would deny its existence. It might be profitable for us to read the account (taken from personal correspondence) of a twentieth-century man, a non-mystic as he himself insists, who has, in his estimation, experienced the Divine:

'One evening, while peacefully seated in my apartment, I was suddenly swept up & beyond my mortal frame & aimed with unerring accuracy & speed towards an indescribable Light. Out of that Light issued a voice which was no voice, & which I understood to be none other than the Divine Presence hidden in the universe. I found myself on the one hand flying with incredible speed through spheres of infinity, while on the other calmly looking down, from the height of the ceiling, at my seated body. This wave of Ascension lasted ten minutes by my estimation. During that period a silent language of pure love, understanding, & forgiveness coursed through my body. The closer I drew towards the Light, an infinity of smaller spheres whirling about it in constant obeisance, the more 'pictures' of my future self, the body seated in the chair, flashed before me. That body was but a shell & without the portion of me which was ready to extinguish itself in the pure flame of infinity it would continue on in the world as a placard-carrying fanatic. I realized then that I could not experience the Divine before experiencing myself. I fought with every available amount of strength to return. I did, only to then ponder the possibility that I was going mad . . . In time, I learned otherwise . . . Since then I have always found meaning in life & have always known it to be a drama, a sacred play. I have learned not to speak of this experience too much. Many have referred to it as a temporary madness. Only I know the substance it has given to my life.'

My correspondent was fortunate that things turned out as they did. More often than not the experience of the transcendent cancels out the mundane reality of everyday existence. This results in as one-sided an attitude as that adopted by those who insist that *only* the mundane reality exists.

Then there is the third & truly mystical reality. It is the reality realized by those who, after experiencing the Other do not deny the existence of the mundane, but in fact take it closer to heart. It is in this reality that the individual is confronted with the fact that there is a tear in the fabric of Being, that the two dimensions, the sacred & the profane, are like a husband & wife separated from one another. It is in willingly experiencing & accepting the tension created by this tear that one experiences this reality.

This reality alone is the one in which man becomes fully conscious of the opposites as they exist in both himself & in the universe, where he realizes that the tension generated by their separation can only be relieved by his attempts, by his efforts to reunite them. It is then that he realizes that the suffering of the mundane world is a suffering growing out of a need for a reconciliation with the transpersonal, & not by a displacement of the human by the transpersonal.

What must be striven after is a unity made up of both realms. The truly mystical experience of life, therefore, is one which has grown out of a purposefully planned entry into the fire of both realities in the individual's attempt to fuse them in the body of himself. The Kabbalah tells us that the upper world does not act until the lower world, the world of man, acts. The one thing the Jewish mystics never lost sight of was the suffering experienced in the arena of the profane. They did not retreat from this suffering, but sought instead to find meaning in it by *living* it. This is the core of mysticism. The temple in which the sacred marriage takes place is the world.

That the work of redemption was understood by the Jewish mystics as an interior process is substantiated by a Zoharic exegesis of Genesis *xxvii*, 27:

'And he came near, & kissed him: and he smelled the smell of his raiment, & blessed him, & said, See, the smell of my son is as the smell of a field

[29] Levertoff, *The Zohar* vol.2, p.53.

which the Lord hath blessed.'

In discussing this section, the *Zohar*[29] states that once a man has entered into the mystery of wisdom & achieved perfection, Solomon comes & says, 'Prepare thy work without, & make it fit for thyself in the field; & afterwards build thine house' (Proverbs *xxiv*, 28). To the Jewish mystic this referred to the cultivation of the soul, the field within the body. The interior process of cultivation & redemption should be the concern of any psychology which claims to heal, for what it is essentially healing is the wound of separation:

'The key to the knowledge of the soul's conscious life is to be found in the dimension of the unconscious. This explains the difficulty of arriving at a real comprehension of the soul's secret. The first objective of a science of the soul is to formulate how Man's spirit is able to descend into these depths.'[30]

[30] C. G. Carus, "Psyche," in *The Discovery of the Unconscious* by Henri F. Ellenberger, p.207.

The first crystallization of the new mythology was the concept of the unconscious. The distinctions of above & below in early mythology came to be called consciousness & unconscious in psychology. Freud's definition of the unconscious clearly made of that domain a hell. Our understanding of the unconscious has since become broader: it is both a heaven & a hell, but more important it is that place through which the Divine may communicate with us. There is no better way to emphasize the validity of this idea than to briefly discuss the Zoharic statements on the nature of dreams. With it I close this work which must in itself be considered but a collection of notes towards a better understanding of Kabbalism, notes hopefully to be taken up & expanded by others.

THE MEANING OF DREAMS IN THE ZOHAR

§Shortly after the kingship was bestowed on Solomon he went to Gibeon & performed a sacrifice of a thousand burnt offerings on the altar. Although not explicitly stated in Scripture, the sacrifice performed by Solomon was a ritual act designed to call the Lord forth for conversation, 'For the tabernacle of the Lord, which Moses made in the wilderness, & the altar of the burnt offering, were...in the high place at Gibeon.' Wherever the tabernacle was located, there the people could perform sacrifice & come into contact with the Lord. We are told that after the sacrifice was performed 'The Lord appeared to Solomon in a dream by night: & God said, Ask what I shall give thee.'(III Kings, *v*). It is with this simple piece of scripture that the *Zohar* begins one of its most revealing expositions.

In an earlier passage[31] we are told that dreams are far more precise than visions, often explaining what is obscure in vision. What is suggested by the brief extract above taken from the Book of Kings is that the dream may be the product of a ritual or sacrifice whose sole purpose is to contact an area of information existing beyond the normal range of consciousness. True, visionary experiences are also arrived at by ritual procedure. In another passage in the *Zohar* we are told that rabbi Hiya strongly desired to communicate with the deceased rabbi Simeon. He fasted for forty days at the end of which time he heard a voice which told him he did not yet have permission to see rabbi Simeon. He continued his fasting for yet another forty days at the end of which time his goal was

[31] I Kings:5.

fully realized. But the effort here is enormous when compared to that of Solomon's, & all that is achieved is a vision of a contemporary, not God himself. What startles one in the exposition is that God comes to speak to Solomon from the *inside*, through a dream which was clearly understood as an interior phenomenon. But the *Zohar* does not stop here. It goes on to say that Solomon had to communicate with God through the dream-world because he had not yet achieved full development.

So then, the communication system of the dream is not the sole property of enlightened men. It is accessible to all men, but the dream is a 'sixtieth part of prophecy,' & a man is shown in a dream only what directly corresponds to the nature of his own character, his soul obtaining the information to be given him by ascending as far into the upper realm as is accessible to that man at that time.

When Solomon asked God he be given an understanding heart that he may discern between good & bad, God replied,

'Behold...I have given thee a wise & understanding heart; so that there was none like thee before thee, neither after thee shall any arise like unto thee...And the Lord gave Solomon Wisdom.' (I Kings *xii*, 12).

That is to say, the epitome of a wise & understanding heart is wisdom. Up until the time of God's gift, Solomon had to rely on dreams. From that time forward until the time of his idolatry & subsequent fall from grace, Solomon could understand the true nature of things by conscious discernment alone, without the use of dreams.

I reiterate that it is obvious that the Kabbalists were aware of the fact that dreams are the phe-

nomena

Von der Seel.

Anima Mercury

The Soul: "The depiction of the Shekhinah takes on many forms in spiritual traditions. Here we find her as symbolic of the spirit Mercury of alchemy. An unusual designation in that Spirit is normally thought of as masculine in form."

A realm close
to the Divine
nomena of a realm contained within man, &
that this realm in some mysterious way sometimes
comes into close contact with the Divine. Here,
we are in the presence of some rather curious
psychological statements:

a. When a man attains full development or perfection, as did Solomon, he achieves the wisdom of
a Solomon.

b. Full development or perfection is achievable
by man via the dream-world, during which time
he may occasionally find himself in the presence
of either Wisdom or God. But it is not until he
achieves full development that he may see Wisdom,
as Solomon did, eye to eye, without the mediating
principle of dreams.

The *Zohar* also tells us that the reason why
Solomon's wisdom excelled was because the moon
had reached its fullness. When he later took many
wives who worshipped strange gods to which he
too eventually offered sacrifices, the Lord told him
of His displeasure with him & his wisdom departed.
The *Zohar* relates the event as follows:

§'When darkness came upon Solomon due to his
many sins, the moon waned because he did not
keep the holy covenant & took up with strange
women.'[32]

And then, the *Zohar* continues, Solomon was
again dependent on his dreams for information,
even as the common men of the time were.

What is absolutely essential for our discussion
here is that we take note of the fact that the gift·
of wisdom is synonymous with the full moon, &
that its loss is synonymous with the waning or
dark moon. It is because Solomon does not keep
his covenant with God in which it was explicitly

[32] Lever-
toff, *The Zo-
har,* vol. 2,
p.80.

asked of him that he keep the commandments &
walk in the way of the Lord that the moon begins
to wane. His ability to consciously discern the heart
of a situation, to communicate directly with the
sphere of wisdom rather than through the sometimes
faulty realm of dream, is taken from him. The
Moon, wisdom, departs & leaves him with the lot
of common men. Throughout the entire *Zohar*,
the nature of Solomon's wisdom is connected with
the nature of the moon, & nothing else.

In an exposition on the scriptural passage, 'And
Solomon's wisdom excelled the wisdom of all the
children of the east country, & all the wisdom of
Egypt,' the *Zohar*[33] tells us that the difference
between Solomon's wisdom & the wisdom referred
to in the passage just quoted lay in the fact that
there was a secret known only to him. That secret
was the name of the moon when it has been blessed
from every possible side. Solomon's wisdom is thus
linked with the moon as a feminine principle in
which was contained knowledge of a supra-personal
nature.

Of the many synonyms given the feminine aspect
of God, the moon is the most important & fre-
quently mentioned. I repeat this here only so that
we might make sense of the following point which
will throw some light on the nature of dreams:
the *Shekhinah*, the feminine principle, withdraws,
hides herself from man to the degree that he sins.
Kabbalistically speaking, the moon (*Shekhinah*)
of the dream world, which is feminine in itself,
wanes or withdraws its light from man when he
sins. The dream world is a sphere of feminine activity through which wisdom may be attained. This
attainment of wisdom is symbolized by the full

33 Lever-
toff, *The Zo-
har*, vol. 2,
p.317.

moon, the feminine principle, without which the Kabbalists insist man is incomplete. Once a man's dream-world is occupied by a full moon he no longer needs the mediating realm of dreams to understand & discern. He is then capable of doing this while awake, conscious & in full control of his senses. His wisdom is the wisdom of the feminine—of the heart, & not just of the mind or the intellect.

The heart as the organ of consciousness is a foreign idea for modern man. We always think of the head, the mind as localized in the brain, as the seat of consciousness. This idea is relatively new in the history of man. The organ of thought was as a rule thought of in ancient times as either located in the heart or in the stomach. In the fourteenth century we find it stated that there are two types of intellect. The one achieves its knowledge by seeing through the eyes, the other by understanding through the heart. Later still the alchemist Paracelsus states that it is in the heart where one finds the true soul dwelling, & that this soul is the breath of God.

In the Kabbalah, it is stated that the messenger of the dream world is a person's soul which leaves him at night & journeys in the realm of the upper worlds. Inasmuch as some souls, according to the Kabbalah, receive their information directly from God, one could equate Paracelsus' statement with that of the Kabbalah. Obviously, souls capable of communicating with God are his very breath in that they carry back his word. In the *Secret of the Golden Flower* we find:

'When men are released from the womb the primordial spirit abides in the square inch which exists between the eyes, but that spirit which we call conscious abides in the heart.'[34]

In Kundalini Yoga the heart center is thought of as the organ of the intuitive mind & that place where the act of meditation is performed.

Finally, from the teachings of the great Hasidic mystic rabbi Baer of Meseritz, the Great Maggid, the most accomplished of rabbi Israel, the Baal Shem Tov's pupils, we have this enlightening & unexpected statement:

'The power of our intelligence has its home in the heart. This corresponds to the saying 'The heart is that which is intelligent.' It is there where it receives its content & the influence from the uppermost level, the unconscious [qidmat-ha-sekhel].'[35]

If we apply this Hasidic statement to the Zoharic statement that the nature of Solomon's wisdom was a discerning heart and that its source was the full moon—moon & heart were generally associated with the feminine sphere of knowledge—then the result we obtain is that Solomon gained his wisdom from the unconscious, the place of dreams

What the Kabbalah presents us with are early intuitions of what now has become a science of the soul. There have been many such sciences throughout the course of history, many of them now viewed as mythical structures, products of imagination or unconscious projection. The most familiar is astrology. Well into the seventeenth century, astrology was taught in universities, a respected science & one which was then thought of as capable of standing the test of time.

Now, from the viewpoint of empirical science, astrology is discredited. The one science which still regards it as containing substance, but substance of an entirely different sort from that which it was

[34] Cary F. Baynes, trans., *The Secret of the Golden Flower*.

[35] Siegmund Hurwitz, "Psychological Aspects in Early Hasidic Literature," in *Timeless Documents of the Soul*, pp.165-6.

36 Dane
Rudhyar, *The
Astrology of
Personality.*

originally thought to have, is psychology.

One of the leading astrologers of this age, Dane Rudhyar,[36] has pointed out that the phenomena with which astrology concerns itself were at first thought of as physiological & elemental. In the twentieth century, we speak of them as being mental & psychological. But, he points out, the work of

From an incantation bowl, two sorcerers invoking powers in turn on the others' behalf. From James Montgomery, *Aramaic Incantation Texts from Nippur.*

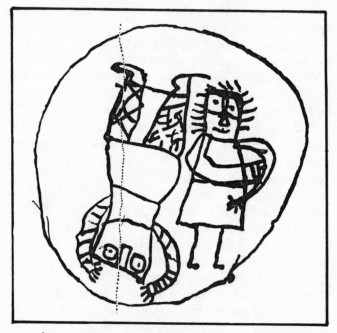

astrology & its methods remain the same. Only man's perspective or awareness has changed.

Much the same may be said of the Kabbalah, as the Hasidic mystics themselves point out. In a work which presents the Kabbalah as it exists today there can be no evading the conclusions of those who have worked in the mainstream of Jewish mysticism. We must therefore give up our magical-mystery explanations of the Kabbalah, our spiritual cloak-&-dagger attitudes, & follow the lead of the masters.

In *Modern Man in Search of His Soul*,[37] Jung wrote wrote that as long as he had to aid anyone in discovering the meaning of the symbols appearing in their dreams, that person was, psychologically speaking, still in a state of childhood. To this he added that unless one is capable of deciphering these symbols he lives in darkness.

Successful dream interpretation requires that the interpreter have at his disposal the archetypal motifs to be found in mythology. It also demands a basic understanding of the structural dynamism of the symbols—the developmental stages of a symbol, its negative & positive expressions, its relevance to immediate reality, & so on. The dreamer is called upon to do nothing less than provide formal expression of the mythology which is uniquely his own. For this task assuredly one needs the wisdom of Solomon.

When we refer the implications of Jung's statement to the collective level, we begin to see the enormity of the problem with which twentieth-century man is confronted. Without a living religious or mythological tradition, ignorant of the message hidden in symbolism (not to mention phantasy), he is still in a state of childhood. This explains a great number of things. Only a child could be so short-sighted as to be unable to visualize the possible outcome of his lighting matches in his bed, beneath his covers—& only a childlike awareness or lack of awareness could fail to see the future of a world busy with the business of an arms-race & with programs for peace which entail the oppres-

sion

[37] C.G. Jung, *Modern Man in Search of His Soul,* p. 67.

The myths & symbols of dreams

The need for the revival of myths

sion of people & the destruction of nations.

The individual on the one hand is being called upon to make real the myth of himself which is to be found at the very core of his being, & he is, on the other, being called upon to revive the myths which lie dusty on the bookshelves of our culture. It is only by reconstructing these myths, by releasing the slumbering & imprisoned spirit in them by means of a reinterpretation based on the findings of the many sciences & disciplines which now view myth as a living force, that each individual may contribute to the reconstruction of a world fallen into darkness. As long as we fail to see that in myth & symbol there is a slumbering spirit capable of transforming the nature of man, & therefore of society & the world, we shall remain children in a paradise where unrecognized evil lives as a beguiling charmer, whispering sweet words of patriotism in the vineyard, aiming arrows of censorship at any who dare attempt programs of equality, & finding in its brother's eye the mote of the beam in his own.

Bibliography & Index

280

Bibliography

Abelson, J. *Jewish Mysticism*. London: Bell, 1913.

Abelson, J. *The Immanence of God in Rabbinical Literature*. 1912. Reprint. New York: Hermon, 1969.

Abrahams, Israel. *Jewish Life in the Middle Ages*. Philadelphia: Jewish Publication Society, 1896.

Adler, Morris. *The World of the Talmud*. New York: Schocken, 1963.

Altmann, Alexander. "A Note on the Rabbinic Doctrine of Creation." *Journal of Jewish Studies* VII (1956): 195-206.

Anderson, Johannes C. *Myths and Legends of the Polynesians*. London: Tuttle, 1928.

Avalon, Arthur [Sir John George Woodroffe], trans. *Kama-Kala-Vilasa*. 3d ed. Madras: Ganesh, 1961.

Baynes, Cary F., trans. *The Secret of the Golden Flower*. Translated from Chinese to German by Richard Wilhelm. New York: Wehman, 1955.

Bowers, Margaretta K., and Glasner, Samuel. "Auto-Hypnotic Aspects of the Jewish Cabbalistic Concept of *Kavanah*." *Journal of Clinical and Experimental Hypnosis* VI (1958).

Box, G.H., and Charles, R.H. *The Apocalypse of Abraham and Ascension of Isaiah*. New York: Macmillan, 1918.

Buber, Martin. *Hasidism*. New York: Philosophical Library, 1948.

Buber, Martin. "Symbolic and Sacramental Existence in Judaism." *Spiritual Disciplines, Eranos Yearbook* IV (1960).

Casanowicz, I.M. "Jewish Amulets in the United States National Museum." *Journal of the American Oriental Society* XXXVI (1917): 154-67.

Cohen, A., ed. *The Soncino Books of the Bible* Surrey, England: Soncino Press, 1947.

Danielou, Alain. *Hindu Polytheism*. N.Y: Pantheon, 1964.

David-Neel, Alexandra. *Initiations and Initiates in Tibet*. New York: University Books, 1959.

Eliade, Mircea. *The Sacred and the Profane*. New York: Harcourt, 1959.

Ellenberger, Henri F. *The Discovery of the Unconscious*. New York: Basic Books, 1970.

Enelow, Hyman G. "Kawwana: The Struggle for Inwardness in Judaism." *Studies in Jewish Literature Issued in Honor of Professor Kaufmann Kohler* (1913).

Epstein, I., ed. *The Babylonian Talmud*. 35 vols. London: Bennet, 1935-52.

Franck, Adolphe. *The Kabbalah*. New Hyde Park, New York: University Books, 1967.

Gaster, M. *The Sword of Moses*. New York: Weiser, 1970.

Gaster, Theodor H. *Customs and Folkways of Jewish Life*. New York: Sloane, 1955.

Ginsburg, Christian D. *The Kabbalah, its Doctrines, Development and Literature*. London: Routledge, 1970.

Ginzberg, Louis. *The Legends of the Jews*. 7 vols. New York: Jewish Publication Society, 1909-38.

Ginzberg, Louis. *On Jewish Law and Lore*. New York: Atheneum, 1970.

Goldmerstein, L. "Magical Sacrifice in the Jewish Kabbalah." *Folklore* VII (1896): 202-4.

Goodenough, Erwin R. *Jewish Symbols in the Greco-Roman Period*. vols. 7 & 8. New York: Pantheon, 1958.

Govinda, Lama Anagarika. *The Foundations of Tibetan Mysticism*. New York: Dutton, 1960.

Heschel, Abraham J. "The Mystical Element in Judaism." In *The Jews*, vol. II. Edited by Louis Finkelstein. New York: Schocken, 1970.

Holmyard, E.J. *Alchemy*. Baltimore: Penguin, 1968.

Hurwitz, Siegmund. "Psychological Aspects in Early Hasidic Literature." In *Timeless Documents of the Soul*. Evanston, Ill.: Northwestern Univ. Press, 1968.

James, William. *The Varieties of Religious Experience*. London: Longmans, 1910.

Jellinek, Adolph, ed. *Auswahl Kabbalistischer Mystik*. Leipzig: 1853.

Jellinek, Adolph, ed. *Philosophie und Kabbala, Erstes Heft, Enthaelt Abraham Abulafia's Sendschreiben ueber Philosophie und Kabbala.* Leipzig: 1854.

Jellinek, Adolph, trans. and comment., *"Sefer Ha-Oth,* Apokalypse des Psuedo-Propheten und Psuedo-Messias Abraham Abulafia." In *Jubelschrift zum Siebzigsten Geburtstage des Prof. Dr. H. Graetz.* Breslau: 1887.

Joseph, Rabbi ben Abraham Chayun. *Sefer Yetsirah.* New York: 1923.

Josten, C.H., trans. "A Translation of John Dee's 'Monas Hieroglyphica' (Antwerp, 1564) with an introduction & annotations." *Ambix* XII (1965): 55.

Jung, C.G. *Modern Man in Search of a Soul.* New York: Harcourt, 1956.

Jung, C.G. *Answer to Job.* New York: World, 1963.

Jung, C.G. *Memories, Dreams and Reflections.* New York: Vintage, 1963.

Kohler, Kaufmann. "The Tetragrammaton and Its Uses." *Journal of Jewish Lore and Philosophy* I (1909): 10-32.

Lauterback, Jacob Z. "Substitutes for the *Tetragrammaton.*" *Proceedings of the American Academy for Jewish Research.* Philadelphia: 1931.

Legge, Francis. *Forerunners and Rivals of Christianity.* New York: University Books, 1965.

Lelut, F., ed. *L'Amulette de Pascal.* Paris: 1846. (Author's translation)

Levertoff, Paul P., trans. *The Zohar.* vols. 2&3. New York: Bennet, 1959.

Levertoff, Paul P., and Simon, Maurice, trans. *The Zohar.* vol. 4. New York: Bennet, 1959.

Lilar, Suzanne. *Aspects of Love.* New York: McGraw, 1965.

Luzzatto, Rabbi Moses. *General Principles of the Kabbalah.* New York: The Press of the Research Centre of Kabbalah, 1970.

Madhavanda, Swami. *The Brhadaranyaka Upanishad.* Calcutta: Advaita Ashrama, 1965.

Mathers, S.L. MacGregor, trans. *The Kabbalah Unveiled.* New York: Weiser, 1968.

Mordell, Phineas. *Sefer Yetsirah.* Philadelphia: P. Mordell, 1914.

Neumann, Erich. "Mystical Man." *The Mystic Vision, Eranos Yearbook* 6 (1968).

Odeburg, Hugo, ed. and trans. *3 Enoch or the Hebrew Book of Enoch*. Cambridge, England: Univ. Press, 1928.

Oesterley. William O. and Robinson, T.H. *Hebrew Religion, its Origin and Development*. London: Society for Promoting Christian Knowledge, 1940.

Rudhyar, Dane. *The Astrology of Personality*. New York: Doubleday, 1970.

Saures, Carlo. *The Cipher of Genesis*. Berkeley: Shambala, 1970.

Saures, Carlo. *The Cipher of Song of-Songs*. Berkeley: Shambala, 1971.

Scholem, Gershom. *Jewish Gnosticism Merkabah Mysticism and Talmudic Tradition*. New York: Jewish Theological Seminary of America, 1965.

Scholem, Gershom. *On the Kabbalah and Its Symbolism*. New York: Schocken, 1965.

Scholem, Gershom. *Zohar: The Book of Splendour, Basic Readings from the Kabbalah*. New York: Schocken, 1968.

Scholem, Gershom. *Major Trends in Jewish Mysticism*. New York: Schocken, 1969.

Simon, Maurice, and Sperling, Harry, trans. *The Zohar*. vols. 1 & 5. New York: Bennet, 1959.

Singer, Isador, ed. *Jewish Encyclopedia*. 12 vols. 1904. Revised edition. New York: KTAV, 1964.

Singer, S., trans. *The Authorized Daily Prayer Book*. London: Eyre and Spottiswood, 1962.

Stenring, Knut. *The Book of Formation*. 1923. Reprint. New York: KTAV, 1968.

Tishby, Isaiah. "Gnostic Doctrines in Sixteenth Century Jewish Mysticism." *Journal of Jewish Studies* VI (1955): 146-52.

Waite, A.E. *The Holy Kabbalah*. New York: University Books, 1965.

Waters, Frank. *The Book of the Hopi*. New York: Ballantine, 1969.

Weber, Max. *Ancient Judaism*. New York: Free Press, 1967.

Weiner, Herbert. *9½ Mystics*. New York: Holt, 1969.

Werblowsky, R. Zwi. "Philo and the Zohar, part one."

Journal of Jewish Studies X (1959): 25-44.

Werblowsky, R. Zwi. *Joseph Karo, Lawyer and Mystic.*
Oxford, England: Univ. Press, 1962.

Westcott, W. Wynn, ed. *Aesch Mezareph or Purifying Fire.*
Trans. by A Lover of Philalethes. New York: Occult Research Press, n.d.

Westcott, W. Wynn, ed. *Sepher Yetzirah.* New York: Occult Research Press, n.d.

Additional notes to footnote 3, page 39: A second Latin version of the *Sefer Yetsirah* appeared in the collection of Pistorius in 1587 and is thought to have been translated by Reuchlinus & Riccius. A third Latin translation appeared in Amsterdam in 1642 accompanied by the Hebrew text & notes. It was published by Friedrich V. Meyer in Leipzig in 1830, & then in a German translation by L. Goldschmidt, in Frankfurt, 1849. The famous occultist Papus translated it into French in 1887, adding to it another short text known as *The Thirty-two Paths of Wisdom.* This was the English title for a work first published in a Latin translation by Rittangelius in 1642.

There are four modern translations of the *Sefer Yetsirah* in English: W. Wynn Westcott, Phineas Mordell, Knut Stenring (under the title *The Book of Formation*) and Rabbi A. Joseph. The only work that is at all easily available is the translation by Westcott. It includes a translation of *The Thirty-two Paths*, but those familiar with the original suggest that it is inferior to the other translations of the *Sefer Yetsirah*.

The absence of any adequate edition of the *Sefer Yetsirah* in English is typical of the state of affairs of Jewish mystical texts in general. While the texts of Hinduism, Buddhism, Taoism, Tantraicism, Shintoism and Sufism are readily available in cheap paper editions, the major texts of Jewish mysticism are mostly untranslated & unpublished.

Additional notes to footnote 6, page 47:

A Latin translation of three sections of the work by Baron Christian Knorr von Rosenroth under the title, *Kabbal Denudata, seu Doctrina Hebraeorum Transcendentalis et Metaphysica,* was published between 1677 & 1684. There is a biographic account of Rosenroth & an assessment of his importance for the kabbalist tradition in A. E. Waite's *The Holy Kabbalah*. In 1887, S. L. MacGregor Mather's translation of Rosenroth's text was published under the title of *The Kabbalah Unveiled*.

Paul Levertoff, Maurice Simon & Harry Sperling's translation in five volumes, 1931-4, has also been reprinted.

These last two editions are the only two readily available in English. In general, when quoting from *The Zohar*, the references will be to the Levertoff, Simon and Sperling edition.

The Index

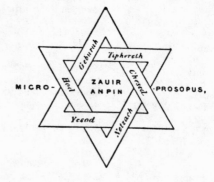

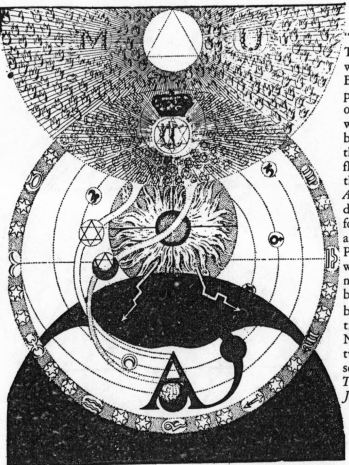

"From the Time in which that Breaker, prophesied of by *Micah*, was come up before us, the Gate flood open, that the First *Adam's* Children could follow him and enter the Paradise, which could not be done by any Soul before that time . . ." Number twelve in a series, from *The Works of Jacob Behmen.*

The hidden
geometry of
Stonehenge:
A hexagon of
66600 sq. ft.;
Solomon's
Seal 66600
sq. ft. in total
area; inner
circle of 6660
sq. yds.; from
John Michell
*A View Over
Atlantis,*
London, 1969

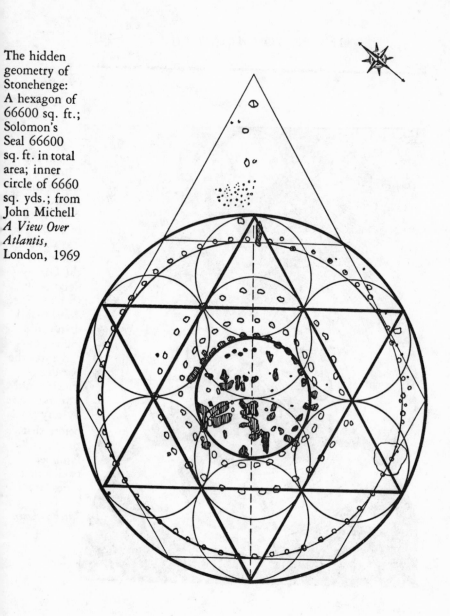

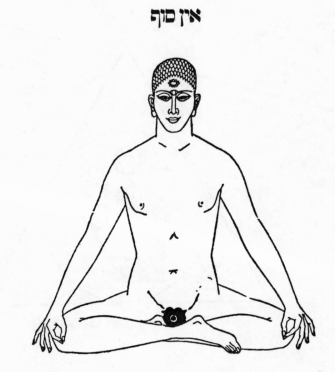

Designed by Jon Goodchild